China's Trade Unions – How Autonomous Are They?

This book examines the status of trade unions in contemporary China, exploring the degree to which trade unions have been reformed as China is increasingly integrated into the global economy, and discussing the key question of how autonomous China's trade unions are. Based on an extensive, grass-roots survey of local trade union chairpersons, the book reveals that although trade unions in foreign-owned firms and in firms dealing with foreign firms are beginning to resemble trade unions in the West, in the majority of firms a state corporatist model of trade unions continues, with chairmen appointed by the party. Many of these chairmen occupy party and trade union positions simultaneously, and, thinking it right to do so, have power bases and networks in both the party and the trade union, with initiatives for protecting workers' interests coming from the top down, rather than the bottom up, and with collective negotiation and democratic participation in union affairs continuing to be a mere formality. The book shows how the state – wishing to maintain political stability – continues to regard itself, legitimated by the concepts of "socialism" and "proletarian dictatorship," as the sole arbiter and protector of workers' rights, with no place for workers protecting their own interests themselves in the harsh environment of the new market economy. The book concludes, however, that because the different model of industrial relations which prevails in foreign-owned firms is formally part of the government system, there is the possibility that this new more Western model will in time spread more widely.

Masaharu Hishida is Professor of Contemporary China Studies and Sociology at Hosei University, Japan. **Kazuko Kojima** is Assistant Professor on the Doctoral Program in International Public Policy, in the Graduate School of Humanities and Social Sciences at the University of Tsukuba, Japan. **Tomoaki Ishii** is Associate Professor in the School of Commerce at Meiji University, Tokyo, Japan. **Jian Qiao** is Dean and Associate Professor in the Department of Labor Relations at the China Institute of Industrial Relations, Beijing, China.

China Policy Series

Series Editor
Zheng Yongnian, China Policy Institute,
University of Nottingham, UK

China's Trade Unions – How Autonomous Are They?

A survey of 1,811 enterprise union chairpersons

Masaharu Hishida, Kazuko Kojima, Tomoaki Ishii, and Jian Qiao

 Routledge
Taylor & Francis Group

LONDON AND NEW YORK

First published 2010
by Routledge
2 Park Square, Milton Park, Abingdon, Oxon, OX14 4RN

Simultaneously published in the USA and Canada
by Routledge
270 Madison Avenue, New York, NY 10016

Routledge is an imprint of the Taylor & Francis Group, an informa
business

Typeset in Times New Roman by
MPS Limited, A Macmillan Company
Printed and bound in Great Britain by
CPI Antony Rowe

British Library Cataloguing in Publication Data
A catalogue record for this book is available
from the British Library

Library of Congress Cataloging-in-Publication Data
China's trade unions : how autonomous are they? /
Masaharu Hishida . . . [et al.].—1st ed.

p. cm.—(China policy series)

Includes bibliographical references and index.

ISBN 978-0-415-49016-0 (cloth : alk. paper) — ISBN 978-0-203-86175-2
(ebook) 1. Labor unions—China. 2. Corporate governance—China.
3. China—Politics and government—2002- I. Hishida, Masaharu, 1950-

HD6837.C4515 2010

331.880951—dc22

2009027616

Contents

v

List of figures

List of tables

Notes on contributors

Masaharu Hishida is Professor of Contemporary China Studies and Sociology in the Department of Law and Director of the Institute of Grassroots at Hosei University.

Before joining the department at Hosei, he taught for 17 years in the Department of International Studies at the University of Shizuoka, where he also served as the Dean of the Graduate School of International Studies and the Executive Board member. He also served as a Visiting Scholar at Japanese Embassy in Beijing, People's Republic of China (1991–2) and as an analyst in the Department of Overseas Economic Information in JETRO (Japan External Trade Organization) (1974–86).

Professor Hishida is recognized as an authority on contemporary China studies, Japan–China relations and the international politics. His books, articles and book chapters have been widely published. He has authored and edited 11 books, including *China: State and Society Symbiotic Relations*, edited (Tokyo University Press, 2003); *The Economic Growth and Social Development*, co-authored with Shigeto Sonoda (Nagoya University Press, 2005); *Fundamental Structure of China from Local/Grassroots*, co-edited with Satoshi Amako (Keiso Shobo, 2000); *Encyclopedia of Contemporary China* (Iwanami Shoten, 1999) and *Foreign Direct Investment and Cross Cultural Management in Northeast Asia,* co-edited with Ku-Hyun Jung (Sasakawa Peace Foundation, 1995). He has also published articles in *Monthly China's Economy, Asia Research, Japan Review of International Affairs, Sekai* (=World) (Iwanami Shoten) and *Toa* (=East Asia) (Kazankai).

Professor Hishida studied at Beijing University (1981–83) after graduating from the Sociology Department, University of Tokyo. He has been teaching at various institutions, including Kyoto University, Aoyama-Gakuin University, Asia University and Kanagawa University.

Professor Hishida has held a number of consultancies, including NIRA (National Institute of Research Advanced), The Premier's Office, JETRO, Institute of Developing Economies, The Japan Institute of International Affairs, Japan–China Association on Economy and Trade, Toyota Foundation, Ministry of Education and Ministry of Foreign Affairs. He also served as a consultant on China for OECD (1992–5). He serves on several boards and is a member of the Japan Association of Asian Studies, Japan Association of International Politics, Japan Contemporary China Association and Japan–China Sociology Association.

Kazuko Kojima is Assistant Professor of Doctoral Program in International Public Policy, University of Tsukuba, Japan (Dr., Keio University in 2006). Her work focuses on public space and civil society in contemporary China. She is the co-author of 'The *Shequ* Construction Programme and the Chinese Communist Party', in Kjeld Erik Brodsgaard and Zheng Yongnian's edited book *Bringing the Party Back In: How China Is Governed* (Eastern Universities Press, 2004); and author of 'The Controversy over the Reform of Chinese Trade Unions under Marketization', *Asian Studies*, 2006 (in Japanese).

Tomoaki Ishii is Associate Professor, School of Commerce, Meiji University, Tokyo, Japan. He was 2007–8 Visiting Scholar at Asia and Pacific Research Center, Stanford University, USA. His publications include *The Socialist State and Trade Unions in China: The Formative Process of Chinese-Style Consultative System*, 2007 and *Labour and Social Dimensions of Privatization and Restructuring: Telecommunication Services*, 1998. He served as an official at the International Labor Organization (ILO) in Geneva, Tokyo and Beijing between 1990 and 2001. He also served as reporter at Kyodo New Service, Japan from 1986 to 1988. He holds M.A. and Ph.D. degrees in political science from Waseda University, Tokyo.

Jian Qiao is Dean and Associate Professor of Department of Labor Relations, China Institute of Industrial Relations (Former China Labor College), China. He is the co-author of *Labor Relations Studies in China*, 2007 and *Labor Relations Studies*, 2005. He served as Editor in Chief of *Industrial Relations and Labor Policies in a Globalizing World*, 2003 and *WTO and Labor Rights Protection*, 2001.

Introduction

For entrepreneurs, China for some time now has been known as an "adventurer's paradise." The reason is that, following the policy of reform and opening adopted in late 1970s, the historical sense of expectancy concerning the Chinese market symbolized by the saying that "if every Chinese added just one inch to his shirt tail, the mills of Lancashire could be kept busy for a generation" has become a reality. More than that, however, for social scientists, present-day China is a paradise for pursuing an "impossible dream." Why? Because for social science, and particularly political science and sociology, which, unlike the natural sciences, are unable to conduct experiments, China is a wonderful laboratory. China's economic growth since late 1970s has been above 9% a year and has continued so for three decades, thereby surpassing the high level of Japan's postwar economic growth, which was described as a "miraculous recovery." As a result, China right now is experiencing a huge transformation on a scale unprecedented in the history of humankind. The operative word here, "unprecedented," has been used time and time again by Chinese researchers. The intellectual study of present-day China is indeed a thrilling treasure hunt, with the discoveries and hypotheses of one moment being suddenly verified by the next by the reality of China itself.

Where is this changing giant of a country heading? What is the nature of China's transformation? Researchers have been seeking answers to these questions from a variety of perspectives. Because of the language problem, relatively little is known in the English-speaking world about Japanese research on contemporary China, and so let us briefly introduce here the steps that Japanese researchers have been taking.

The first full-fledged research on contemporary China in Japan was the priority area research project "Structural Change in Contemporary China" (1996–8), headed by Professor Kazuko Mori and bringing together more than 80 Japanese researchers. Under an overall team for this priority area research project, subgroups were set up on the topics of economics, history, environment, and international relations. We made up a subgroup on the theme of "State–Society Relations in Contemporary China." The aim of this project was to analyze, from a long-term perspective, the abrupt social changes occurring in present-day China as a result of the advance of the reform and opening program and, transcending the simplified approach of conventional individual research, which focused on observation of the situation, to study the process of various structural changes in society, such as spatial and stratified movements, social attitudes, and social integration principles, from the analytical paradigm of "state–society relations." The results of this project were compiled in a six-volume series titled *Structural Change in Contemporary China*, published by the University of Tokyo Press (in Japanese). The research results of our subgroup are presented in volume five of the series, *Society–State Cohabitation* (edited by Masaharu Hishida, June 2000, 323 pages; in Japanese). As suggested by the title, the subgroup argued that contemporary Chinese society is cohabiting with the state.

In order to complement this perspective through field studies, in 1997 we carried out village, enterprise, and community surveys and other fieldwork designed to ascertain the progress of marketization in China, which is in a phase of transition; the progress of linkage with the international economy; and the impact on political and social systems. Through interviews with Chinese policymakers, researchers, and others, direct questionnaires to company workers, and so on, we obtained empirical data and micro information that directly hinted at the scale of the impact of internationalization and marketization on the political and social systems of present-day China in various areas, including movement at the primary city and village levels and among regions. At the same time, we reached the conclusion that since this impact was bringing about irreversible changes, the program of internationalization and marketization itself, adopted by China as a national policy, had reached the point of no return.

In particular, as the primary society of present-day China is in a process of transformation due to the promotion of marketization policies by the state, we noted the emergence of a new wealthy class enjoying the benefits of marketization and internationalization and the significant development of primary elections and the activities of village committees in rural villages.

Therefore, in 1998, on the basis of our research interest about whether the new wealthy could be seen as a newly formed class or a social group sharing specific values, we collected data on these people and conducted an analysis of their attributes as a joint project with Chinese researchers (the Institute of Sociology of Tianjin Academy of Social Sciences, Chongqing Academy of Social Sciences, Guangdong Province Academy of Social Sciences, etc.). In addition, from 1999 to 2002 we conducted surveys on the advancement of village autonomy, focusing on the election of village mayors, and the political development of China. The purpose of this research was to accurately grasp the institutional arrangement system and practical implementation of rural government based on our awareness of the fact that, as a result of permeation of the system of electing the heads of village committees (the village mayor) in what are called primary elections, democratization might be advancing in China at a much faster tempo than ordinarily assumed.

Specifically, we engaged in wide-ranging research exchange with the Chinese Comparative Politics Research Center of the Communist Party of China's Central Bureau of Translation, the School of Government of Beijing University, the Rural Problems Research Institute of China Agricultural University, the

Institute of Sociology of Tianjin Academy of Social Sciences, Anhui Academy of Social Sciences, South China Agricultural University, the Institute of Sociology of Shanghai Academy of Social Sciences, the Institute of Tibetan Studies of Qinghai Academy of Social Sciences, and others. In particular, we concluded an agreement with China Agricultural University, the Central Bureau of Translation, Anhui Academy of Social Sciences, South China Agricultural University, and the Qinghai Academy of Social Sciences for the joint implementation of a questionnaire survey of village leaders and ordinary villagers; we retrieved around 1,000–1,200 samples of analyzed data as a result.

Making use of these survey methods and our network with Chinese researchers, we next implemented a project titled "An Academic Survey of Social Autonomy in Contemporary China" (2003–7). The aim of this project was to clarify the impact of an autonomous society on the state, a theme that had not been clearly demonstrated in existing research so far. That is to say, the state–society cohabitation argument mentioned above put the emphasis on the process of penetration to a society dependent on the state as a consequence of the state's withdrawal. By contrast, in our project, from the perspective of societal corporatism, we put the focus of analysis on such factors as the awakening of rural *citizens* in village communities, the autonomy of residents in cities, and the resurgence of civil society, such as the trend toward workers expressing their interests in action and the formation of a middle class. The results are presented in this book, which focuses especially on the role of trade unions in representing the interests of workers.

On reflection, why was it that we became interested in corporatism? The reason was the emergence of new organizations in China in the "era of the private sector." Originally in China, after the communist revolution of 1949, society was swallowed up by the state under a policy of social group management. In other words, social organizations could only exist as part of the state structure or with the approval of the state. The adoption of market forces through reform and opening and introduction of competitive relations brought about a contraction of the planned economy space and withdrawal of the principle of planning and increased social spheres that were relatively independent from the state. This led to a rapid rise in the number of nonpublic enterprises, nongovernmental organizations, and nonprofit organizations and their increased presence in Chinese society.

However, these social organizations were certainly not approved as independent bodies with their own decision-making powers. It appeared only that some governmental powers were being gently transferred to regional and private-sector groups and organizations. So the question is whether this movement now will take the form of *societal corporatism* (autonomous from the state and penetrating through to the state), or *state corporatism* (dependent on the state and penetrated by the state), or something in between these two concepts.

Next, why should we be interested in trade unions? In China, trade unions are part of a political consultative setup positioned as "mass organizations" under the national center of workers, the All-China Federation of Trade Unions (ACFTU). In the Chinese socialist system, they have the role of coordinating the interests of three parties – the state, enterprises, and workers. However, since the policy of reform and opening has created new conditions, such as the end of ideology and the diversification of interests among workers themselves, one wonders whether the trade unions, which previously were supposed to represent the interests of workers, are properly fulfilling that role today. Immediately after the Tiananmen Square incident in 1989, Deng Xiaoping is reported to have said that the formation of an independent union like Solidarity in Poland would be a nightmare for China. And at a meeting of party leaders in February 2000, Jiang Zemin pointed to the problem of the quasi-religious sect Falun Gong that had erupted in the previous year as a destabilizing factor in society and, likening Falun Gong to Solidarity, declared a sense of alarm. If the present trade unions are not fulfilling their conventional role as representatives of the interests of the workers, then workers need a new channel and new means to express their interests. If union leaders are tied into the party and state setup as an elite, then the unions are bound as organizations within the establishment of state corporatism.

In light of the labor disputes and spontaneous acts of violence that have been occurring frequently in recent years, in order to avoid such incidents, a political determination is required for a shift from the present state corporatism to a type of societal corporatism (neo-corporatism) premised on the parallel existence of government organizations, semi-government organizations, and independent groups.

Outline of survey

Given this interest in the various problems of trade unions, we selected as our counterpart the China Labour College (now the China Institute of Industrial Relations, CIIR; name changed in 2003) and commenced joint research with it. As suggested by its former name of the China Labour College, the CIIR is a body for grooming leaders of trade unions belonging to the ACFTU. In May 2003, after ratification by the Chinese Education Ministry, the CIIR did spread its wings into the fields of higher vocational education and adult higher education. But just as the Central Party School engages in the grooming and retraining of the party elite, the principal objective of the CIIR is to groom and retrain the trade union elite (http://www.ciir.edu.cn/). In other words, selected chairs and deputy chairs of trade unions throughout the country gather at the CIIR.

Our team for the project "An Academic Survey of Social Autonomy in Contemporary China," which received a grant from the Japanese Ministry of Education, Culture, Sports, Science, and Technology, discussed problems of interest to the two sides with CIIR President Li Deqi and Researcher Qiao Jian and finally reached agreement on the implementation of a questionnaire survey for primary trade union leaders. After concluding a memorandum, we commenced the necessary work. On a sweltering day in Beijing in 2003, wiping away the sweat that was trickling down our faces, the Japanese and Chinese sides engaged in a heated discussion of the contents of the questionnaire. In the end, the two sides agreed to conduct a questionnaire centered on finding out the extent to which trade unions today are organized by workers of their own accord, the extent to which they protect the interests of workers from the bottom up, and whether they are trying to expand. With the cooperation of CIIR researchers Fu Lin, You Zhenglin, and others, the questionnaire was conducted from March 2004 to June 2006 targeting primary trade union leaders in cities around China. (The original questionnaire is shown in Appendix 1.)

The results of the survey are presented in this book. We ended up with a total of 1,811 samples from Liaoning Province (226), Beijing (223), Shanghai (400), Zhejiang Province (309), Guangdong Province (425), Gansu Province (189), Guizhou Province (16), Henan Province (22), and no reply (1). Since it would have been difficult to conduct the questionnaire through random sampling, we implemented it by means of a group reply format following explanations by the CIIR staff using such occasions as meetings and training sessions held at each place. By the type of enterprise to which they belonged, the respondents were from state-owned or state-owned joint-stock enterprises (957), collective companies (60), private companies (61), joint-stock partnership enterprises (33), limited liability public corporations (150), joint-stock limited liability public corporations (90), companies with investment from Hong Kong, Macao, or Taiwan (15), foreign-capital companies (32), and others (292). This was the first-ever questionnaire directly targeting primary trade union leaders in China and focusing on trade unions as a point of contact between the state, enterprises, and workers in that country. We decided to publish an English version of the results because of the special features of the data obtained through the project. We hope that sharing these rare and valuable survey results with researchers around the world will contribute to the debate about the party-state establishment in China.

Composition of the book

Needless to say, the highlight of this book, as stated above, is our compilation of a questionnaire and the survey results, which represent the first-ever primary data sets relating to Chinese trade unions. These two materials are presented at the end of the book in Appendices 1 and 2. Consideration has been given so that, in the case of electronic printing, readers can set their own formats for the materials as Excel charts and thereby engage in their own analysis of the data.

The chapters in the book can be seen as guides for deciphering the data, although each chapter represents an analysis of the questionnaire results from the standpoint of the author. As explained above, we carried out the research from the perspective of corporatism, but what are the movements in contemporary Chinese society related to this corporatism? The first chapter, "Trade Unions and Corporatism under the Socialist Market Economy in China" (Tomoaki Ishii), analyzes this question. In this chapter, Ishii examines what role the ACFTU is fulfilling as a mediator in state–society relations in the China of reform and opening, and the significance and limits of the trade union reform line that has been set as a goal. Ishii postulates that when Zhao Ziyang, in his political report to the 13th party congress in October 1987, called for a separation of power between the party and the government, there was a possibility of a shift from the "party-state" regime to a relatively free form of institutional pluralism. After the 1989 Tiananmen Square incident, however, this societal corporatism suffered a setback and is in the process of regressing to state corporatism. The enactment of trade union and labor legislation is described to illustrate the trend. Ishii concludes that although the political consultative setup in China, including the ACFTU, appears to be stable, there is a possibility that the setup and the role of the ACFTU could become quite unsteady depending on the escalation of labor autonomy.

The second chapter, "Direction of Trade Union Reforms and Corporatism in PRC: Based on a Survey of Primary Trade Union Chairmen (2004–6)" (Kazuko Kojima), places the spotlight on the debate about trade union reform, which was shelved after the 1989 Tiananmen Square incident, and classifies the form of corporatism that China is aiming for. Specifically, it attempts an analysis of the questionnaire results after considering the qualifications for trade union membership, leadership personnel affairs, and financial affairs from the perspective of trade unions as an interest group. First of all, Kojima notes that a difference clearly exists in the form of the trade union and the desire for reform among trade union leaders depending on the type of enterprise to which the union belongs. And second, she notes that a disparity is arising concerning the role of trade unions between the coastal provinces and the inland provinces. From now on, Kojima predicts, Chinese workers are going to look more critically at trade unions, and also the internationalization of labor problems is building up pressure for change. She suggests that the present state of primary trade unions and trade union leaders, which has been clarified by our survey, is pressing for speedier and more drastic reform.

The third chapter, "Between the Party-State, Employers, and Workers: Multiple Roles of the Chinese Trade Union During Market Transition" (Qiao Jian), analyzes the role that trade unions should play based on the reality of Chinese politics, namely, single-party rule, centered on the concept of social capital. In China, where traditionally the party plays a bonding role with the workers and the masses, the author, a Chinese researcher, rejects arguments for a civic society, since this would mean independence from the "party-state" regime. Therefore, Qiao selects social capital, that is, the existence in the social network of a number of organizational resources that people acquire and use, as his main tool for analyzing the questionnaire results. In consideration of the tendency for trade union leadership to be a full-time job, the fact that trade unions increasingly see themselves as separate entities from the enterprise, and other factors, Qiao points to a heightening trade union consciousness and expresses the hope that a solid ideological base will be formed in the shift and development of the trade union movement in China from now on. In particular, Qiao makes special mention of the improved role of trade unions in protecting the rights of members and gives a positive appraisal of trade union reform.

In these chapters, the authors have attempted an analysis of the questionnaire results, our common property, from their respective standpoints. Perhaps some readers will be surprised at the diversity of conclusions arising from the differences in basic perspectives. Or maybe readers in English-speaking countries will again sense the difference in academic rhetoric that exists between Japan and China, two neighboring countries in the Far East.

However, one might venture to say that the possibility of these diverse interpretations regarding trade unions and trade union leaders itself is proof of the enigmatic existence of trade unions in China. Whatever the interpretation, though, be it Ishii's political consultative setup or Qiao's multidimensional role of trade unions, in the background there is the ubiquitous presence of the Communist Party of China (CPC). Of the primary trade union leaders who responded to our questionnaire, 90.3% were party members, and 96.5% of the enterprises to which they belonged had party organizations. Thus, the final chapter of this book, "The Morphogenesis of the CPC: Organizational Issues" (Masaharu Hishida), takes a look at the CPC, the biggest player in present-day Chinese politics. The author considers the CPC as a political and social organization and analyzes its characteristics from the point of view of organization theory, and in particular the evolutionary theory of organizations and the theory of self-organization. Specifically, Hishida looks at the results of official questionnaire surveys conducted by China itself and poses such questions as why do people participate in this organization? What are their motives in joining the party? Are there any differences in the meaning of the organization and its image between party members (and potential members) and nonparty members ("the masses")? How far do these motives for joining the party actually function in the real world? And are there really any practical merits in becoming a party member? Finally, as a background factor to trade union reform, Hishida illustrates the state of morphogenesis in the party (the process of transformation of an organization from confusion and chaos to a new order).

Whatever the case, as stated at the beginning, contemporary China is experiencing tremendous social changes as a result of its unprecedented scale of economic growth, the kind of changes that have never before been seen in any society. At a time of financial instability and increasing uncertainty in the global economy, the world inevitably is closely watching the outcome. What is certain is that social unrest triggered by warps in the conventional regime of state corporatism, that is, socialism and the democratic dictatorship of the people, is reaching a critical point, and the leadership of the party, which is the sole actor capable of finding a solution, is going to be tested.

Masaharu Hishida

1 Trade unions and corporatism under the socialist market economy in China

Tomoaki Ishii

Introduction

Since the founding of the People's Republic of China (PRC), trade unions under socialist systems have maintained the classic dualism formulated by Lenin whereby trade unions functioned as the "transmission belt" between the communist party and workers, serving the "top-down" function of increasing productivity by organizing labor for the purpose of developing the economy, as well as the "bottom-up" function of communicating workers' demands for realizing better working conditions and benefits.[1] The basic function of this relationship is symbiotic, intermediating between the mutual needs of the state and society. On the one hand trade unions are legally institutionalized autonomous organizations, but on the other hand they are characterized as mechanisms to lure the masses into order. In China, however, trade unions have not placed the state and society on equal footing, but existed in a patron–client hierarchy where the state needed the worker to realize its nationalistic objectives. The worker needs the state to protect a privileged status and income against the background of an oversupply of cheap labor and extremely restricted life chances for the overwhelming majority of the population.[2] Hence, the state and society in socialist China, much like in advanced nations such as Northern Europe, Central Europe, Japan, etc. have formed a certain type of corporatism, namely a system of labor interest representation in which the constituent units are organized into a limited number of singular, compulsory, noncompetitive, hierarchically ordered, and functionally differentiated categories, recognized or licensed (if not created) by the state and granted a deliberate representational monopoly within their respective categories in exchange for observing certain controls on their selection of leaders and articulation of demands and supports.[3] Based on this definition, it seems that the relationship between trade unions and the state in China also constitutes a certain type of corporatism. The subcategory of this corporatism would also follow P. Schmitter's definitions: corporatism that "autonomously permeates the state" can be considered as societal corporatism and corporatism that is "dependent on the state for its establishment" as state corporatism.[3]

In the process of adopting corporatism approach, however, it is important to take into account historical backgrounds under Chinese socialism in contrast to those of Soviet Russia or socialist states in Eastern Europe, since China seems to have yielded its specific relationship of power among workers, the state, and the Party, and it is not difficult to imagine that this made it possible for the relationship between labor and management to develop in a uniquely Chinese way. In this connection, J. Wilson pointed out that, according to Mao Zedong's understanding of a farmers society that recognized the value of agriculture more than that of the proletariat, Chinese trade unions represented a weak working class of limited numbers, and when compared to unions in Eastern Europe or the former Soviet Union, they operate in an environment of considerably reduced influence and increased uncertainties.[4] Thus, there has been no change in the fact that relationship between labor and management in China developed from an agonistic relationship between the governmental objective of securing integration or reorganization of workers, and the workers' objective of realizing their individual interests. Furthermore, it is also important to note that the concept of orthodoxy has been drifting between the state and society, and it has therefore become the presumption that the influence exerted by the alliance between workers and the Party has been a decisive factor in the retention of Party's legitimacy, and that any threat to the authority of the Communist Party since 1949 would have required the involvement of the industrial workforce to succeed.[5]

Looking back on the history of Chinese workers' movement from this perspective, it is easy to understand what has consistently formed the fulcrum in the balance of the relationship between workers and the Party-state is the model of dual enterprise management system adopted by the "factory management committee" and the "workers' representative congress," with the exception of the period from 1953–6 during the first Five Year Plan and the midst of 1980s during the Deng Xiaoping era when China experimented with the Soviet-styled "factory director responsibility system."[6] As A. Chan described, labor and management relations under the Chinese socialist system developed under the model of communist state corporatism with a dynamic that moves cyclically in circles.[7] Thus, even if there have been times when labor and management relations have demonstrated some aspects of societal corporatism along with occasional changes in the government or economy, they have not basically deviated from the framework of state corporatism.

Against the backdrop of the post-Tiananmen incident era, the Chinese government has approved 1,400 national associations, while 19,600 associations and branch organizations have been registered at the provincial level, as well as 160,000 groups at the county level by 1993.[8] The common thread in the establishment of these associations is that, while a certain degree of self-reliance with a limited level of freedom has been temporarily granted to these societal groups, they are not always recognized as independent social organizations which contain decision-making mechanisms in and of themselves like those set forth in the theory of pluralism. Instead, they are more likely to fulfill "top-down" policies as part of the national governmental organization than to fulfill social functions in areas that are closer to actual conditions. Therefore, there is a strong implication that there has been a state-led corporatist reorganization of social groups rather than an abrupt flourish of "civil society."[9] Since trade unions have played its important role as social groups or organizations, it is more effective to adopt a corporatist approach rather than civil society approach, when analyzing the development of workers' movement and industrial relations in China.[10]

As a matter of fact, the major findings of our research undertaken between 2004 and 2006 at trade unions of some 1,800 companies in Shanghai, Beijing, and other smaller cities in Liaoning, Zhejiang, Guangdong, and Gansu provinces also confirmed that the basic nature of relationship between labor and management, or workers and state, seems to remain unchanged even today. Asked in what type of job trade union's chairman was engaged before taking up his/her incumbent post, for example, the largest number of respondents (36.4%) answered "middle class curdle (chief at section, or department level)," and the second largest (15.8%) answered "secretary of the party committee," and then 11.7% responded "director of enterprise (or president of factory)." As for the procedure to become chairmen of trade unions, the largest number of respondents (47.3%) answered "by the election of workers representative after the recommendation of organizations," and the second largest (21.6%) answered "appointment from upper organizations," while only 2.3% answered "by an election after open competitive selection." In addition, among these "upper organizations," the majority of respondents (22.9%) was found to be from "Party organization at unit level," while the second largest (7.7%) was from "trade unions at higher level." These data clearly indicate that the Part-state still plays a decisive role in the process of trade unions activities in which even the management seems to be trying to become an "insider" in some particular cases. It is therefore highly doubtful to what extent trade unions are organized as their own autonomous and independent body free from the political power from outside, with a view to protecting and expanding workers' interests from the bottom.

As "management autonomy" has been promoted considerably with the development of market economy, however, it is quite natural that the call for "autonomous trade unions" to oppose this trend is also rapidly growing, and workers themselves have once again begun to question from the "bottom-up" why the All China Federation of Trade Unions (ACFTU) is there to take up an urgent task of reorganizing a certain type of corporatist system. Therefore, this chapter will adopt the concept of corporatism with a view to focusing on the major role of the ACFTU which still finds its basic function as an intermediary between the state and society, while looking back on the workers' movement before and after the Tiananmen incident, as well as inquiring into the implication of its history from 1980s, and the present status of trade unions in China.

The initial movement toward societal corporatism

The recovery of the Worker's Representative Congress and the ACFTU

When the Gang of Four was arrested and the Cultural Revolution came to an end, the Ninth Trade Union Congress was held at the ACFTU's regular national conference in October 1978 to officially announce that China's union movement had entered into a new stage. During his speech at the congress, Deng Xiaoping emphasized the importance of trade unions which are conducive to improving the level of their administration, economy, management, skills, and culture:

> Trade unions ought to protect workers' benefits; aid and direct enterprise managers and regional administrators to whatever extent possible; and improve workers' conditions, including their residences, diet, and general health and safety. Trade unions are for the workers, and they should exist as an exemplar of democracy.

Deng Xiaoping went on to add that "enterprise's most important problems ought to be debated at the worker's representative congress or the workers' congresses." Furthermore, he emphasized the importance of the democratic management of enterprise by the workers. As a result, in 1981 the "Provisional Regulations Concerning Workers Congress and Staff Members in State-owned Industrial Enterprises" were announced, and by the end of 1982 approximately two hundred thousand workers' representative congresses had been revived in large and mid-scale enterprises throughout China.[11]

After the Third Plenum of the Eleventh Party Congress (December 1978), which became a turning point in the nation's history, directives were issued for trade unions to further develop the workers' movement. The focus of discussion was the relationship between the trade unions' interests and obligations, and it touched on the unions' duties to the socialist revolution and overall construction of the state; their duties form the standpoint of technology, organization, and institutions to realize the economic strategy of "Four Modernizations"; their duties as the working masses representatives to strengthen international and domestic ties between the working classes, worker education, and the protection of the interests of the state and associations; and their duties as the Party's "supporters." Following this recovery of the trade unions' position and the reinvigoration of their activities, the numbers of their branch organizations also increased from 329,000 locations in 1979 to 447,000 locations in 1983; and among the entire country's one hundred fifteen million urban workers, union membership reached seventy-seven million.[12]

These instructions reinvigorated the economy and moved enterprise one step closer to independence, and as "democratic" management of enterprise was put into practice, the ACFTU's social status recovered to a large degree. However, many commentators believe that the extent of this recovery was limited and that the rebirth of the trade unions must surely be interpreted as rather more symbolic than substantial despite any merits in claims that the union structure at that time was part of an overall pattern of industrial democracy.[13] For example, the right to strike, which was included in the 1975 constitution, was removed in a 1982 amendment, demonstrating the symbolic nature of the changes.[14] It should have been possible to nurture the democratic management of an enterprise or factory as long as the expansion of industrial democracy does not become a potential threat to the Party-state, but this compromise did not occur without conceding the freedom to strike. At this stage, it was more likely that the government may have considered the workers' movement as a potential anti-establishment strategy by workers, and therefore the expansion of a new, centralized bureaucratic power in place of the Party would be approved by the establishment. This concealed an ambivalent evaluation of its own authority's legitimacy in establishing a state corporatist framework.[15]

In October 1983 at the Tenth Trade Union Congress, the significance of trade unions as interest representation groups was raised once again. At the meeting, President Li Xiannian described how the trade unions had borne the duty of protecting the interests of the working class, as well as that of improving workers' qualities. He also emphasized the importance of the role which trade unions played as a "bridge" and a "belt" connecting the Party and the working masses. To clarify the workers' interests and responsibilities under the Party's new "Four Modernizations" initiative, Ni Zhifu, the chairman of the ACFTU, presented "three duties" for trade unions as organizations of the masses: (1) Under the leadership of the Communist Party of China, trade unions should reflect workers' demands in their policies and arouse the workers' enterprising spirit; (2) trade unions should protect workers' legitimate rights and interests, and to fulfill their duties to the state and society, they should support justice and investigate errors; and (3) they should connect with workers in fringe enterprises and at the association level, build a close relationship with them, represent their interests and demands, and become their true "home."[16] In 1984, to establish a "correct relationship" between "the State, industry and workers," the "Decision of the Central Committee of the Chinese Communist Party on Reform of the Economic Structure" asserted the principle of "separation of economic and property rights" in the relationship between the state and enterprise. This contributed to the foundation for the expansion of enterprise's managerial autonomy under the market economy.[17]

As if symbolizing a series of movements toward corporatist reorganization, China sent representatives from the tripartite system: government, workers, and employers to the ILO's International Labour Conference for the first time in 1983.[18] According to G. White, these changes represented an important move from the position of putting the state's interests first, as in the past, to a position where workers' individual interests are protected by relatively autonomous organizations.[19] There was apparently a move from the direct management of enterprise by its Party-state "owners" to democratic governance by workers who began to participate in management and administration with the factory director as "managers," and the Party also stepped down from its position as an advisory council.[20] However, it should be noted that in the process of groping toward democratic trade unions, the Party-state utilized the traditional Chinese value of the "home" (the workers' home) in organizing and mobilizing workers' organizations at grass roots workplaces toward achieving the "Four Modernizations." It was no doubt the Communist Party of China which played the father's role in executing the leadership inside "workers home." Even if the Party-state no longer directly managed enterprise under the guise of "party guidance," it remained unchanged under the new name of "governmental guidance."

Progress toward societal corporatism and the momentum of trade union reform

The Thirteenth National Congress of the Communist Party of China (October 1987) once again affirmed the basic posture that the trade unions' functions fulfilled an important role in the socialist democratic lifestyle as a "bridge" or "belt" between the working class and the Party in a corporatist framework. In October of the following year, the Eleventh Trade Union Congress emphasized the importance of trade unions fulfilling their role as pluralistic groups, and stated that as a social power for promoting reform, trade unions should get actively involved in multileveled political participation, and implement supervision of the state and society. Regarding those activities, the emphasis was placed on low-level fringe organizations, and it was decided that they should achieve more results in cities to expand external cooperation, while preserving their independence.[21]

The climax of trade union reform before the Tiananmen incident came in July 1988 at the Thirteenth Leadership Conference of the Tenth All-China Trade Union Congress. The debate focused on how trade unions themselves could participate in trade union reform. As a result of this discussion, the "Basic Thoughts on Trade Union Reform" was adopted in outline, and the plan was formally adopted at the Sixth Executive Session of the Tenth All-China Trade Union Congress in September 1988. First, the plan demanded further reform at trade unions against the backgrounds of complicated social contradictions and the diversification of social interests caused by the reform of the economic system, and called upon trade unions to realize their social role in promoting ambitious and appropriate reform. Second, the plan clarified the trade unions' social role in advocating workers' legitimate interests as well as democratic rights in participating in workers reform. It also emphasized the importance of fulfilling the duties of economic and social development, participating in the management of the state and society, as well as participating in the democratic management of enterprise business units. Third, the plan assigned Chinese trade unions to establish independent, democratic working class mass organizations that could be trusted by workers under the leadership of the Communist Party. It also advocated that the goal of trade union reform was to create a socio-political organization that would fulfill the important duties of civil and state life. Fourth, as an immediate reform, the plan proposed to change the trade unions' external relationships with a particular focus on correcting the relationship between the administration and the government, as well as the unions' relationship with the Party. Finally, the plan also called for the trade unions to develop a closer relationship with the masses for the purpose of promoting a deeper commitment to trade unions' self-reform.[22]

The Tiananmen incident in 1989, however, brought all of the reform processes to an abrupt halt, including the factory director responsibility system and the "Basic Thoughts on Trade Union Reform." The daily activities of grass roots trade unions were never systemized, and trade union reform ended with no major achievements. It is true that the trade union reform process played an important role in widening the area of relatively free activity and increasing the level of independence in trade unions until it reached its peak in 1989. However, it should be noted that this initiative was originated in the "upper realm" of the ACFTU and Party hierarchy. It was not independently and autonomously set in motion from "the bottom." The entire process was consistently placed "under the leadership of the Communist Party of China," and therefore this should not be understood as an experiment with a formula for civil society which permits a certain type of political pluralism. Instead, it was to the end no more than one process in a movement toward societal corporatism permeated by the Party-state. In addition, the movement was no more than a tentative trial promoted within the larger framework of state corporatism. In short, it is not appropriate to view the process as having established a societal corporatist system between workers and Party-state.

Industrial relations in nonstate-owned enterprises

After the Tenth Trade Union Congress (1983), the development of the Party's policy of opening the country to foreign businesses was accompanied by an accelerated establishment of trade unions in nonstate-owned enterprises such as the three-capital enterprises (Chinese–foreign joint venture, joint production, foreign-funded independent business), township enterprises, etc., and by 1985 approximately 2,000 three-capital enterprises had been established. Union organization rates reached 70% in the Xiamen Special Economic Zone, 60% in Shantou, 40% in Zhuhai, and 72.4% in Shenzhen. At the same time, 30,000,000 people were employed in township enterprises by the end of 1993, but only 19,600 enterprises had organized unions, and the organization rate for the country's 123 million urban workers had not exceeded a paltry 1.5% (1,830,000 people).[23] Furthermore, there was a close relationship between the township enterprises' union leaders and managers, and it was exceedingly rare for them to come from the general pool of workers. In the majority of cases, they came from among assistant factory directors or middle managers who overlapped with the Party cadre.[24] According to a fact-finding survey by the Chinese Academy of Social Sciences, in 63% of town enterprises the local government chose the factory director, in 17% the workers' enterprise congress elected the factory director, and in the remaining 20% the enterprise's board of directors appointed the factory director. Looking at these figures, it is clear that direct or indirect intervention by local government accounted for the majority of these appointments.[25] In 1993, 1,958 enterprises established labor dispute arbitration systems, but only 586 locations actually dealt with labor disputes. Only a few trade unions answered that they had exercised the worker's fundamental rights to collective bargaining and labor agreements.[26]

From the very beginning, township enterprises were created with a view to eliminating the surplus labor pool of 150,000,000 persons which was concentrated in rural villages, and a policy was adopted in 1984 based on the principle "leave the farm, not the village" which recognized the migration from rural villages to small industrial cities. Due to the economic squeeze in 1989, however, township enterprises were faced by bankruptcy and economic slowdown, and farmers left the agricultural industry and farming villages to rush into the cities.

As symbolized by the paralysis of its functions, it was clear that the economic effectiveness and flexibility of its labor-absorbing system was insufficient.[27] Furthermore, the farming villages' surplus labor caused a partition of the socio-economic system into center and periphery, city and country, haves and have-nots, and this problem known as "Latin Americanization of China" was identified across the country with a widespread attention around the world.[28] The farmers, who at first entered the cities in a disorderly fashion, were soon organized by domestic labor delivery contractors, and within this organizational structure began to work as "agricultural migrant workers." This caused the social phenomenon known as the "migrant worker flood," and the three rural problems (farming villages' slow development, the impoverishment of farmers, and the agricultural industry crisis) came under close scrutiny.

In the later half of the 1990s, however, the reform of state-owned enterprises caused increasing numbers of layoffs among urban workers. In cities, the "agricultural migrant workers," the unemployed, and the newly laidoffs began to compete among themselves for their own interests, and a "race to the bottom" expanded to a large extent.[29] In 1993, the agricultural migrant work force numbered 70,000,000, but it had skyrocketed to 140,000,000 by 2003. This was not just because the majority of these workers pursued low-wage work on construction sites and at other 3D (difficult, dirty, dangerous) jobs that urban workers normally avoided. Even if the agricultural migrant workers' employment agent had signed an individual contract with the employer, there existed no contract between the agent and the worker in most of the cases. As a result, most of the agricultural migrant workers were used by urban workers as virtually "second class citizens," and as seen in discriminatory treatments such as wage defaults and kickbacks, poor working conditions, work-related accidents and occupational diseases, and the denial of education for women and children.[30]

At the ACFTU's Fourteenth Trade Union Congress in September 2003, agricultural migrant workers were officially granted social recognition as "new members of the urban working class," and the problem of introducing farmers into trade unions was addressed as an urgent topic for trade unions. In areas such as Shanghai, Guangdong, Xinjiang, Suzhou, and Hangzhou where the migrant flood was concentrated, approximately 40 trade unions for agricultural migrant workers (migrant workers' associations) were established. Each was placed under the leadership of the local branch of the ACFTU, and at each location about 34,000,000 migrant workers were enrolled in these trade unions each month.[31]

The Fifteenth National Party Congress in September 1997 had taken a positive position on the ownership economy and a nonplanned economy, while advocating the reorganization and curtailment of the managed economy. Afterwards, profits continued to increase by downsizing, not by state-owned enterprise reform. This decision caused a large number of workers to become unemployed, and therefore the number of petitions, strikes, demonstrations, and other cases of agitation by workers' organizations increased very quickly. With the systematic adjustments that came with China's 2001 entrance into the World Trade Organization (WTO), the number of incidents continued to grow. At nonstate-owned enterprises which mainly employ migrant workers, conflicts between labor and management were intensified daily, since they often developed into strikes due to the fact that labor laws were not effectively applied.[32] In the first half of 2002, for example, incidents of agitation involving over 100 people, including enterprise workers, staff, and retirees, increased 53% across the country over the same period in 2001, and the number of participants reached 162,000, 2.6 times more. Among those, there were 39 incidents involving organizations of over 1,000 people, 3.9 times larger than 2001. The number of participants in these incidents was 102,000, 4.4 times more than 2001. In 2003, participation in labor incidents by laidoff workers and retirees' associations topped 1,440,000 people. Combined participation in labor agitation by various organizations across the country reached a high record of 46.9%. It was much easier to strike in enterprises that were not state-owned, and frequent protests against unpaid wages, low wages, and unfavorable working conditions became quite common. In October 2004, for example, 4,000 people went on strike and blockaded the roads to protest low wages at Shenzhen's Hong Kong owned Meizhi Haiyan Electronics Factory. In addition, strikes among taxi drivers quickly spread across China. The strikes were not just directed against the government agencies that presided over transportation policies. The striking drivers in certain parts of the country even attempted to enforce a socially effective unified group action, which resulted in destructive activities against drivers who continued with regular business operations instead of participating in the strike.[33]

This sudden increase in the trend toward labor agitation by Chinese workers' groups caused a great deal of social unrest which resulted in a serious problem accompanying an unhealthy influence on coordinated socio-economic development. These protest activities by a few workers' groups greatly exceeded the framework of societal corporatism, and some may argue that this can be seen as a manifestation of a concrete trend toward the formation of civil society that makes it possible for the working poor to take initiative from the "bottom-up." The most important point, however, is that these fierce strikes were mostly "autonomous" decisions by the working poor, not strikes organized by trade unions. As discussed above, the ACFTU certainly took a first step toward organizing agricultural migrant labor, but even if the ACFTU had been helpful in doing something for the neglected and socially unempowered, "unorganized" workers such as the unemployed, laidoff, and migrant workers, their priority should have been given to protecting the interests of "organized" urban workers. For ACFTU, therefore, protecting and developing the concrete interests of "organized" urban workers and the interests of "unorganized" workers at the same time created contradictory results that were fundamentally opposed. Thus, the reward of "organized" urban workers for submitting to "a certain amount of control" by the Party-state and the government authorities was that they received representational monopoly under the umbrella of the ACFTU, whereas the overwhelming number of unorganized migrant and unemployed workers existed outside of the corporatist interest exchange system and were completely excluded from the "privileged status and income"[2] that was available only through trade union membership.

Societal corporatism or civil society?

The Tiananmen incident and the role of trade unions

It was in June 1989 around the time of the Tiananmen incident that autonomous trade unions were born for the first time in the history of PRC. Their influence on the course of the movement was significant, and the most famous group among them was the Beijing Workers' Autonomous Federation (BWAF). In May 1989 at Tiananmen Square, staff from the ACFTU called for the increased independence of trade unions and put up posters stating that "trade unions should work and speak for the workers and masses." They also held a "dialogue meeting" with the students to support the students' hunger strike by contributing 100,000 RMB to the Red Cross.[34] However, the advent of alternative trade unions which suggested the insufficiency of the existing trade unions and symbolized the extent of the workers' sense of neglect set off alarms among the upper echelon of the Party's leadership and within the ACFTU.[35] As soon as the Beijing Workers' Autonomous Federation was established, the authorities promptly cracked down on the "illegitimate use of the working class's name, and the plans to overturn the people's government." Regarding this decision, the AFCTU's president, Ni Zhifu, announced on one hand an opinion that reflected a "top-down" inclination: "China's trade unions must work under the leadership of the CCP, and no trade unions in opposition to the CCP are allowed to be established." But on the other hand, he strove to reconcile "top-down" concerns regarding the dangerous situation caused by the advent of autonomous trade unions with an emphasis on the importance of protecting workers' interests and rights, stating that "the trade unions must avoid simply acting as agents of the government and work independently so as to increase their attractiveness to workers and enjoy more confidence from the workers, leaving no opportunity for those who attempt to organize 'independent trade unions'."[36] However, the ACFTU's activities before and after the Tiananmen incident did nothing more than "cement" the bond between workers and the Party, and after June 4, the ACFTU resumed its role as a voluble supporter of Party policy and the mounting discussions of independence for the trade union movement that had been conducted for the previous year or two were completely silenced.[37]

In 1992, the Trade Union Law was passed, and this allowed a certain level of independent activities for trade unions, while it also affirmed ACFTU as the only legal trade union without the right to strike.[38] It made it possible for trade unions to operate with government activities by participating in the management of the state, economy, and cultural enterprises. The law also stipulated that trade unions should defend the interests of all the people while simultaneously protecting the legal interests of workers. They are also entitled to supervise the "democratic" management of enterprise in possessing the right of disagreement, mobilizing workers, extending competition between workers, and increasing the labor productivity.

From the start, the new trade union law originated from a movement to demand new regulations after a few trade union executives had complained about the Party's interference in a 1987 enterprise-level trade union election. At the Thirteenth

Party Congress, Zhao Ziyang's reformist faction had supported the movement for increased trade union autonomy and reform of the unions' political framework, and at the Eleventh Trade Union Congress in 1988, the ACFTU demanded a readjustment of the relationship between the trade unions, the Party, and the government. At the same meeting, the beginning of a leadership system in seek of more reforms was announced, and several actual experimental reforms were launched, but the Tiananmen Square incident forced these events into retreat.[39] Consequently, the 1992 Trade Union Law enacted after these events has turned out to be half-hearted. In the case of management, considerable progress has been made through enterprise legislation and regulation to enhance its autonomy, but in the case of trade unions, it is most probable that their subjection to Party domination has been increased since the turmoil of 1989, because their rights to act industrially seem to have been weakened by the Trade Union Law of 1992.[40] In that sense, it is difficult to dismiss the impression that the nature of the 1992 Trade Union Law was completely different from the original intentions that inspired the law before the Tiananmen incident.

Reversion to national corporatism

During the drafting of the 1994 Labour Law, which followed the passage of the Trade Union Law, a tripartite meeting was held among the China Enterprise Directors Association (the current China Enterprise Confederation), the government, and the ACFTU. As social partners, each group's ideas were largely represented.[41] The resulting law assigned the state to carry out measures in promoting employment opportunities, developing and maintaining labor standards, social security, labor and management relations, improving workers' living standards, promoting competition between workers, and carrying out constructive proposals to increase work productivity. For the workers, the law established the right to protect the legal rights of workers which allowed workers to participate in equal consultation with employers.[42]

According to the Labour Law, the trade unions' primary duties were set to mobilize, organize, and educate union members in order to increase enterprise productivity by promoting labor competition. The main emphasis was put on increasing productivity by strengthening the management system. It is true that the individual interests of union members were protected, but those interests were normally understood as a secondary benefit that would only be realized after achieving all of the interests for both the enterprise and the state. With a view to planning for a reorganization of the economy for the post-Tiananmen environment, the ACFTU retreated into an original position of state corporatism that maintained and protected the Central Party's leadership policies in encouraging workers to "spontaneously" mobilize. In 1994, for example, the newly formed "League for the Protection of Working People's Rights" demanded that the right to strike be incorporated into the text of the new law. It was perhaps a foreseeable development that the authorities did not recognize the groups' registration under the "Provision on the Registration of Social Organizations," and the group was denounced as a "counter-revolutionary organization."[43]

Unlike state-owned enterprises, foreign-owned enterprises had exempted from the obligation to institute the workers' representative congress in the workplace, and therefore trade unions acted as the workers' only representatives. A Party branch cannot function as an official organ in a joint venture, and so the Party secretary or deputy secretary usually serves instead as the trade union chair. In other words, the joint venture's trade union has basically incorporated the functions that are normally performed by the Party branch.[44] At the Twelfth Trade Union Congress in 1993, the ACFTU decided that trade unions would protect the rights and political status of workers in foreign enterprises at the time of signing collective agreements in cooperation with managers for the purpose of enterprise development. It also assigned trade unions to supervise the observation of laws and rules regarding wages, working hours, social insurance, etc. in view of promoting the early stages of trade union development in existing enterprises. The result of this effort was that by 1990 unions had been established in 41.9% of the foreign-funded enterprises in Guangdong's three special economic zones, 43% of those enterprises' employees had joined unions, and in the Shenzhen special economic zone, unions had been organized in 96% of foreign-funded enterprises employing over 25 people.[45] By 1993, there were only 8,260 trade unions in foreign-funded enterprises, and the organization rate did not exceed a modest 10%, but by 1994, organization of trade unions was refocused on and began to be prompted, and new trade unions were organized at 24,700 (37%) of the country's 75,500 foreign-funded enterprises. Over 90% of the strikes that occurred at that time were said to have been at privately owned enterprises that had not yet organized trade unions.[46] Amidst the increase and intensification of labor disputes, the "Temporary Provisions Concerning the Handling of Labour Disputes in State Run Enterprises" was replaced with the "Regulations of the People's Republic of China Concerning the Handling of Labour Disputes in Enterprises" (1993), a unified standard which explicated principles, mechanisms, and methods for labor dispute resolution, regardless of ownership including foreign-funded enterprises.[47]

In the second half of 1990s, the ACFTU vigorously expanded its labor dispute arbitration activities, and 74.6% of unions across the nation had set up by 1997 just under 290,000 grass roots labor dispute arbitration committees. Labor dispute arbitration committee organization rates for state-owned enterprises reached over 80%.[48] Following 1998's activities, emphasis was placed on strengthening relationships between labor and management. Above all, emphasis was placed on management activities that promoted democratic conferences with each enterprises' workers' enterprise congress, and new progress was seen in the conclusion of labor agreements, the regulation of industrial relations, and the establishment of equitable negotiations between labor and management.[49] At the Thirteenth Trade Union Congress in October 1998, there was an announcement about the leadership policy for the next five years and the unions' historical duties. Due to the substantial changes in labor and management relationships, it was decided that trade unions should improve supervisory systems which enable workers' democratic participation in encouraging legislation regarding the establishment of cooperative systems between workers and management. It was also considered significant to promote the reemployment of laidoff workers, construction of a social security system, and the organization of workers.[50]

By increasing the activities of fringe unions, ACFTU as well as the government attempted to create both the stability of "top-down" state corporatism, and simultaneously a "bottom-up" system that took into account workers' dissatisfaction. Of the approximately 200 million Chinese urban workers, about half were not unionized, and the majority of these worked in newly established nonpublic enterprises. In November of 2001, the government undertook a plan to raise the number of unionized workers in private industry from 14,300,000 to 36,000,000 by 2002. The invigoration of trade union activity was no longer just "top-down," but had also spread to the field.[51] By June 2002, the number of enterprise-level trade unions across the nation had climbed to 1,660,000, with 600,000 new unions in state-owned enterprises and 1,030,000 in new nonstate-owned enterprises. The number of union members reached 131,540,000, with 88,110,000 coming from state-owned enterprises and 39,620,000 from newly established private enterprises.[52] In 2001, the 1992 Trade Union Law was amended, and the changes added legal procedures for making management complaints against employers and even more regulations concerning workers rights. On the other hand, articles concerning workers' obligations such as "trade unions shall . . . uphold leadership by the Communist Party of China, and Marxist-Leninism, Mao Zedong Thought and Deng Xiaoping Theory" were also newly incorporated. It can therefore be inferred that the government once again attempted to achieve the stability of state corporatism by placing ideological limits on social rights of workers.[53]

In November 2001, when China joined the WTO, its already cheap labor force was exposed to global market competition, and inevitably the domestic employment situation and guarantees of workers' rights and interests came under even more pressure.[54] Recorded urban unemployment rates in the years from 1999 to 2002 were 3.1%, 3.1%, 3.6%, and 4.0%, respectively. At the end of March 2003, they surpassed the historical high to become 4.1%. The number of urban unemployed for the entire country increased from 750,000 to 7,750,000[55] between 2002 and 2003. The number of labor disputes across the nation also increased. The number of labor disputes received by labor dispute arbitration committees at every level reached 184,000 by 2002, with the number of participating workers climbing to 610,000, respectively 19.1% and 30.2% higher than the previous year.[56] China's participation in the WTO propelled economic development, trade system reform, adjustment of the economic structure, and privatization of enterprise, and as a result, labor and management relations again fell into an uneasy state of affairs. In November 2004, amid concerns about deteriorating working conditions at foreign-funded enterprises, the ACFTU confronted Chinese locations of WalMart, which is well known for obstructing the establishment of trade unions. The ACFTU declared: "They [WalMart] are in violation of the Trade Union Law, and we are prepared to sue them." WalMart yielded, conceding that, "if workers ask to establish a trade union, we will respect that request, and fulfill our duties and responsibilities under the Trade Union Law." This landmark event demonstrated not only the ACFTU's power in a direct confrontation, but also its opposition to the intensifying WTO-driven competition in the Chinese labor market. Thus far, the power of trade unions in general and the ACFTU in particular has been felt primarily at foreign-funded enterprises.[57]

The implication of "Asian" corporatism

The Chinese Party-state system of state corporatism was created even before 1960, but it is important to note that it was established as a "moving body," and that it has also shown some movements toward societal corporatism. Therefore, it cannot truly be described as a "system," but nor can we speak of a Chinese corporatism as some stable institutional *fait accompli*.[58] This is a substantial difference between China and other socialist nations such as the former Soviet Union. The authoritarian and subordinate character of Chinese corporatism is not always identical with Schmitter's definition of state (or societal) corporatism, which has mainly been applied in analyzing western societies. Instead, it has an Asian bias and is perhaps a unique system that should be called "East Asian corporatism." As in A. Walder's analysis of Chinese industrial bureaucracy which makes use of Max Weber's concept of "traditional authority," it could be called "neo-traditionalism," the unification of patrimonial control and modern bureaucratic control.[59] From early on, East Asia's Confucian culture has regarded individual and private interests as "selfish." These personal interests were transcended by the greater good, and therefore a "father-knows-best" type of moral paternalism had been predominant in this region.[60]

It is generally thought that Confucianism as a social ethic lies at the root of East Asian traditional and family values. H. Zeigler who analyzed the relationship between Confucianism and corporatism pointed out that the idea of Confucian was to use the paradigm of the family to construct the ideal government, and that a harmony occurs when all esteem the legitimate authority and superior moral position of the male head of the family, and therefore there is in Confucian thought a strong sense of "consensus politics," rather than the conflict so central to pluralism. The emphasis is on hierarchical relationships, and there is no need for balancing power between competing groups, since such groups were by definition "usurpers of legitimate authority."[61] It was exactly for this reason that even those autonomous trade unions that appeared during the Tiananmen Square crisis behaved contrary to Schmitter and O'Donnell's general prediction. In the majority of cases, Schmitter and O'Donnell considered that the biggest challenge to a transitional system was a new or revived sense of solidarity and ability to act collectively among the working class and lower class employees organized by trade unions, but what followed in China was not the creation of institutions that represent class in a "civil society." Instead, the goals of the movement in China were limited to a certain level of independence from the Party-state, and a better negotiable system in societal corporatism that would realize personal demands for "higher wages, improved working conditions, and the cessation of arbitrary employment and dismissal policies."[62] It is therefore extremely difficult to demonstrate a correlation between the institutional framework of corporatism and Confucianism. Nevertheless, there seems no choice but to acknowledge that behind this sense of familial values lies a Chinese traditionalism that has long been normalized as a system of social ethics as described earlier.

China's Party-state and corporatism

The legitimacy of rule and trade unions as a variable

Starting in the 1980s, the nation shifted toward Deng Xiaoping's modernization policy, which was adopted as part of democratization process that received a substantial setback at Tiananmen Square in 1989. There was apparently a workers' movement to reestablish an independent (autonomous) ACFTU, but the governmental position has not been appraised as having had the potential to create a breakthrough to a "civil society." It is even difficult to regard the autonomous trade unions that appeared during the peak of the Tiananmen Square protest movement as an indication of the development of an independent society.[63] Analysts' opinions are therefore divided on whether or not the state of affairs surrounding the Party and ACFTU after the peak of the democratization process should be understood as a type of state corporatism.[64] However, as has been seen so far, if there was any deviation from state corporatism, the only thing is that the ACFTU's path was split between the decision to regard its mediation structure of interest as a "dependent variable" or to regard it as an "independent variable." It was precisely for this reason that a strongly independent trade union movement like syndicalism (independent variable) has been prevented by all of China's authorities. Moreover, the only political body that held the power to decide whether the ACFTU was a "dependent variable" or "independent variable" was the legitimate Party-state. For this reason, the longevity of pluralistic groups that depended on the state was effectively limited. Societal corporatism would develop and become stable to the point of institutionalizing government's involvement in a limited number of autonomous groups or organs, but the question of what groups will be allowed to exist under what conditions is ultimately limited by the authorities.[65] Conversely, during the times when control by the Party-state was relaxed, the corporatist institutions that had already existed in society may lose their original stabilization functions, and they might reach a crossroads whether or not to expand their independence, as well as whether civil society be established or corporatism be maintained. In the history of industrial relations in China, however, the ubiquitous Chinese Communist Party-state suppressed the blooming of civil society, and because the formation of cooperation between the classes was difficult and considered even dangerous, a tripartite system of corporatism constituted by the Party-state, enterprise, and the ACFTU (workers) has remained unchanged until today.[66]

Comparison between Chinese and Eastern European trade unions

When compared with some cases of democratization in Eastern Europe, China-related questions seem to become especially salient. What made the Polish democracy movement possible, for example, was the combination of the "bottom-up" demands for democratization from the autonomous trade union "Solidarity," and the "top-down" or "counter-reformation" plan (tolerance for societal corporatism) for reorganization of the entire system which brought about social initiatives to the state. To become "free trade unions," "Solidarity" concluded the Gdansk Agreement (1980) which forced the government to recognize civil society which should not be controlled by the Party in exchange for recognizing "the role of Party's leadership" in the domain of the state. This established a paradoxical mechanism firmly embedded in the state, which was developing societal corporatism to some degrees, but finally rolling back the state by breaking through into civil society.[67] In comparison, because union leaders in China had a vested interest (monopoly of representation) in receiving the same treatment as government bureaucrats, there was a tendency for them to represent the "enterprise" instead of the "workers." The pact concluded between the Party and the ACFTU, which had been forced to change after the Tiananmen incident had no substantial effect other than to secure a degree of influence over the reform policy for trade union leaders. Therefore, their own positions would not have been endangered, as it was almost impossible for them to lose the vested interests which they had gained by living in the iron cage of the Chinese government.[68]

If the ideological roots of Poland's civil society can be found in "Catholic personalism," then this formed the basis of the movement that called for a "third way" founded on social solidarity and deep interpersonal relationships which criticized both depersonalized "liberalistic individualism" and "Marxist-Leninism." In comparison, as M. Weber said, this Christian personalism (persönlichkeit) finds its antithesis in China's Confucian humanism (menschlichkeit), since a "Confucian code of conduct" is deeply rooted in Chinese society which ultimately knows no social duty other than the duty of human deference (menschliche Pietätflichten) created by "the friendly relationships between one person to another, lord and vassal, superior and subordinate, father and child, teacher and student." Therefore, "there existed no middle way to provide guidance from the Confucian ethics which, like Christianity, had put down strong roots to a civil way of life."[69] Nevertheless, after a series of Eastern Europe's democratic revolutions, industrial relations began to change along with the expansion of the EU starting from the case in Poland. Regardless of the country, the workers' movements have been stagnated, and the cause of this stagnation is now considered to be the result of consolidation of tripartism, or a type of neo-corporatism that encouraged peaceful compromise between workers and employers.[70] This is especially important when considering the two-faced political function of corporatism which may differ from region to region to some degree according to the actual conditions.

The possibility of civil society in China

If the state's support of movement "from the bottom to the top" is one of civil society's important roles, it is difficult to find evidence of the Chinese state's active movement toward this goal up to this point. It is normally understood that the relationship between the state and society is intermediated by the concept of legitimacy, in other words, the fact that whether the "state's existence is predicated on its submission to the representatives of the society" or "the state substitutes itself for society and legitimates itself through some political project such as social revolution or economic development."[71] In China, however, the "representational doctrine" of the state standing-in for society has been predominant until today. In contrast with the rapidly changing "economic system," the "political system" has maintained a strong Party-state framework. The ACFTU has suffered from a painful dilemma of their own by calling for a careful "top-down" move to corporatism, while simultaneously meeting the "bottom-up" demands of workers whose eyes have been opened to protecting their own interests under the harsh environment of the market economy. However, the right to distribute social and state legitimacy is still limited to the function of the state. As referred to A. Chan, the state is so powerful that the top-down transmission of party directives regularly suppresses the bottom-up transmissions relating to workers' interests.[72] Nevertheless, industrial relations in foreign-funded enterprises have been characterized clearly closer to the West's than those in state-owned enterprises, since they are not state employers, nor the unclear employers in township enterprises, but employers whose class is clearly defined as capitalists who are engaged in bargaining. For instance, from 1988 to 1994, the number of strikes recorded at foreign-funded enterprises (primarily Asian) rose to 250,000.[73] Moreover, it is important to note that, because industrial relations in these foreign-funded enterprises were tied into the governments' official system, they may become a "blessing in disguise."[74] In other words, there is a paradoxical mechanism in the process of creation of civil society which makes it possible for pluralist groups such as independent trade unions to come into being, as the more stable rule the authorities may desire by completing the formation of corporatism, the more will they be on the brink of breaking through to a civil society.

Conclusion

What has become clear in this chapter is that the existence of "labor autonomy" still remains questionable at this stage in Chinese trade unions. Analysts both in and outside of China agree that democratic reform from the perspective of improving relationships between the workers' enterprise congress and the ACFTU has greatly contributed to the improvement of "labor autonomy." Even if one can positively assess the meaning of internal reform from an "appointment system" to an "elective system" at the workers' representative congresses, it should be noted that Party's democratic centralist system has not been discarded, and it has enormously negative implications for trade unions' autonomy.[75] An even more fundamental problem, therefore, is the actual condition of the Party-state's authority which still resides inside the trade unions to control the workers' representative congresses. As long as the ACFTU does not institute some kind of internal reform, it will be difficult to deny workers' demands for autonomous trade unions. Consequently, it is possible that authorities would allow the ACFTU to expand trade unions' freedom all the way from the central administration to the regional grass roots in a fashion close to societal corporatism. What is important to note in this respect is the relationship between China and the ILO, the international social democratic organ that functions as an external international norm.

After 1985, the Chinese Department of Labour and Social Security, the ACFTU, and the China Enterprise Management Association (the current China Enterprise Confederation) carried out ILO technical cooperation projects in the fields of employment, working conditions, industrial relations, social security, etc., and in recent years high priority has been placed on the "establishment of a sound industrial relations system," and there has been an aggressive expansion of related activities.[76] Even though it is a western-style system free from a direct political relationship with the government, the neo-corporatist tripartism proposed by the ILO is very attractive to the Chinese authorities, because it would stabilize industrial relations by putting them into a fixed framework, and it could proactively disarm the potential threat posed by an outbreak of informal trade unions. However, the Chinese government has either simply not ratified or has shown no intention of ratifying the ILO conventions that enshrines basic rights such as the "Freedom of Association and Protection of the Right to Organize" (Convention 87) and the "Right to Organize and Collective Bargaining" (Convention 98) as fundamental principles. As a result, it is difficult to deny the impression that the government is only utilizing a corporatist facade to maintain stable industrial relations.

In the 1990s, a tripartite system (government, trade unions, employers' associations) of participation was institutionalized in the legislative process regarding labor-related issues, and the ACFTU has represented the rights of workers around the nation actively in participating in labor legislation. In 1999, the Chinese Enterprise Confederation was officially established and assumed a role in the tripartite system as China's representative employers' association. It is true that the National Tripartite Consultative Committee was established in 2001,[77] but as is the case with Japan's "enterprise unions," the activities of workers' congresses at individual workplaces are limited to inside factories and enterprises without external and unified behavior or actions around the nation and industries. Furthermore, unlike Germany's "codetermination system" and "joint management council" or France's "enterprise associations" and "employee representatives," they do not have the power to legislate as a group independent of government control in negotiating with the management in China.[78] As discussed above, the workers' representative congresses and trade unions under the umbrella of the ACFTU are not linked together in a politically independent system, and they are isolated from the outside like Japan's "enterprise-based unions."[79] Therefore, the Chinese industrial relations system can be interpreted like the revisionist statement that "workers do not participate in the country's policy decisions"[80] or the position that "corporatism without labor" remains exclusive from participating in all policy formulations,[81] despite the fact that ACFTU has represented workers in participating in labor legislation process through a "top-down" approach. J. Shen and J. Benson also point out that, although tripartite consultation has become widely established in China, enterprise-level unions are still considered to be a part of enterprise management and that they tend to protect the economic interests of employers, since unions and workers' representatives at that level are dependent on enterprise management. This often results in the situation in which the tripartite consultation system has hardly been in a position to act as impartial mediators in labor dispute resolution.[82]

Although it seems that the extent of the current ACFTU's political influence on government is quite limited, it will become impossible to escape from demands to increase "trade union autonomy" from the bottom, as "management autonomy" expands with the development of socialist market economy. In fact, a substantial change between managements and workers has been seen in an enactment of the Labour Contract Law, which came into effect in 2008. It mainly set out the formation, amendment, and termination of employment contracts between employers and employees, with a view to strengthening in particular the protection of workers' interests against the background of increasing number of agricultural migrant workers in an extremely weak position. The law is normally interpreted as contributing to improvement of their deteriorated working conditions as well as strengthening the position of other ordinary workers. Some may argue here if the adoption of new labor laws is much more useful and effective in protecting and enhancing the workers' independent status than doing something through trade unions' activities, but it is also true that the ACFTU has played a positive role in the drafting and adopting procedure of this law "from above."

In any case, the rationale of the ACFTU as a coordinator between state's and workers' interests will most probably be questioned sooner or later, since trade unions in a more liberalized society should serve exclusively for workers. Contrary to the intentions of authorities who hope to use the corporatist framework for the purpose of achieving political integration and stability, there are no geographical limitations on the paradoxical mechanism which may accomplish the breakthrough to a civil society, and this will make it possible for autonomous trade unions and other pluralist groups to come into being. Therefore, even if China and Eastern Europe do not share the same political (cultural) system, it is too early to assert that China will not undergo the same political transformation as in Poland.

Notes

1 Alex Pravda and Blair A. Ruble (ed.), *Trade Unions in Communist States* (London: Allex & Unwin, 1986), p. 2.
2 Alan P. L. Liu, *Mass Politics in the People's Republic: State and Society in Contemporary China* (Boulder, Colorado: Westview Press, 1996), p. 90.
3 Philippe C. Schmitter and Gerhard Lehmbruch (ed.) (translated by Sadashi Yamaguchi), *Gendai Corporatism I* (Modern Corporatism I), (Tokyo: Bokutakuhsa, 1984), pp. 34–5. The attempts to use the concepts of corporatism in understanding the state

and society's relationship through the analysis on the status of trade unions under the Chinese socialist system were pioneered by Jonathon Unger, Anita Chan, and Gordon White. Unger and Chan held the position that after the establishment of modern China, the All China Federation of Trade Unions (ACFTU) had basically occupied a position consistent with state (Party-state) corporatism, and that there had been essentially no periods of social corporatism (Anita Chan, "Revolution or Corporatism? Workers and Trade Unions in Post-Mao China," *The Australian Journal of Chinese Affairs*, vol. 29, January 1993; Jonathan Unger and Anita Chan, "Corporatism in China: A Developmental State in an East Asian Context," in Barrett L. McCormic and Jonathan Unger (ed.), *China after Socialism in the Footsteps of Eastern Europe or East Asia?*; New York: An East Gate Book, 1996). While White accepts Chan's argument, he puts some distance between himself and her by arguing for corporatism from a position that is close to the theory of civil society (Gordon White, *Chinese Trade Unions in the Transition from Socialism: The Emergence of Civil Society or the Road to Corporatism?*; Brighton: Institute of Development Studies Working Paper, no. 18, 1995). On the other hand, Margaret Pearson, basing her argument on those of Chan and White, claims that socialist corporatism has two faces (Janus-faced): an organization similar to an enterprise management team is monopolized by the state, while maintaining a fixed autonomy, and is neither completely autonomous nor completely controlled by the state, thereby creating a "third domain" that exists between the state and society (Margaret M. Pearson, "The Janus Face of Business Associations in China: Socialist Corporatism in Foreign Enterprises," *The Australian Journal of Chinese Affairs*, no. 31, January 1994, pp. 25–46). In this respect, Steven Goldstein claims that in the theories of corporatism posited by Chan, White, *et al.*, there is an ambiguous separation between societal corporatism and democracy, and therefore the framework of the analytic paradigm asserting that economic change leads to pluralism and civil society is not sufficiently valid (Steven M. Goldstein, "China in Transition: The Political Foundations of Incremental Reform," in Andrew G. Walder (ed.), *China's Transitional Economy*, Oxford, New York: Oxford University Press, 1996, pp. 143–69). In China, Zhang Jing, Feng Tongqing, Zhang Yingyan, etc., also make reference to corporatism theory in connection with labor issues, but only to introduce the viewpoint of western researchers, and to this day the corporatism approach is not established as a general methodology in analyzing the relationship between state and society in China. (See Zhang Jing, *Fatun Zhuyi* (Corporatism), Beijing: Zhongguo Shehuikexue Chubanshe, 1988; Feng Tongqing, *Zhongguo Gongren de Mingyun* (Destiny of Chinese Workers), Beijing: Shehuikexue Wenxian Chubanshe, 2002; Zhang Yingyan, *Dangdai Zhongguo Ladongzhidu Bianhua yu Gonghui Gongneng Zhuangbian* (Change in the Contemporary Chinese Labour Institutions and Transformation of Trade Union's Function), Baoding: Hebei Daxue Chubanshe, 2004). One probable reason is that even if the concept of corporatism is defined by P. Schmitter's original theory, in the case of a practical application to China, it is always accompanied by the ambiguity noted by Goldstein. Regardless of the theorist, the question of whether corporatism is a part of the Chinese administrative system or an independent institution cannot yet be presented clearly enough.

4 Jeanne L. Wilson, "The People's Republic of China," in Alex Pravda and Blair A. Ruble (ed.), op. cit., p. 219.

5 Greg O'Leary, "The Making of the Chinese Working Class," in Greg O'Leary (ed.), *Adjusting to Capitalism: Chinese Workers and the State* (New York: M. E. Sharpe, 1998), p. 53.

6 Hiroshi Nakanishi, "Chugoku ni okeru Kigyo to Rodo" (Enterprise and Labour in China), in Yoshiyuki Sekiguchi (ed.), *Chugoku no Keizai Taisei (Reform of Economic System in China)* (Tokyo: University of Tokyo Press, 1992), pp. 236–7.

7 Anita Chan, "Revolution or Corporatism? Workers and Trade Unions in Post-Mao China," *The Australian Journal of Chinese Affairs*, vol. 29, January 1993, p. 37.

8 Jonathan Unger and Anita Chan, "Corporatism in China: A Developmental State in an East Asian Context," in Barrett L. McCormic and Jonathan Unger (ed.), op. cit., p. 105.

9 For example, B. Michael Frolic adopts a new concept of "State-Led Civil Society," but it is actually used in the same implication as corporatism. See B. Michael Frolic, "State-Led Civil Society," in Timothy Brook and B. Michael Frolic (ed.), *Civil Society in China* (New York: M. E. Scharp, 1997).

10 Atul Kohli and Vivienne Shue, "State Power and Social Forces: On Political Contention and Accommodation in the Third World" in Joel S. Migdal, Atul Kohli, and Vivienne Shue (eds), *State Power and Social Forces: Domination and Transformation in the Third World* (New York: Cambridge University Press, 1996), pp. 293–326.

11 Wang Yongxi (ed.), *Zhongguo Gonghuishi* (History of Chinese Trade Union) (Beijing: Zhonguo Dangshi Chubanshe, 1992), pp. 410–23.

12 Ibid., p. 426.

13 Ng Sek Hong and Malcolm Warner, *China's Trade Unions and Management* (London: Macmillan Press, 1998), p. 27.

14 Ibid., p. 74.

15 Ibid., p. 27.

16 Wang Yongxi (ed.), op. cit., pp. 430–1; Ng Sek Hong and Malcolm Warner, op. cit., pp. 28–9.

17 Li Shousei, *Chugoku Kokueikigyou no Keiei to Roshikankei: Tekkou Sangyou no Jirei 1950–90 Nendai* (Management and Industrial Relations of Chinese State-owned Enterprises: 1950s–90s Examples of Steel Industry) (Tokyo: Ochanomizu Shobo, 2000), p. 286.

18 Dangdai Zhongguo Congshu Bianji Weiyuanhui, *Dangdai Zhongguo Gongrenjieji he Gonghui Yundong* (Contemporary Chinese Working Class and Trade Union Movement), (Beijing: Dangdai Zhongguo Chunbanshe, 1997), vol.1, p. 615.

19 Gordon White, op. cit., p. 11.

20 Cf. Ken'ichi Imai, "Corporate Governance," *Gendai Chugoku no Kouzou Hendou* (Structural Transformation of Contemporary China) (Tokyo: University of Tokyo Press, 2000), vol. 2.

21 Wang Yongxi (ed.), op. cit., p. 448.

22 Ibid., pp. 450–52.

23 Ng Sek Hong and Malcolm Warner, op. cit., p. 49.

24 Chang Kai, *Laodongguanxi, Laodongzhe, Laoquan* (Labor Relations, Workers, The Right of Work) (Beijng: Zhongguo Laodong Chubanshe, 1995), p. 149.

25 Nihon Rodo Kenkyu Kikou, *Chugoku no Rodo Seisaku to Rodoshijou,* (Labour Policies and Labour Market in China) (Tokyo: Japan Institute of Labor, 1997), p. 255.

26 Chang Kai, op. cit., p. 151.

27 See my paper on the relationship between international labour market and Chinese domestic labour market. Katsu Yanaihara and Tatsufumi Yamagata, *Ajia no Kokusai Rodo Ido* (International Labour Migration in Asia) (Tokyo: Institute of Developing Economies, 1992).

28 See Xia Lian, *Fazhan zhong Guojia de Zhengzhi yu Fazhi* (Politics and Rule of Law in the Developing Countries) (Jinan: Shangdong Renming Chubanshe, 2003).

29 See Bai Nansheng and He Yupeng, "*Huixiang, haishi jincheng? Zhongguo Nongmin Laodongli Huiliu Yanjiu,*" in Li Peilin (ed.), *Nongmingong – Zhongguo Jincheng Nongmin de Jinji Shehui Fenxi* (Analysis on Social Economy of Working Farmers in China) (Beijing: Shehuikexue Wenxian Chubanshe, 2003).

30 Chui Chuanyi, "*Er Yuan Jiegou Xia de Nongmin Quanyi yu Shehui Guanli Gaige,*" *Souhu Caijing* (Souhu Finance Daily), 31 July 2003.

31 *Zhongguo Qingnian Bao* (China Youth Daily), 23 September 2003; *Shenzheng Shangbao* (Shenzheng Commerce Daily), 25 September 2003.

32   As for the current status of labor disputes in China, see Changkai, *Laoquan Lun – Dangdai Zhongguo Laodongguangxi Tiaozheng Yanjiu* (Right of Labour, Research on the Adjusting System of Labour Relations in Contemporary China) (Beijing: Zhongguo Laodong Shehuibaozhang Chubanshe, 2004), p. 293.

33   Qiaojian, "*Zhongguo Shichanghua Jinchengzhong de Laogong Qunti Shijian Fenxi* (Analysis on the Incidents of Working Mass in the Age of Marketization in China)," paper presented at 11th Social Asian Forum, October 2005, Taibei.

34   Gordon White, op. cit., p. 13; Ng Sek Hong and Malcolm Warner, op. cit., p. 54.

35   Jude Howell, "Trade Unions in China," in Greg O'Leary (ed.), op. cit., p. 160.

36   Ng Sek Hong and Malcolm Warner, op. cit., p.55.

37   Greg O'Leary, op. cit., p. 53. The International Confederation of Free Trade Unions (ICFTU) appealed the case of violent oppression exerted to the Beijing Workers' Autonomous Federation (BWAF) in the Tiananmen incident to the ILO's Committee on Freedom of Association in November 1989. As a result, the committee affirmed that in the registration system in which all the Chinese trade unions were registered, permission of the authorities went ahead of it, and that this was not simply the matter of procedure, but something against "freedom of association." Therefore, the committee strongly recommended suspension of death penalty to nine members of the BWAF. After this, a long political confrontation between the Chinese government and ICFTU through ILO continued for years. See *A Moment of Truth: Workers' Participation in China's 1989 Democracy Movement and the Emergence of Independent Unions* (Hong Kong: Hong Kong Trade Union Education Centre, 1990), pp. 155–79. In addition, a considerable number of papers have been published to analyze the Tiananment Square incident from the viewpoint of labor. Of these, about the delicate relations between workers and students in the incident, see E. Perry, "Intellectuals and Tiananmen: Historical Perspective on an Aborted Revolution," in Daniel Chirot (ed.), *The Crisis of Leninism and the Decline of the Left: The Revolutions of 1989* (Seattle and London: University of Washington Press, 1991); Andrew G. Walder and Gong Xiaoxia, "Workers in the Tiananmen Protests: The Politics of the Beijing Workers' Autonomous Federation," in op. cit.; Anita Chan, "Revolution or Corporatism? Workers and Trade Unions in Post-Mao China," op. cit.; Gordon White, "Prospects for Civil Society in China: A Case of Shaoshan City," *The Australian Journal of Chinese Affairs*, vol. 29, January 1993.

38   Ibid.

39   Jude Howell, "Trade Unions in China," in Greg O'Leary (ed.), op. cit., p. 159.

40   Greg O'Leary, op. cit., p. 61.

41   Anita Chan, op. cit., p. 53.

42   Ng Sek Hong and Malcolm Warner, op. cit., p. 60.

43   Masatsugu Matsuda, *Kaikaku Kaihou Seisaku ka no Roudojijyo* (Labour Affairs under Reform and Open-Door Policies), Rodo'undo, October 1995, p. 217.

44   Anita Chan, "Industrial Relations in Foreign-funded Ventures, Chinese Trade Unions, and the Prospects for Collective Bargaining," in Greg O'Leary (ed.), op. cit., p. 127.

45   Ng Sek Hong and Malcolm Warner, op. cit., p. 116. As for a case study on industrial relations in Guangdong province, see Stephen W. K. Chiu and Stephen J. Frenkel, *Globalization and Industrial Relations in China* (Bangkok: Regional Office for Asia and the Pacific, ILO, 2000); Anita Chan, *China's Workers under Assault – The Exploitation of Labour in a Globalizing Economy* (New York: M. E. Sharpe, 2001).

46   Chang Kai, *Laodongguanxi, Laodongzhe, Laoquan*, op. cit., p. 209.

47   Ma Chengsan, *Chugoku Shinshutsu Kigyo no Rodo Mondai; Nichibeiou Kigyo niyoru Kensho* (Labour Issues at Japanese Enterprises Investing in China: In Comparison with U.S. and European Countries) (Tokyo: JETRO, 2000), p. 58.

48   Gao Aidi, *Xin Zhongguo Gonghuishi: 1948–1998* (New History of Trade Union 1948–1998), Zhongguo Jingji Chubanshe, 1999, p. 153.

49   Ibid., p. 184.

50 Ibid., pp. 195–6.
51 *Gongren Ribao* (Workers' Daily), 12 November 2000.
52 Qiao Jian, *"Rodosha ni yoru Danketsuken no Houteki Hoshou to Jissen – Chugoku no Hi-kouyusei Kigyo niokeru Rodo Soshiki wo Reini ni"* (Legal Protection of Freedom of Association and its Practice – Example of Labour Organizations at Nonstate-Owned Enterprises), paper presented at 10th Social Asian Forum, October 2004, Seoul.
53 Akira Chishima, *"Chugoku no Rodohou Kaisei"* (Amendment of Chinese Trade Union Law), *Kaigai Rodo Jiho* (Overseas Labour Bulletin), April 2002.
54 As for the impact of China's joining WTO on the field of labour, see Chang Kai and Qiao Jian (ed.), *WTO: Laodong Quanyi Baozhang* (WTO: Protection of Workers' Rights) (Beijing: Gongren Chubanshe, 2001), Chan Kai (ed.), *Laozi Guangxi yu Laogong Zhengce* (Labour Relations and Labour Policies) (Beijing: Zhongguo Gongren Chubanshe, 2003).
55 National Bureau of Statistics, *Official Statistics on the Development of Labour and Social Security-related Activities 2002*; Ministry of Labour and Social Security, News Bulletin for the First 4 Months of 2003.
56 Qiao Jian, *"Xin Yilun Jiegou Tiaozhengxia de Laodong Guangxi ji Gonghui de Yinying Duice"* (Labour Relations and Response of Trade Union under a New Structural Adjustment), paper presented at 9th Social Asian forum, Shanghai, September 2003.
57 Anita Chan, "Recent Trends in Chinese Labour Issues: Signs of Change," *China Perspectives*, vol. 57, Jan–Feb 2005, pp. 15–17.
58 Gordon White, Jude Howell and Shang Xiaoyuan, *In Search of Civil Society: Market Reform and Social Change in Contemporary China* (Oxford: Clarendon Press, 1996), p. 213.
59 Andrew Walder, *Communist Neo-Traditionalism: Work and Authority in Chinese Industry* (Berkeley: University of California Press, 1988), p. 251.
60 Jonathan Unger and Anita Chan, "Corporatism in China: A Developmental State in an East Asian Context," Barrett L. McCormic and Jonathan Unger (ed.), *China after Socialism in the Footsteps of Eastern Europe or East Asia?* (Armonk: M. E. Sharpe, 1996), p. 99.
61 Harmon Zeigler, *Pluralism, Corporatism and Confucianism: Political Association and Conflict Regulation in the United States, Europe, and Taiwan* (Philadelphia: Temple University Press, 1988), pp. 24–5.
62 Schmitter and O'Donnell (translated by Hideko Magara and Masanobu Ido), *Minshuka no Hikaku Seijigaku: Ken'ishugi Shihai Igo no Seiji Sekai* (Comparative Politics of Democratization: The World of Politics after the Authoritarian Rule), pp. 135–6.
63 Elizabeth J. Perry, op. cit., p. 142.
64 Gordon White, op. cit., p. 20.
65 J. Linz (translated by Susumu Takahashi) *Zentaishugi Taisei to Ken'ishugi Taisei* (Totalitalian and Authoritarian Regimes) (Kyoto: Horitsubunkasha, 1995), pp. 143–4.
66. Anita Chan, "Revolution or Corporatism? Workers and Trade Unions in Post-Mao China," op. cit., p. 36.
67 Akira Kawahara, *Tou Chuou no Minshuka no Kouzou* (Structure of Democratization in East–central Europe) (Tokyo: Yushindo, 1993), pp. 16–29.
68 Gordon White, Jude Howell and Shang Xiaoyuan, op. cit., p. 64.
69 Max Weber, *Gesammelte Aufsätze zur Religionssoziologie* 1 (Tübingen: J.C.B. Mohr, 1920). E. Perry also referred to the same point. (Elizabeth J. Perry, "Intellectuals and Tiananmen: Historical Perspective on an Aborted Revolution," in Daniel Chirot ed., *The Crisis of Leninism and the Decline of the Left: The Revolutions of 1989* (Seattle and London: University of Washington Press, 1991), p. 142.
70 Stephen Crowly, "Explaining Labour Weakness in Post-communist Europe: Historical Legacies and Comparative Perspective, *East European Politics and Societies*, vol. 18, no. 3, pp. 394–429.

71   Chalmers A. Johnson (translated by Yoshihiko Nakamoto), *Rekishi wa Futatabi Haji-matta: Ajia ni okeru Kokusai Kankei* (History has Resumed: International Relations in Asia (Tokyo: Bokutakusha, 1994), p. 189.

72   Anita Chan, op. cit., p. 37.

73   Anita Chan and Irene Norlund, "Vietnamese and Chinese Labour Regimes: On the Road to Divergence," in Anita Chan, Benedict J. Tria Kerkvliet and Jonathan Unger (eds), *Transforming Asian Socialism: China and Vietnam Compared* (Lanham, Maryland: Rowman & Littefield Publishers, 1999), p. 213.

74   Ng Sek Hong and Malcolm Warner, op. cit., p.121.

75   Anita Chan, op. cit., p. 51.

76   *Brief Information on ILO Beijing Office* (Beijing: ILO Beijing, 2000).

77   Anita Chan, "A New China? Some Hope for Optimism for Chinese Labour," *New Labour Forum*, vol. 13, no. 3, Fall 2004.

78   Yoshiyuki Sekiguchi (ed.), *Chugoku no Keizai Taisei* (Reform of Economic System in China), op. cit., p. 242.

79   For example, T. W. Leung also identifies the same nature of the Japanese enterprise-based trade union in that of Workers Representative Congress in China. See Trini Wing-Yue Leung, "Trade Unions and Industrial Relations under Socialism in China," Gerd Schienstock, Paul Thompson and Franz Traxler (ed.), *Industrial Relations between Command and Market: A Comparative Analysis of Eastern Europe and China* (New York: Nova Science Publishers, 1997), p. 267.

80   Karel Van Wolferen (translated by Masaru Shinohara), *Nippon Kenryoku no Kouzou* (The Enigma of Japanese Power: People and Politics in a Stateless Nation) (Tokyo: Hayakawa Shobo, 1990).

81   T. J. Pempel, Tsunekawa and Keiichi Tsunekawa, "Corporatism without Labour," in Philippe C. Schmitter and Gerhard Lehmbruch (ed.), op. cit.

82   Jie Shen and John Benson, "Tripartite Consultation in China: A First Step towards Collective Bargaining?," *International Labour Review*, vol. 147, no. 2–3, pp. 231–48, 2008.

2 Direction of trade union reforms and corporatism in PRC: Based on a survey of primary trade union chairmen (2004–6)

Kazuko Kojima

Introduction: Corporatist theory and the Chinese trade union

The purpose of this chapter is to analyze the position and the functions of Chinese trade unions under marketization from both sides: the arguments for trade union reform and the actual condition as illustrated by a survey of primary (basic-level) trade union chairmen conducted between March 2004 and June 2006. The analyses will provide useful materials for considering the direction in which the Chinese corporatist system is going.

It was in the mid-1990s that the corporatism approach began to be applied in analyses of the Chinese socio-political structure. The optimism that once identified the social diversification in the age of reform and open-door policies as the germination of civil society stumbled upon the Tiananmen incident in 1989.[1] Instead, the corporatism approach has been adopted to pay more attention to the state' s initiatives in the formation and development of social groups, or to the state's control over society, and it has successfully offered a more plausible framework in analyzing China. For example, Tony Saich (1994) cautioned against the easy-going use of the civil society approach, and called the current system in China "Quasi state corporatism."[2]

Prior researches on the Chinese trade union have traced the above-described development of study on China. Although some analysts have presented favorable prospects concerning the trade unions' change into an interest group for workers or an important component of the civil society in the near future,[3] most of the studies since the mid-1990s have been more pessimistic about the trade union's reforms. For example, Andrew Walder (1992) analyzed the workers' participation in pro-democracy movements in 1989, and concluded that workers had not been given effective channels to transmit their interests despite the increasing necessities to institutionalize new channels adaptable to the new situation under reform and liberalization.[4] Anita Chan (1998) and Jude Howell (1998), who undertook research on the actual state of the trade union's activity at foreign-funded enterprises (FFEs), also reached restrained conclusions about the possibilities for the existing trade unions' role.[5] Ng Sek Hong and Malcolm Warner (1998) also examined the current situation, where trade union cadres were too involved in the privileged class of power elites to implement innovative ideas for fundamental reform.[6] Feng Chen (2003) analyzed the limitations of the trade unions' role as the representative of workers' interests in the mediation and arbitration process for labor disputes, and concluded that the behavior of the trade union was still constrained as an apparatus within the state corporatist structure.[7]

Regarding the future of the trade union and Chinese political regime, Chan (1993) warned that social disorder could result if the existing political structure was not innovated into the more democratic state corporatism within the next ten years. However, at the same time, she also suggested the possibility that a drastic change in the Chinese communist party (CCP) and in the government could realize the transition to a kind of societal corporatism (neo-corporatism) based on the coexistence of governmental, semi-governmental, and bottom-up organizations.[8] Chen (2003) also concluded that the only way to prevent violent direct action by the workers and the formation of other voluntary organizations by workers was to enhance the autonomy of the existing trade unions by transforming the state corporatist structure into centralized societal corporatism.[9] Gordon White (1996) put more emphasis on the trade union's own initiative than on the initiative of the CCP in reform and warned that if the trade unions and other social organizations hold firm to the vested interests resulting from their close bond with the party and the government, severe conflicts between the trade union and new voluntary organizations would lead to social disorder.[10]

However, the application of corporatist theory leaves the following problems. First, we cannot adequately depict the core aspects of one country's political structure by using the concept of corporatism, which can be used in the wider sense. Moreover, it still remains uncertain what factors define the transition from state to societal corporatism, although more than a few scholars expect such a transition as a result of trade union reform. In fact, different opinions have been raised about the evolution of the Chinese political structure from state to societal corporatism. For example, Bruce Dickson (2001) concluded that the incremental and gradual evolution from state to societal corporatism would not be realized without the end of the party's monopoly and decay of the communist system.[11] Mary Gallagher (2002) concluded that it is the rifts between the "official civil society" incorporated in state corporatism and the "real civil society" (e.g. fluid population, folk religion) that would bring about change in Chinese politics.[12]

The second problem of applying corporatist theory is that the changes and dynamics of the power balance among the state and social groups tend to be disregarded under the framework of corporatism. Tony Saich warned that the explanations using the notion of corporatism may take the risk of obscuring important elements of change as well as oversimplifying the complexities of the dynamics of the interaction between state and society.[13] In my viewpoint, corporatist and civil society theories are not necessarily mutually exclusive. In analyzing the Chinese trade unions, we need to draw mixed pictures of the state–union relationship of mutual dependence, guidance, and conflict by balancing these two theories.

In this chapter, the ongoing reforms of Chinese trade unions will be analyzed from both sides of the arguments and practices, with the aim of providing dynamic analyses of the Chinese corporatist system. Concrete arguments related to the trade union's personnel and financial affairs from the ongoing arguments over trade union reform are extracted and categorized into two directions. In Chapter 3, the data from a survey of primary trade union chairmen will be analyzed based on the categorization.

Arguments on trade union reform under marketization

Points of issues over trade union reform

The debates on trade union reform, which stagnated because of the Tiananmen incident in 1989, have revived under full-scale marketization. Hereinafter, the points of the ongoing debates over trade union reform will be introduced from three aspects: membership eligibility, personnel arrangement of trade union cadres, and financial affairs of the primary trade unions.

Membership eligibility of trade unions

The biggest issue of trade union reform is distilled into one basic question: Whose interests should the trade unions represent in facing diversification and obvious inequality inside the "working class."?[14] On one hand, socialist ideologues maintain the standpoint that trade unions in a socialist state should represent the interests of all social strata, including the administrative managers of the public sector, because all social strata belong to the "working class" in a broad sense. Some proponents even insist that private entrepreneurs' interests should also be represented by the trade union, because they have been officially identified as important contributors to the construction of "socialism" and qualify to enter the CCP under the "Three Representatives" theory given by the former General Secretary of the CCP Jiang Zemin.[15] On the other hand, there is opposition to admitting management personnel into trade unions. The proponents take the standpoint that the trade unions should focus on representing the interests of blue collar workers in labor disputes. For example, Wu Yaping (Associate Professor of Trade Union Affairs at the China Labor College) insists that although the management personnel of public enterprises are included in the category of the "working class" in the sense that they, unlike the management personnel of private enterprises, are not owners of production capital, they still should not be eligible to join trade unions, since they stand to represent the employers in negotiating collective contracts or for the arbitration of labor disputes. Moreover, Wu proposes that all CEOs and management personnel of public enterprises, including vice factory directors, labor relations managers, heads of accounting departments, and heads of planning departments, should not be eligible to be members of trade unions while in office.[16]

Personnel arrangement of trade union cadres

Regarding the assumption of management personnel and their close relatives to positions in the trade union cadres of nonpublicly-owned enterprises, negative opinions are predominant. They are concerned about the fact that many trade unions are put under the control of the management and are prevented from safeguarding the workers' rights and interests effectively.[17]

On the other hand, many individuals accept the current situation of the management staffs of publicly-owned enterprises concurrently serving as the chairpersons of the primary trade unions, in spite of the prescript in the Trade Union Law (2001) that states: "For a trade union in an enterprise or institution with two hundred and more workers and staff members, there may be a full-time chairman" (Article 13). For example, in 2002, Chen Yiping (Jilin Province Trade Union School) and Qiu Limin (Marxism Leninism Research Institute of Jilin University) wrote: although party or administrative cadres' serving as chairpersons of trade unions is inconsistent with the goal of trade union reforms aiming at "popularization," "democratization," and "legalization" and with the Party's guidelines on the autonomy of trade unions, this way may be advantageous provisionally for the trade unions to increase organizational power and influence, under the current difficult situation that the reforms have not been completed and trade unions have no prestige and power to be recognized as their interest group by workers.[18] There are, however, many negative views. A logical conflict of interest cannot be avoided if the same person represents both the management and workers. As a result, the rights and interests of vulnerable workers would inevitably be neglected. Liu Yuanwen and Gao Hongxia (Shanxi Labor Affairs Institute) assert that management personnel serving as chairpersons of trade unions would definitely put the Equal Consultation and Collective Contract System in jeopardy, and mistrust toward trade unions would be amplified.[19]

There are few opinions that advocate separating the personnel arrangement of trade union cadres from the CCP-controlled cadre management system. While many trade union cadres recognize the necessity to remake trade unions into workers' self-government associations, they still cling to their posts as bureaucrats and try hard to secure the maximum vested interests by staying within the framework of the CCP-controlled cadre management system. They, at the same time, recognize that the CCP-controlled cadre management system is the last and most important frontier for the one-party dictatorship and that trade union reforms are also prohibited from challenging it.

However, we should note the following attempts being made concerning the selection of primary trade union cadres. First is the movement to give substance to the election of chairmen of primary trade unions. While Trade Union Law stipulates that trade union committees at various levels shall be democratically elected at members' assemblies or members' congresses (Article 9), the elections have become a dead letter, and most chairmen have been commissioned by the CCP. In this context, the election conducted in Lishu County, Liaoning Province in the late 1990s is unique in that it accepted candidates from a broad range of its membership in the first stage, and decided on the official candidates based on the number of votes each candidate obtained in a preliminary election. Actually, this way was officially recommended by the All China Federation of Trade Unions (ACFTU) as a model case for the election of primary trade union chairmen. As to the case of Lishu County, it is also epoch-making that the Lishu County trade union council was given authorization to manage the primary trade union cadres (screening, selection, appointment/dismissal, transfer, training, and administration of *dang'an*) by the Party Committee and its organizational personnel division.[20]

Second, the regional trade union councils' dispatching trade union cadres to nonpublicly-owned enterprises could also be regarded as a movement for trade unions to become autonomous in personnel affairs. In recent years, some local city and country-level unions established a professional trade union chairman storehouse system.[21] Under this system, the local union councils select good candidates for primary trade union chairpersons through public recruitment and examination, register them in the storehouse, and dispatch them at need to nonpublicly-owned enterprises. After a probation period, they can be formally voted in as trade union chairmen by the Union Members' Assembly. Furthermore, the two cases of Ningdu County, Jiangxi Province, and Taiyuan City, Shanxi Province, are remarkable in that the county/city trade union councils demonstrated a willingness to provide for the payment and welfare of all the chairmen they dispatched. Who pays the trade union chairmen? This is an important question in consideration of the autonomy of the trade union in personnel management. It is still not realistic for most of the regional trade union councils, which face financial difficulties, to pay all the wages and benefits of the chairmen of primary trade unions; however, some critics insist that the wages and benefits of the cadres and full-time staffs of primary trade unions should be paid by regional trade union councils, as long as they are financially capable.[22]

Third, the proposal of enhancing the "Federation and Representation" system is also a noteworthy movement for personnel affairs reform of the trade union. Federation and representation is an idea for reforms presented at the 11th National Congress of Chinese Trade Unions held in October 1988. The system proposed was to select county and higher-level trade union cadres from the cadres of industrial unions at the correspondent administrative level and regional/local trade unions at the next lower level, including the primary level, by democratic election. In fact, Article 11 of the "Constitution of the Trade Unions" (1998) states, "Committees of national industrial unions, local industrial unions at different levels, township trade unions and neighborhood trade unions in cities may, in accordance with the principles of federation and representation, consist of the chief leading members elected by the lower trade union organizations in a democratic way and representatives from the parties concerned according to an appropriate proportion." However, although the system has been adopted in industrial unions and townships or lower level trade unions, it has not been practiced at higher than county-level trade unions. The organization department of the Nantong City Trade Union Council in Jiangsu Province considers the system to be "advantageous to make trade union organization healthy and to popularize and democratize trade unions."[23] Once the system is used widely, the representation of trade unions at all administrative levels will be improved and legitimatized.

Financial affairs of primary trade unions

Regarding the financial affairs of primary trade unions, it is notable that work units' contribution to trade union expense has been open for discussion. While the obligation of enterprises, institutions, or governments to allocate the money, equivalent to two percent of the monthly payroll of all the workers and staff members, is stipulated in Article 42 of "Trade Union Law," some critics have begun to point out the negative effects on the trade unions' autonomy in recent years. For example, Song Deqiang (China Institute of Industrial Relations) expresses his fear that the trade union might degenerate into a subordinate entity of the enterprise, by depending for its expenses upon the enterprise; and asserts that the dues equivalent to two percent of the monthly payroll of all workers should be first paid to employees and the employees should pay trade union dues directly.[24]

Besides the above-mentioned arguments over the pros and cons of work units' contributions to trade union expenses, there exists a debate on the measures to cope with unpaid or delinquent payment of dues by enterprises. Actually, arrears in trade union dues by enterprises have posed serious problems in recent years. According to a survey in Henan Province in the period of March–April 2001, only one to two percent of private enterprises (PEs) with trade unions have been paying dues.[25] In Heilongjiang Province, 90 percent of nonpublicly-owned enterprises have not paid dues.[26] Nonpayment of dues at the primary level directly causes financial crises at higher-level trade unions as they collect money from the primary-level trade unions. There is a report that one-third of 60 county-, city-, and district-level trade union councils in Jilin Province are facing difficulties in paying trade union cadres their wages and benefits.[27] Article 43 of the Trade Union Law states: "Where an enterprise or institution delays allocating or refuses to allocate the contribution to the trade union without justifiable reasons, the basic-level trade union or the trade union at a higher level may apply to the local People's Court for an order of payment; if it refuses to obey the order, the trade union may, in accordance with law, apply to the People's Court for compulsory enforcement."

Although legalizing and enforcing payment of union dues is now an established practice under the jurisdiction of the People's Court, however, a way to prevent arrears is still an issue. One of the arguments that have developed concerns the pros and cons of entrusting the collection of the contribution to the taxation affairs department of the government. Actually, in some areas, local trade union councils started outsourcing the job of collecting the contribution to taxation affairs offices in order to improve the financial situation. For example, since 2002, the Jinhua City Trade Union Council in Zhejiang Province has commissioned the taxation office to collect the contribution in Dongyang City and Pujiang County.[28] The Luliang Prefecture Trade Union Council in Shanxi Province issued a notice in conjunction with the Luliang taxation office, "Notice Concerning Collection of Union Dues from all area enterprise work units by the area tax department," and started to impose union dues on all enterprise and business work units in 13 counties (cities) in Luliang Prefecture.[29] Furthermore, a more drastic proposal exists to change union dues into a "Workers and staff members' Rights and Interest Protection Tax." According to the proponents of the idea, the introduction of this tax would make it easier to collect union dues and would help unionization by making dues mandatory regardless of whether a trade union existed or not.[30] Of course, objections have been posed to these methods of collection. Many objections are based on the concern that commissioning the taxation office to collect trade union dues would create the impression that the trade union expenses belonged to public finance and damaged the principle of trade unions' financial independence.[31]

Concerning trade unions' financial independence, another argument is being developed over the necessary procedures for primary trade unions to become a legal person in the capacity of a public organization. Although many critics agree that it is necessary to grant legal personality to basic-level trade unions in order to prevent the widespread diversion or embezzlement of trade union funds by management and to promote trade unions' financial independence, the actual rate of primary trade unions with a legal personality is low. One of the reasons is the different opinions regarding the procedures. The regulations of the Trade Union Law are not clear in this regard. Although Article 14 states, "A basic-level trade union organization which has acquired the qualifications of a legal person as prescribed in the General Principles of the Civil Law, shall, in accordance with law, be granted the status of a legal person as a public organization," concrete procedures are not clarified in the article. It is common opinion that as long as primary trade unions go through the evaluation, ratification, registration, and certification issued by higher-level trade unions, it is not necessary to go through the special process of obtaining the status of a legal person as a public organization.[32] However, some still insist that primary trade unions need to be evaluated, ratified, and registered by a governmental agency to obtain the status.[33]

Two thought patterns on trade union reform:
From a corporatist approach

The above-mentioned arguments on trade union reform can be categorized into two thought patterns based on the directions toward which corporatism aims.

The first is a viewpoint that promotes the trade union's functions to safeguard workers' rights and interests without changing the close ties or integrated combination with the CCP and the government, which are legitimated by the ideology of "socialism" and "proletarian dictatorship." The history of the People's Republic of China proves that it was specifically for the purpose of strengthening the CCP's guidance toward workers that most of the central leaders promoted the trade union reforms in the 1960s and in 1980s.[34] Many trade union cadres, who enjoy a privileged political status and economic treatment as bureaucrats, have also been following this viewpoint. Even though the proponents of this viewpoint are positive about establishing institutional frameworks for the trade union to participate in the policy-making process as a representative of workers (e.g. the system of equal consultations and collective contracts; the system of the congress of workers and staff members; the system for the election of representatives from among the workers and staff members to the board of directors or the board of supervisors of a company; the system of mediation and arbitration of labor disputes; and the system of joint meeting of trade unions, enterprises, and the government), they are quite negative about separating the trade union from the party in its personnel and finance. Instead, they insist that, in order to strengthen the negotiating power of a trade union, the position of trade union chairman should be filled concurrently by the managements of publicly-owned enterprises or vice-posts of the party, who have power and networks in the CCP. They also propose that the function of collecting the contribution from enterprises should be entrusted to the taxation affairs department of the government in order to solve the problem of arrears in payment. The "Workers and staff members' Rights and Interests Protection Tax" is the ultimate proposition by the proponent.

The second viewpoint is to increase the trade union's autonomy from the party and the government (administration) by limiting the CCP's guidance in personnel and fiscal affairs. The proponents of this view emphasize the need to revive the trade union as a real interest group of blue collar workers. Although they share the same views as the former in that they do not approve of the freedom of association in denial of existing trade union organizations, they strongly recognize the necessity to change the seriously bureaucratized trade unions to deal with the ever-intensifying labor disputes under a market economy. If their political intentions could be expressed in a single phrase, it would be to aim at the conversion from a "socialist" and "proletarian dictatorship" type of state corporatist system to a state corporatist system in the normal sense. Based on such political intentions, they show negative opinions about the practice of administration executives of publicly-owned enterprises, as well as private entrepreneurs and their relatives, concurrently serving as a trade union chairman. They are also negative about administration executives' holding membership eligibility in a trade union. Regarding the fiscal affairs, they insist on changing the current way that depends on contributions by enterprises, and build a new system financed by dues that the members pay directly. The reform ideas advocated by Li Lisan immediately after 1949, including strengthening the personnel and financial independency of the trade union from the CCP,[35] have been adopted by some cadres and intellectuals since then. Actually, some reforms aiming to strengthen the personnel independency of trade unions, such as democratic elections of primary trade union cadres and the establishment of a professional trade union chairman storehouse by county-level trade unions, have been executed since the 1980s.

The analysis of the data from a survey of primary trade union chairmen (2004–6)

This section examines what perception the primary trade union chairpersons hold in terms of the above-mentioned issues of trade union reforms by providing some survey data. I frequently used the data about the enterprise's form of ownership in the following analyses, in order to illustrate the transformation of the trade union under marketization. Although the number of the samples for enterprises with funds from Hong Kong, Macao, and Taiwan (EFHMTs) (15) and that of FFE (32) were limited, I didn't except the data, which show the features of the trade unions under a market economy. In addition, the data of each province is also introduced to examine the different conditions under different levels of economic development.

Analysis of the survey data

Hereinafter, I illustrate two findings regarding the current situation of the primary trade unions.

First, it is obvious that differences exist regarding the current situation and the reform intention of the trade union chairmen, by the form of ownership of the enterprise. Under the current situation, state-owned/state-holding enterprises (SOEs) are embedded in the above-mentioned "socialist" and "proletarian dictatorship" type of state corporatist system. As for SOEs, it was found that no less than 24.5 percent of the chairmen were still being appointed by the party organization at the work unit (see Figure 2.1); even in cases where they assumed the post through elections or open selective examinations, 35.1 percent of them participated in the election or examinations following the recommendation of the party organization of the work unit (see Figure 2.2). Both the ratio of the chairmen who are CCP members and the ratio of the chairmen who serve concurrently as "Secretary," "Vice-secretary," or as a member of the Party committee at the corresponding level reached high percentages, 90.0 percent and 46.4 percent, respectively (see Figures 2.3 and 2.4).

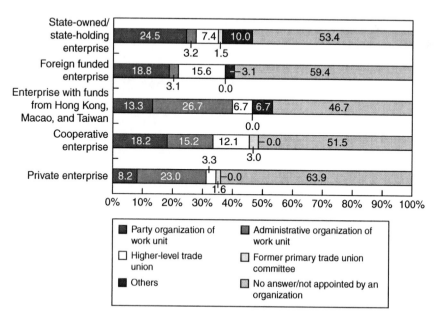

Figure 2.1 (If you are appointed by an organization) Which organization appointed you?

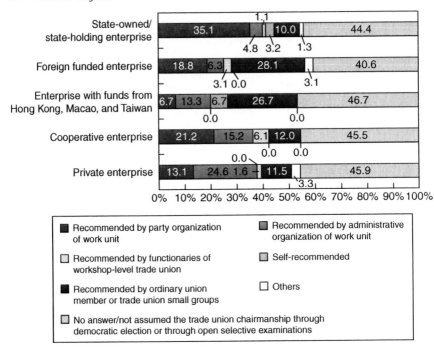

Figure 2.2 (If you assumed the trade union chairmanship through a democratic election or through open selective examinations) What was the reason for your taking part in the election or examinations?

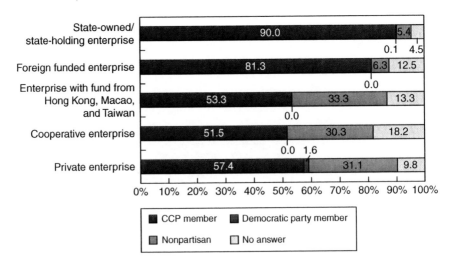

Figure 2.3 Political appearance.

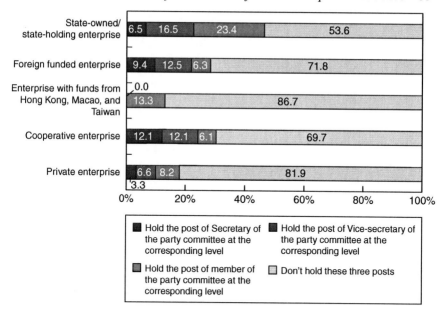

Figure 2.4 What are the specific posts you hold concurrently?

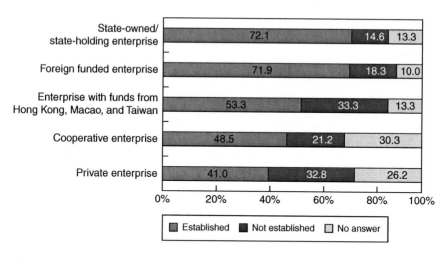

Figure 2.5 Has your primary trade union committee established a party group or party branch in it?

Moreover, no less than 72.1 percent of the chairmen of SOEs answered that their union committee had established a party group or party branch in it (see Figure 2.5). All of these data suggest the fact that the primary trade unions of SOEs tend to be subordinate to the party on the personnel side.

PE, EFHMT, and cooperative enterprise (CE) show contrasting characters compared to an SOE. As for these types of enterprises, the proportions of the trade union chairmen who were appointed or recommended by the party organization of the work unit are low (see Figures 2.1 and 2.2). The percentages of the chairmen who are CCP members and the percentages of the chairmen who serve concurrently as secretary, vice-secretary, or as a member of the Party committee at the corresponding level are also relatively low (see Figures 2.3 and 2.4). The percentages for the establishment of a party group or party branch in the primary trade union committee are also low (see Figure 2.5). These data suggest that the trade unions of PEs, EFHMTs, and CEs are relatively separated from the existing cadre management system controlled by the CCP. However, it does not necessarily mean that these trade unions hold stronger intentions to become interest groups of workers by acquiring more autonomy. In fact, as for the trade union chairmen of these types of enterprises, the ratio of being appointed or recommended by the administrative organization of the work unit, the ratio of serving concurrently as CEO or in a vice-post of the administrative organization at the corresponding level, and the ratio of a factory manager's or a president's transfer to the post are remarkably high (see Figures 2.1, 2.2, 2.6, and 2.7).

These data suggest that the trade unions of these types of enterprises tend to be controlled by the management, which is autonomous from the Party. Consequently, the trade union's autonomy of fiscal management or activities as an interest group of workers tend to be less promoted in these enterprises than in SOEs. For example,

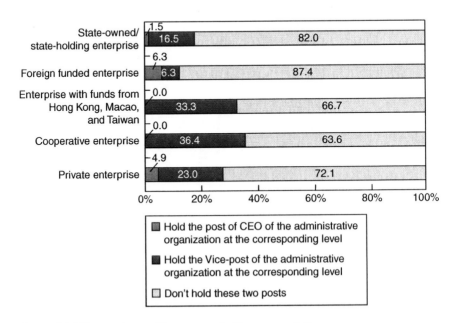

Figure 2.6 What are the specific posts you hold concurrently?

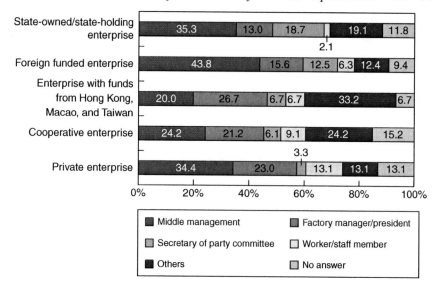

Figure 2.7 What was your last position before being the trade union chairman?

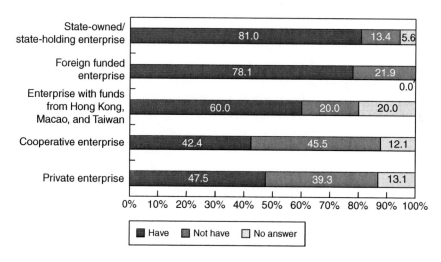

Figure 2.8 Does your trade union have its own account for managing funds independently?

to the question "Does your trade union have its own account for managing funds independently?", no more than 47.5 percent of PEs and 42.4 percent of CEs answered "Yes," while the average percentage was 74.8 percent (see Figure 2.8).

Moreover, 52.5 percent of PEs and 60.6 percent of CEs need to get the approval of the administrative manager of the work unit for using the union funds (see Figure 2.9).

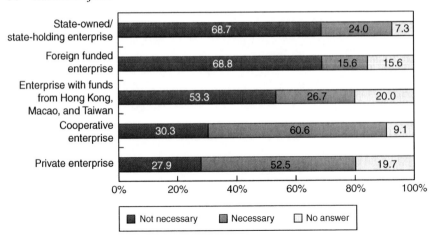

Figure 2.9 In using the union funds, is it necessary to get the approval of administrative manager of work unit?

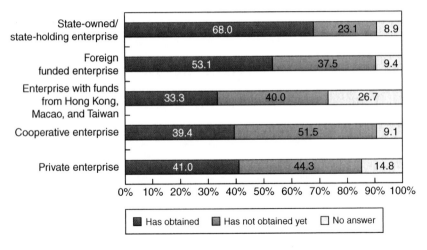

Figure 2.10 Has the union obtained the status of a legal person as a public organization?

The acquisition rates of the status of a legal person as a public organization are low in these enterprises (see Figure 2.10). Moreover, a positive answer to the question "Are there any cases where delegations of over 10 representatives bring in a bill at members' congress/members' assembly?" showed 13.1 percent for PEs, and 13.3 percent for EFHMTs, both of which were lower than the average rate (32.1 percent) (see Figure 2.11). When we focus on the actual functions of labor protection, the ratios for signing collective contracts with the administration of a work unit for EFHMTs (60.0 percent) and CEs (57.6 percent) were lower than the ratio for SOEs (74.7 percent) (see Figure 2.12).[36]

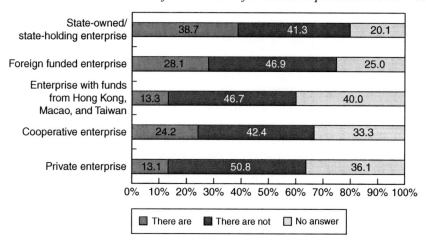

Figure 2.11 Are there any cases where delegations of over 10 representatives bring in a bill at members' congress/members' assembly?

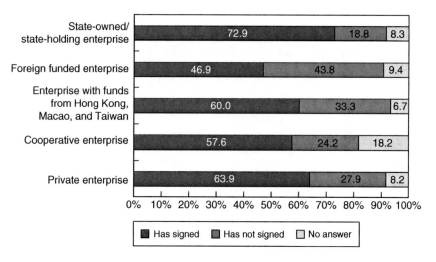

Figure 2.12 Has your union, on behalf of the members, signed collective contracts with the administration of your work unit?

According to the data, it can be concluded that it is not the trade union chairmen of PEs or of EFHMTs, but those of the SOEs that hold a strong awareness of the trade union's autonomy or the trade union's role as an interest group. For example, regarding the establishment of a professional trade union chairman storehouse by county-level unions, the agreement ratio for the proposition "Disadvantage in developing trade union activities because dispatched chairmen or cadres are not familiar with the inside details of the enterprise" was high in FFEs (37.5 percent), PEs (36.1 percent), and EFHMTs (33.3 percent) (see Figure 2.13).[37]

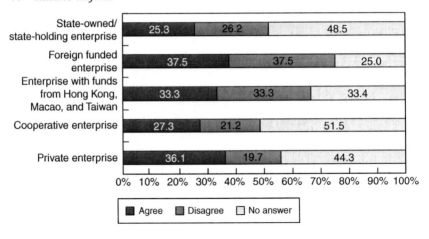

Figure 2.13 Do you agree to the proposition "the establishment of Professional Trade Union Chairman Storehouse disadvantages in developing union activities because dispatched union cadres are not familiar with the inside details of the enterprise"?

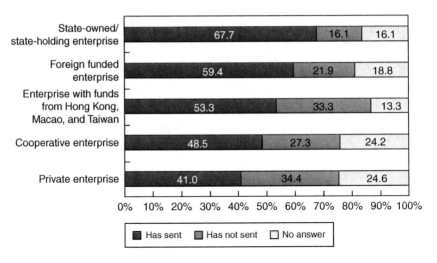

Figure 2.14 Has your primary trade union ever sent delegates in the next higher-level congress of trade unions?

The difference in ownership was also seen in the answers to the questions about a "federation and representation" system. While the proportion of the trade unions that have ever sent delegates to the next higher-level congress of the trade union was 67.7 percent in SOEs, it was no more than 41.0 percent, 48.5 percent, and 53.3 percent in PEs, CEs, and EFHMTs, respectively (see Figure 2.14). In addition, when agreement or disagreement on the system was asked, the proportion of

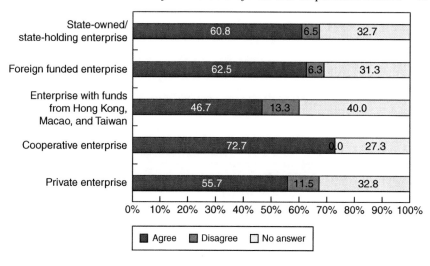

Figure 2.15 Do you agree with federation and representation system?

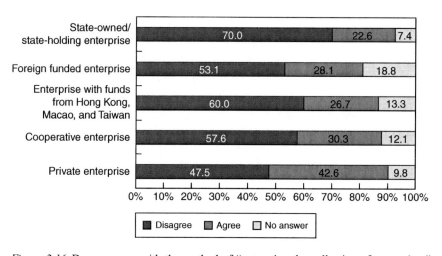

Figure 2.16 Do you agree with the method of "entrusting the collection of enterprises" contribution to taxation affairs department disadvantages in the trade union's displaying its financial independency from government finance"?

agreement was low in order of EFHMTs (46.7 percent), PEs (55.7 percent), and the proportion of agreement was low in EFHMTs (46.7 percent) and PEs (55.7 percent) (see Figure 2.15). Regarding fiscal management, in contrast to the chairmen of SOEs, the majority of whom disagreed with the method of entrusting the collection of the enterprises' or undertakings' contribution to the taxation affairs

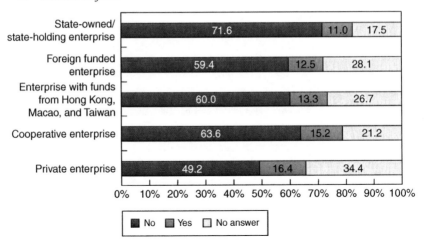

Figure 2.17 Are you going to use the method of entrusting the collection of the enterprises' contribution to taxation affairs department?

department the ratio of disagreement was relatively low in PEs (47.5 percent), FEs (53.1 percent), and CEs (57.6 percent) (see Figure 2.16). To the question "Are you going to use this method in the future?", while the rate of answering "No" was no less than 71.6 percent in SOEs, it was low in CEs (63.6 percent), EFHMTs (60.0 percent), FFEs (59.4 percent), and PEs (49.2 percent). As for PEs, the rate of answering "Yes" reached 16.4 percent (see Figure 2.17).

When the above-mentioned results are considered, we have to conclude that the expectation that trade union reform is roused from the nonpublicly-owned sector is limited at this point. The trade unions seem to be facing a harsh reality, that is, to maintain limited functions as an interest group by being incorporated into the "socialist" "proletarian dictatorship" type of state corporatist structure, or to fall into being a nominal interest group by unification with the management.

Second, we can observe the differences in trade union chairmen's stances on the reform among different regions. These regional disparities were shown by the data on the fiscal affairs of the trade union. For example, the proportion of the trade unions that have their own accounts for managing funds independently was low in Guizhou (56.3 percent) (see Figure 2.18). The ratio of the trade unions that need to get the approval of the administrative manager of the work unit for using the union funds was high in Guizhou (43.8 percent) and Gansu (42.3 percent), and low in Shanghai (17.0 percent) (see Figure 2.19).

To the question "Have you ever experienced the situation of nondistinctiveness of union expense and administrative expense?" the highest ratio was marked in Henan (31.8 percent), and the lowest was marked in Shanghai (14.0 percent) (see Figure 2.20). The ratio of the trade unions that face a greater or lesser revenue shortfall in conducting union activities reached 87.6 percent in Guizhou and 81.0 percent in Gansu, while the average was 60.0 percent (see Figure 2.21).

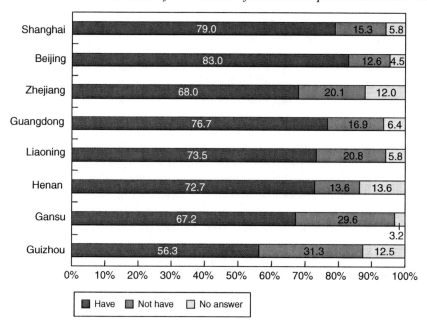

Figure 2.18 Does your trade union have its own account for managing funds independently?

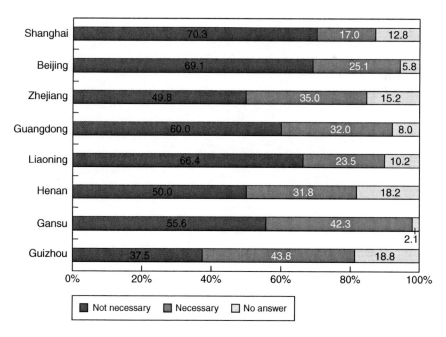

Figure 2.19 In using the union funds, is it necessary to get the approval of administrative manager of work unit?

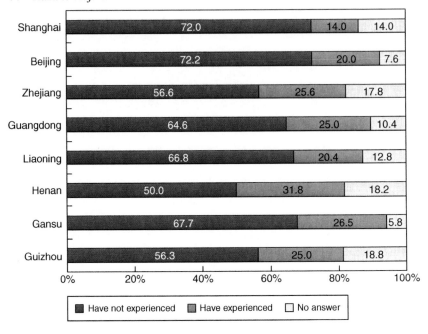

Figure 2.20 Have you ever experienced the situation of nondistinctiveness of union expense and administrative expense?

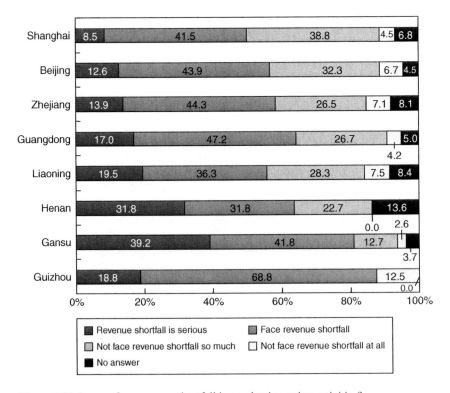

Figure 2.21 Do you face revenue shortfall in conducting union activities?

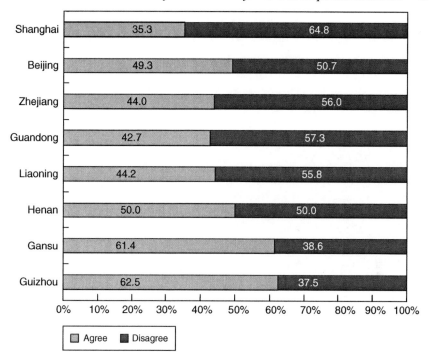

Figure 2.22 Do you agree to the proposition "Financial difficulty is one of the major impediments of the development of trade union work"?

Moreover, regarding the major impediments to the development of trade union work, the proportion answering "financial difficulties" was high in Guizhou (62.5 percent) and Gansu (61.4 percent), and low in Shanghai (35.3 percent) (see Figure 2.22). "Financial difficulties" are actually supposed to influence the trade union work; the ratio of the trade unions that provide mutual aid supplementary insurance for union members was exceptionally high in Shanghai (68.8 percent), and low in Henan (13.6 percent), Guizhou (18.8 percent), Gansu (23.8 percent), Liaoning (24.3 percent) (see Figure 2.23). It is remarkable that the trade unions in the provinces, where tight financial conditions are expected, are supposed to be faced with giving priority to securing their income even at the expense of their financial autonomy. As for entrusting the collection of enterprises' contribution to the trade union to the taxation affairs department, the trade unions in Henan showed a relatively positive attitude; 45.5 percent of them agreed with this way, 13.6 percent have never used this way, 31.8 percent answered that they were going to use this way in the future. To the proposition "Collection by the taxation affairs departments would create the image that trade unions' funds belong to government finance, posing a disadvantage to the trade unions' displaying their independency," while the proportion of "agree" and "disagree" were almost equal in Shanghai (48.3 percent and 51.8 percent) and in Beijing (45.7 percent and

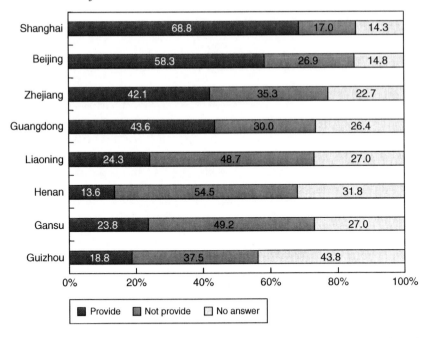

Figure 2.23 Does your trade union provide mutual aid supplementary insurance for union members?

54.3 percent), the "agree" ratio was far below the "disagree" ratio in Guizhou (12.5 percent and 87.5 percent), in Henan (27.3 percent and 72.7 percent), and in Gansu (33.3 percent and 66.7 percent) (see Figure 2.24).

Social pressures for trade union reform

As observed above, the nonpublic sector does not necessarily function as a space promoting trade unions' autonomy and dissolving the "socialist" "proletarian dictatorship" type of state corporatist structure.[38] And the trade unions in interior areas tend to prioritize the continued existence of trade unions over autonomy, in facing severe financial standing.

Frontline workers cast a cold eye at the unchanged situations of the trade unions. In the survey, we asked the primary trade union chairmen's perception of the image of their trade union among the members. The results showed that 11.8 percent of the chairmen answered "very good," 50.9 percent answered "good," 29.7 percent answered "fair," and 1.3 percent answered "bad" or "very bad." When we pay attention to the total percentage of "very good" and "good", FFEs (71.9 percent) had the highest score; in contrast, CEs (33.3 percent), EFHMTs (33.3 percent), and PEs (47.6 percent) had the lowest scores (see Figure 2.25). It can be easily imagined that the images of the trade unions among frontline workers are not better than the self-perceptions of trade union chairmen.

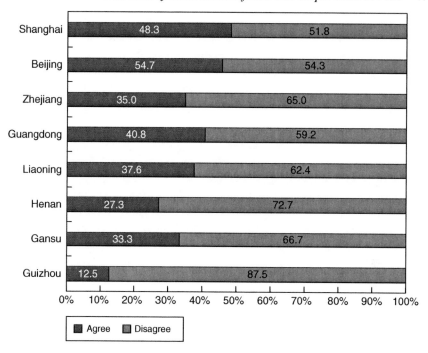

Figure 2.24 Do you agree to the proposition "entrusting the collection of enterprises' contribution to taxation affairs department is a disadvantage to the trade union's displaying its financial independency from government finance"?

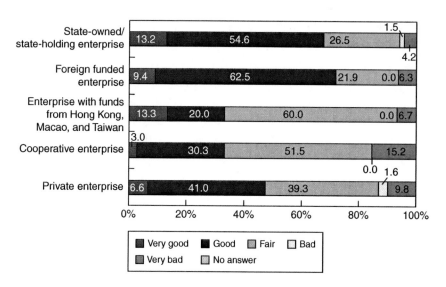

Figure 2.25 According to your understanding, how is the image of the trade union among the members?

As a consequence, the grievances of workers are not expressed through trade union-mediated routes but are vented through petitions, lawsuits, strikes, and demonstrations. And it is noteworthy that the frequent labor troubles and labor disputes are becoming increasingly organized and sophisticated, with assistance provided by legal experts, intellectuals, NGOs, media, and other social powers. This reflects the widely rising concern over the socially vulnerable these days. As is shown by a case in which 83 migrant workers in Chongqing appointed a famous lawyer, Litai Zhou, their attorney to file a class action suit accusing the Chongqing Municipal Trade Union Council of negligence of duty,[39] workers' protests are sometimes directed against the trade unions, which do not work as the workers' interest groups. Additionally, bottom-up organizations voluntarily organized by the workers are emerging outside the existing trade union organizational hierarchy. For example, in Shenzhen, the "Shenzhen Migrant Workers' Association" was established by a migrant worker named Zhiru Zhang in March 2004.[40] The Association, in the constitution put in its homepage, emphasized that it was an interest group for migrant workers that migrant workers in Shenzhen had formed voluntarily with the aim of safeguarding their own legal rights and interests, in contrast with existing trade unions, which depend for their expenses on the managements and become dysfunctional under the Party's direct control. Concerning the relation between the Association and the trade union, it reiterated that the Association would not challenge the existing framework centered around the trade union, by stating "In safeguarding migrant workers' rights and interests in an enterprise with a trade union, we positively cooperate with the trade union by providing rearguard support"; at the same time, however, it also declared that the "Shenzhen Migrant Workers' Association" was not a subordinate organization of the trade union but an independent social organization that stood on an equal footing with the trade union.[41] Qiao Jian (China Institute of Labour Relations) insists that the trade union should incorporate the voluntary organizations by workers (e.g. Association for Migrant Female Workers *Dagongmei Jingjie*, Employee's Association *Guyuan Xiehui*, and Countrymen's Association *Tongxianghui*), which emerged in facing the functional decline of the trade union, into the existing trade union system through guidance and education, rather than disfavor or attack them.[42] However, there is a persistent resistance against accepting new organizations into the existing framework, within the trade union and the party state. The above-mentioned Shenzhen Migrant Workers' Association was eventually cracked down on as an illegal NGO in November 2006, and brought to a standstill.[43]

It is not only the expansion of internal social forces but also the ongoing internationalization of labor issues that form pressure on Chinese trade unions to push through further reforms. For example, concerning WTO agreements, the governments, trade unions, and consumers' organizations in relevant countries, as well as United Nations' organizations, are working to insert into WTO agreements a provision for guaranteeing basic labor rights, including freedom of association, right of collective bargaining, prohibition of forced labor and child labor, etc., with the aim of enhancing mutual monitoring of the labor environment among countries. If such provisions are contained in the agreements, China has to abide by the provisions as a member country. In fact, the Internal and Judicial Affairs Committee of the National People's Congress has initiated comprehensive exams on the conformity of domestic labor legislation with international commitments.[44]

Reality always precedes the arguments. In reality, workers are pressing for more rapid and drastic reforms of the trade union than most primary trade union chairmen recognize. The stability of Chinese society depends on whether the CCP can perceive the recognition gap and respond flexibly and effectively to the dysfunction of the existing "socialist" and "proletarian dictatorship" type of state corporatist system.

Endnotes

1   The surge of the pro-democracy movements in the late 1980s was positioned in the same tide as the ongoing democratic reforms in Eastern Europe, and raised expectations among China watchers that the social forces, which seemed to be emerging and developing in China, would form a "civil society" to counter the authoritarian regime, just as in East European countries.

2   Tony Saich, "The Search for Civil Society and Democracy in China," *Current History*, vol. 83, no. 584, September 1994, p. 262.

3   See, e.g. Kevin Jiang, "The Conflicts between Trade Unions and the Party-State: The Reform of Chinese Trade Unions in the Eighties," *Hong Kong Journal of Social Sciences*, vol. 8, Autumn, 1996, pp.121–58.

4   Andrew Walder, "Urban Industrial Workers: Some Observations on the 1980s," in Arthur Lewis Rosenbaum (ed.), *State and Society in China: The Consequences of Reform*, Boulder: Westview Press, 1992.

5   Anita Chan, "Labor Relations in Foreign-funded Ventures: Chinese Trade Unions and the Prospects for Collective Bargaining," and Jude Howell, "Trade Unions in China: the Challenge of Foreign Capital," in Greg O' Leary (ed.), *Adjusting to Capitalism: Chinese workers and the State*, London: M.E. Sharpe, Inc., 1998.

6   Ng Sek Hong and Malcolm Warner, *China's Trade Unions and Management*, London: Macmillan Press Ltd., 1998, pp. 165–6.

7   Feng Chen, "Between the State and Labour: The Conflict of Chinese Trade Unions' Double Identity in Market Reform," *The China Quarterly*, vol. 176 (Dec. 2003), pp. 1006–28.

8   Anita Chan, "Revolution or Corporatism? Workers and Trade Unions in Post-Mao China," *The Australian Journal of Chinese Affairs*, vol. 29, January 1993, pp. 31–61.

9   Feng Chen, op. cit., p. 1028.

10 Gordon White, Jude Howell and Shang Xiaoyuan, *In Search of Civil Society: Market Reform and Social Change in Contemporary China*, Oxford: Clarendon Press, 1996, pp. 212–14. Gordon White, "Chinese Trade Unions in the Transition from Socialism: The Emergence of Civil Society or the Road to Corporatism?," Institute of Development Studies Working Paper, vol. 18, May 1995, p. 28.

11 Bruce Dickson, "Cooptation and Corporatism in China: The Logic of Party Adaptation," *Political Science Quarterly*, vol. 115, no. 4, 2001, pp. 517–40.

12 Mary E. Gallagher, "The Ties That Bind: Civil Society and the State in China," paper prepared for presentation for the Project on Civil Society and Political Change in Asia, Phnom Penh, Cambodia, October 24–27, 2002, pp. 124–41.

13 Tony Saich, "Negotiating the State: The Development of Social Organizations in China," *The China Quarterly*, vol. 161, March 2000; Tony Saich, *Governance and Politics of China*, New York: Palgrave Macmillan, 2001, pp. 209–10.

14 Lu Xueyi (Social Science Institute of the Chinese Academy of Social Sciences) clearly showed the substantial inequality inside the "working class" by classifying it into ten

social strata. Lu Xueyi, "Research Report of Social Strata of Today's China," Beijing: Social Sciences Academic Press, January 2002.

15 Wu Shenyao (Vice-Chairperson of Shanghai Municipal Trade Union Council) revealed the following understanding on the matter: "Private entrepreneurs play an important role in constructing socialism, as do workers and farmers. Therefore, trade unions should not treat them as we used to, i.e. exploit the ones who exploit. To protect the rights and interests of blue-collar workers is the basic duty of trade unions; however, trade unions should not focus their activities only on the issues of blue-collar workers. They should also consider the interests of private entrepreneurs." See Gu Changshen and Wang Xiaolong (eds), "Spirit of the 16th Party Congress and Trade Union Activities – Chairperson of Province/City Trade Union Speaks His Mind Freely," Beijing: Chinese Workers Publishing Co., March 2003, pp. 60–3.

16 Wu Yaping, "Eligibility of Trade Union Members," *Theory and Practice of Trade Unionism*, vol. 13, no. 5, October 1999, pp. 44–6.

17 Article 9 of the Trade Union Law (2001) stipulates: "No close relatives of the chief members of an enterprise may be candidates for membership of the basic-level trade union committee of the enterprise." However, there are many cases of tacitly allowing the management staffs of enterprises and/or their family members to serve as committee members of the trade unions.

18 Chen Yiping and Qiu Limin, "Opinion on Party Administrators serving as Trade Union Chairpersons," *Theory and Practice of Trade Unionism*, vol. 16, no. 4, April 2002, pp. 47–8.

19 Liu Yuanwen and Gao Hongxia "Basic Activities of Trade Unions after Reforms," *Theory and Practice of Trade Unionism,* vol. 17, no. 6, pp. 18–20.

20 Lishu County Trade Union Council, "Direct Elections of Chairmen of Primary Trade Unions enhance the reform of the Trade Union," *Chinese Workers' Movement*, vol. 2, 1998, p. 21.

21 The attempts of some city and county level trade union councils in Hebei, Jiangxi, and Shanxi have been reported. *Workers' Daily*, March 29, 2002; August 13, 2002; August 14, 2002; December 7, 2004.

22 *Workers' Daily*, November 12, 2004.

23 Li Shichun and Cheng Fei, "Issues and Thoughts That Trade Union Leadership Management System is Facing Currently," *Shandong Province Trade Union Management Institute News*, vol. 5, 2000, p. 17.

24 Song Deqiang, "Trade Union Fees Should Be Paid Directly By Members Instead of Being Deducted and Paid By Enterprises," *Theory and Practice of Trade Unionism*, vol. 17, no. 6, December 2003, pp. 29–30.

25 Zhang Dinghua, "Report on Unionization and Safeguard of Rights and Interests By Trade Unions of Private Enterprises in Henan Province," *Report on Activities of Trade Unions*, no. 15, June 15, 2001, p. 3.

26 *Workers' Daily*, December 21, 2004.

27 *Workers' Daily*, December 21, 2004.

28 *Workers' Daily*, November 7, 2003.

29 *Workers' Daily*, June 13, 2003.

30 Guo Yongqi, "Market Reform of 2% Trade Union Contribution," *Trade Union Financial Affairs of China (Zhongguo Gonghui Caikuai)*, vol. 11, November 2001, pp. 38–9.

31 *Workers' Daily*, September 19, 2002; November 7, 2003.

32 The legal interpretation of the Supreme People's Court agrees with this idea in the "Opinion on issues concerning industrial trade unions and basic-level trade unions to have the status of a legal person in the capacity as a public organization and on possibility of freezing trade union accounts" issued in May 1997.

33 Jiang Ying, "Verification and Its Process of Trade Unions to Be a Legal Person," *Theory and Practice of Trade Unionism*, vol.13, no. 5, October 1999, pp. 47–8.

34 For details, please refer to Kojima Kazuko, "The CCP and the Trade Unions: The Trade Unions under the Socialist Education Movement," *China 21*, vol. 8, May 2000,

pp. 99–120; Kojima Kazuko, "The Chinese Communist Party and the Trade Unions: *Gonghui* under Economic Reform," *The Tsukuba University Journal of Law and Politics*, vol. 33, September 2002, pp. 71–102.

35 For details, please refer to Kojima Kazuko, "The Chinese Communist Party and the Trade unions: The Intra-Party Disputes over the Trade Unions (1950–1951)," *Asian Studies*, vol. 42, no. 3, September 1996, pp. 83–114.

36 Among nonpublicly owned enterprises, the trade unions in FFEs have a particularity in that they combine two conflicting features: the feature of a "socialist" "proletarian dictatorship" type of state corporatism and the feature of autonomous control. For example, the rate of having party groups or party branches in the primary trade unions is relatively high (FFE: 71.9%, average: 69.1%). At the same time, a relatively high rate of trade unions were established by "workers and staff members' voluntary request" (FFE: 28.1%, average: 13.3%). As to the way of assuming the trade union chairmanship, a relatively high rate of chairmen answered that they were "elected by a members' congress or members' assembly" without any organization recommendations (FFE: 31.3%, average: 18.3%). A relatively low proportion of them need to get the approval of the administrative manager of the work unit for using the union funds (FFE: 15.6 %, average: 28.4%).

37 Regarding the method of a professional trade union chairman storehouse by county-level unions, 41.0% agreed with the opinion "this way is worth promoting nation-wide," while 13.9% disagreed.

38 It is also worth noting that private enterprise showed a higher percentage (13.1%) than the average rate (3.7%) in ordinary workers' becoming trade union chairmen.

39 Eighty-three migrant workers of Chan'an Automobile Limited Company filed a collective lawsuit with Chongqing No. 1 Intermediate People's Court against Chongqing Municipal Trade Union Council for negligence of duty in January 2005. According to their attorney, Litai Zhou, Chongqing Municipal Trade Union Council denied to issue a "Certification of Poverty," which is necessary for the workers to be exempted from arbitration fees in applying for arbitration at the Chongqing Labor Dispute Arbitration Committee.

40 Zhiru Zhang (born in 1974) is a migrant worker from Hunan Province. He was prepared to organize a migrant workers' association in Dongguan city, Guangdong, in 1995, but failed to get government approval of the registration. Then, he established a primary trade union organization and assumed the chairmanship at the Weifeng Shoe Factory, a Taiwan-funded factory in Dongguang City. Afterwards, he went back to Hunan, and established the Young Men's Mutual Aid Society in Chetang village, which was ratified by the government. After working at the Guanlanyuanxing Electronics Factory as a migrant worker from February 2000, he again prepared to organize a trade union there, but couldn't obtain permission from the management. According to Zhang, it was his grueling experiences as a migrant worker that drove him to establish the "Shenzhen Migrant Workers' Association."

41 http://www.szwlg.com/ (accessed on August 10, 2006).

42 Qiao Jian, "Workers: Legal Protection for Labor Organizations," in Ru Xin, Lu Xueyi and Li Peilin, *Analysis and Forecast on China's Social Development (2006)*, Beijing: Social Sciences Academic Press (China), 2005, pp. 320–1.

43 According to Zhiru Zhang, the direct reason for the crackdown was its association with 11 other grass roots workers' organizations that carried out a large-scale signature collection campaign in March 2006 in a bid to abolish labor dispute arbitration fees. Liu Yi, "Pay Attention to the Crackdown against Shenzhen Migrant Workers' Association," *Boxun News Sight*, November 16, 2006. http://www.peacehall.com/news/gb/pubvp/2006/11/200611160111.shtml

44 Feng Tongqing, "China's WTO Accession Will Influence Its Labor Relations," *Theory & Practice of Trade Unions (Journal of China Labor College)*, vol. 16, no. 4, August 2002, pp. 8–10.

3 Between the party-state, employers and workers: Multiple roles of the Chinese trade union during market transition – A survey of 1,811 enterprise union chairpersons[1]

Jian Qiao

Proposed questions and research hypothesis

Introduction to questions

Following the economic reform and restructuring in 1980s, several tendencies and factors about China's labour relations are being experienced:

First of all, the former interest-integrated labour–capital relations, in which the state stood for the entire society, has transferred to employment relations between two independent interest groups, namely the employers and the workers. Under command economy, labour relations merely composed of the state and the employees. The latter had no independent identity besides the citizenship of the state. Such a relationship determined an administrative-dominated industrial relation system that emphasised the only difference between management and workers was the difference of socialist division of labour. However, under the market transition, interest segregation between the state and market has taken place, with market evolution characterising a separation of interests between the employers and the employees as well. Employment relations become dominant so that workers undertake a subordinate role, compared to the capital, in the labour market.

The operational mechanism of labour relations has shifted from state's administrative control to enterprise-centred market adjustment. On the one hand, firms are gaining their authority at the workplace, as the state withdraws. On the other hand, the state endeavours to establish a labour law system to safeguard the market functioning and puts the contract system as the centre of its labour institution. The separation between individual and collective labour relations is then established.

In addition, marketisation intensifies the interest divergence among all actors. 'Downsizing for efficiency and implementing reemployment' reform of the state-owned enterprises (SOEs) in 1997 led to 'separation of principal and auxiliary work' and further 'change of auxiliary industry' in large-scaled SOEs in 2002. Around 30 million employees, or half the total SOE workforce, were removed from SOEs. Consequently, SOE reform has become a 'Winner-Take-All' game

(Qiao and Jiang 2004: 315). Meantime, in the fast-growing non-public sectors, the differentiation and divergence between capital and labour is getting even greater.

Furthermore, employment flexibility brings about a massive growth of informal labour, which proposes new challenges to the task of protecting labour rights and benefits. Since the middle of 1990s, the state has encouraged employment and re-employment of the workforce in various forms of flexible employment. As a result, a variety of employment means, such as labour dispatch or secondary employment, hourly work, temporary work, seasonal work and student work, are widely seen.

In 2002, a statistical gap of 39% emerged between the number of employees directly hired in enterprises and the aggregate number of employed persons. This gap means 96.42 million people were under flexible employment (Yue 2005: 46). On these grounds, a tendency of short-term labour relations can be seen, and labour standards are hardly able to stay high. No doubt, these social problems have aggravated the instability of labour relations.

In consequence, market-oriented labour relations cause escalation of labour–capital contradictions and intensification of conflicts that also lead to tension between workers and the state. Since the beginning of twenty-first century, the focus of labour disputes in China has shifted from individual labour disputes to collective ones (see Table 3.1). This shows labour-related conflicts have become the most serious social problem, which may threat current construction of a harmonious society (Globe 2005).

Table 3.1 Numbers of collective labour disputes and workers involved from 1994 to 2006

Year	Numbers of collective labour disputes (Piece)	Annual growth rate (%)	Numbers of workers involved in collective labour disputes (Person)	Numbers of workers involved in labour disputes (Person)	Ratio of workers involved in collective disputes to all workers involved in labour disputes (%)
1994	1,482	—	52,637	77,794	67.66
1995	2,588	74.63	77,340	122,512	63.13
1996	3,150	21.72	92,203	189,120	48.75
1997	4,109	30.44	132,647	221,115	59.99
1998	6,767	64.69	251,268	358,531	70.08
1999	9,043	33.63	319,241	473,957	67.36
2000	8,247	−8.80	259,445	422,617	61.39
2001	9,847	19.40	287,000	467,000	61.46
2002	11,024	12.00	374,956	608,396	61.60
2003	10,823	−1.80	514,573	801,042	61.60
2004	19,241	77.80	477,992	764,981	62.50
2005	16,217	−15.72	409,819	744,195	55.07
2006	13,977	−13.81	348,714	679,312	51.33

Sources: China Labour Statistics Yearbook 1995–2006, Statistical Communiqué on Labour and Social Security Undertakings in 2006.

According to the 'Report of Standing Committee of National People's Congress to Examine Implementation of Labor Law', it is widely seen that labour contracts are rarely signed; short-termed and unregulated contracts prevail; standards of minimum wages have never been completely implemented; back wages still exist; mechanism of regular pay increases has not yet formed; long overtime work and bad working conditions commonly exist; social insurance system has problems of narrow coverage, low-level overall plan and severe arrears of insurance premium; labour inspection is far from sufficient and the settlement of labour disputes has too long a cycle and low efficiency. All of these problems are primary causes of the present intensified labour conflict (He 2007).

Historical evolution of trade union identity in China and theoretical hypothesis

Right after the establishment of the People's Republic of China, Chinese trade union established the guideline of 'production-centred trinity' which included production, livelihood and education. In fear of the possible accusation of the 'economy-oriented', trade unions disregarded any function in coordinating labour relations or protecting workers' interests. Therefore, such a 'detached' role from the masses leads to the dispensable role of trade unions.

Since the Chinese state conducted market reform in 1978, trade unions began to explore and strengthen its own identity and function as the representatives and protectors of employees. On the Ninth Trade Union Congress in 1978, Deng Xiaoping proposed the major role of trade unions as an organisation for enterprise democratic management and grassroots supervision. The Communist Party of China (CPC) demanded the All-China Federation of Trade Unions (ACFTU), along with its hierarchical branches, closely contacting the masses, speaking and working for employees, so as to gain the trust of workers. These became the characteristics, fundamental functions and legitimacy of the then union movement.

The Eleventh Trade Union Congress in 1988 brought up the protection function of trade unions and a tentative idea of reform. This was the first time that the four social functions of trade unions were proposed, namely 'to safeguard, to construct, to participate and to educate', which took the place of the former 'trinity' guideline under the command economy. The same Congress also put forward 'the primitive tentative plan of trade union reform', which defined the goals of union reform as 'abiding by the guiding principle and political route of the Party, to build the trade unions as independent, autonomous, fully democratic working class organisations trusted by employees, as well as influential social political group in the whole nation and society'.

The political turmoil in 1989, however, postponed such union initiatives indefinitely. In the 1990s, SOE restructure caused large-scale layoffs. Mr. Wei Jianxing, the then president of ACFTU, proposed a thorough review of union works and doctrines by requiring the union to push the implementation of the Labour Law of China[2] as the breakthrough point for union transformation. Labour rights were the focus, and Wei concentrated on collective contract to achieve the interests and rights of workers. The amendment of Trade Union Law in 2001 further defines the basic responsibility of Chinese trade union as the protection of employees' legal rights and interests.

This study aims at exploring the impacts of Chinese economic market reform on the relationship:

- between grassroots trade unions and their hierarchical upper-level union leaders;
- between trade unions and the state;
- between trade unions and employers; and
- between trade unions and Chinese workers.

The theoretical hypothesis is that following the market reform and consequently increasing labour–capital conflicts, to a certain degree, trade unions would become independent and autonomous from enterprises, and even from the party and the state (Chen 2003). Both in theory and practice, grassroots trade unions would view representation and protection of legal rights and interests for workers as their basic duty, so as to tighten the nexus between ACFTU and union members.

Methodology and basic information of the target group

Process of questionnaire survey and research methods

The target group of this questionnaire investigation is the enterprise union chairpersons and deputy chairpersons. The sample areas cover both developed and underdeveloped regions in China.[3] For the areas, some are SOE-centred and others host mostly private business. Meanwhile, different development models can also be spotted, since some provinces focus on labour-intensive manufacturing and others target at high-tech firms.

This survey lasted from March 2004 to June 2006. In total, 2,000 questionnaires were distributed to enterprises' union presidents, among which 1,811 were valid. We concluded the overall situation and variable interaction analysis through Statistical Package for Social Sciences (SPSS).

Basic information

In terms of gender, males account for 67.4% of all target persons, while females 32.6%, which reflects the fact that the majority of grassroots union chairpersons are male. As to age structure, 9.2% are from 21 and 35 years; 63.6% 36–50 and 27.2% 51–60 years. This shows middle-aged persons in the prime of life comprise the main part of union presidents. Meanwhile, since the average age of enterprise employees is getting younger, the percentage of young union chairpersons has grown to a certain degree. From the perspective of educational background, 3.4% of all union chairpersons are junior-middle-school[4] graduates, while 19.6% of them graduate from senior middle school, secondary technical school or occupational school, 41.7% from junior college, 31.6% from undergraduate university and 3.8% from postgraduate schools.

This demonstrates that the education level of union chairpersons has improved a lot in recent years, since the majority of them are at least university graduates. As a whole, the gender, age structures and educational level of grassroots union chairpersons enable them to understand union policies in more depth. They also have higher capacities of conducting their work goals.

Regarding the types of ownership, the majority of enterprises in this survey are SOEs or state-holding public-listed companies, which is 57.1%. It is followed by limited-liability companies 8.9%, joint-venture companies limited 5.4%, private firms 3.6%, collective-owned enterprises 2.9%, joint-venture companies cooperative 2.0%, foreign firms 1.9%, Hong Kong, Macao or Taiwan invested companies 0.9% and the rest of 17.4% selected as 'other ownership'. There are 15 industries in total, among which manufacturing ranks at the top with a percentage of 23.2%, followed by transportation, post and telecommunications 15.1%; electricity, coal and water 10.5%; public institution, political and social groups 8.8%; construction 8.4%; farming, forestry, herd and fishing 5.5%; education, culture, art and broadcasting 4.9%; social service 4.7%; sanitation, sports and social welfare 4.3%; mining 3.9%; wholesale, retailing and catering industry 3.5%; financing and insurance 2.2%; real estate 1.9%; geological survey and water management 1.8%; as well as scientific research and integrated technical services 1.4%.

From the perspective of history, 5.6% of the sample enterprises were established before People's Republic of China was founded in 1949; 35.8% before the 1978 market reform; 28.8% between 1980 and 1995 and the rest 29.8% after 1996.

In terms of the scale of employment, 57.8% of the firms are small, employing 10–500 people; 12.5% of the sample enterprises hire 501–1,000 employees; 21.5% 1,001–5,000; 4.2% 5001–10,000; and 4.0% more than 10,000 employees.

As a whole, this survey gives consideration to enterprises established at different historical periods, and mainly focuses on medium and small-sized enterprises, which also fit for the general feature of corporate development in the Chinese market.

Several key features of this survey

Both organising grassroots union and election of chairpersons are carried out under the close control of the CPC

Since 1978, development of Chinese trade unions has closely linked to the economic reform and economic restructuring. Most grassroots unions were either eliminated or merged in the process of SOE restructuring in 1990s. From 1999, ACFTU strengthened organising in non-public enterprises. In consequence, the number of grassroots unions rose. This survey illustrates that only 28.4% of the sample firms had union branches before the market reform, while unions in the rest enterprises were organised afterwards, among which 41.3% of the grassroots unions were founded between 1996 and 2005.

According to the Trade Union Law, Chinese trade unions are mass organisations 'formed by the working classes of their own free will' (Article II). Nevertheless, only 14.3% of union chairpersons in this survey agree with such a statement, while 82.1% of them believe the organising of their union is the 'decision of the organisation'. On the daily Chinese labour political language, 'organisation' refers to both upper-level trade union hierarchies and their equivalent CPC organs. It is almost unanimously recognised among Chinese enterprise union leaders that unions are formed from the top to the bottom.

Among the surveyed unions, 67.2% have obtained legal status as an independent social organisation separate from firms and the state. By the end of 2003, 62.2% of the unions had a membership of 5–500, 12.4% 501–1,000, 19.0% 1,001–5,000, 3.2% 5,001–10,000, and 3.1% over 10,000 members.

Regarding the ways employees joined unions, 61.5% of grassroots chairpersons believe that employees join unions with their own will, 26.9% consider all employees of their firms becoming members automatically and 10.1% think employees first receive advice from shop-stuarts and then apply for membership. Contrary to the nearly unanimous opinions on union establishment, it seems union chairpersons hold more inconsistent ideas on the question of how employees join unions.

The difference among enterprises with different ownerships in membership recruiting is also distinctive (see Table 3.2). A higher percentage of employees in SOEs or state-holding public-listed companies voluntarily join trade unions, while this percentage is lower in private enterprises. Fewer employees in the SOEs choose to join the union because of the advices from union staffs, but the advices of shop-stuarts in non-public enterprises are quite successful in recruiting members. In collective-owned enterprises, the proportion of voluntary assembly is also relatively high.

As to personal profiles of union chairpersons, 90.3% are CPC members; only 0.4% join democratic parties[5] and the remaining 9.3% do not belong to any political organisation. Before holding the position of trade union heads, most of them have acquired certain professional status in relevant enterprises or institutions. Among them, 40.6% hold positions of middle-level managers, 17.9% of union presidents serve concurrently as directors or deputy directors of CPC committees, another 13.3% are retired factory heads or managers, and 6.6% of union chairpersons are re-elected. In addition, only 4.2% of current chairpersons were ordinary employees before being elected. Regarding the tour of duty, 74.8% have taken on the very position since 2000, while 21.4% have started to hold the office from 1990s.

For the election procedure, 51.7% of the union chairpersons are nominated by the organisation,[6] and then elected by the enterprise general member assembly or representative assembly (Table 3.3). Besides, 23.3% are assigned by the organisation. Only 2.6% are elected through the general member assembly or representative assembly following open competitive screening tests.

Interestingly, when the answers are related to 'the organisation', 51.0% of 'the organisation' actually means CPC branches in the very enterprise or institution, and 17.2% refers to upper-level trade unions. 10.7% is enterprise administration, and merely 2.9% of the interviewees believe it is the grassroots union committee.

When looking at the different ways of selecting union presidents (Table 3.3), most of the union chairpersons in state-controlled companies are appointed by the organisation, while the number is relatively fewer in highly marketised enterprises.

Table 3.2 Comparison of enrolment in enterprises with different types of ownership (%)

	Types of ownership									Total
	SOEs/state-holding public-listed firms	Collective-owned enterprises	Private enterprises	Joint-venture cooperative firms	Limited-liability companies	Joint-venture companies limited	Hong Kong, Macao or Taiwan invested firms	Foreign-invested firms	Others	
Voluntary participation	64.6	52.2	46.4	55.2	57.4	60.0	61.5	65.5	58.5	61.5
Application on advice	7.8	8.7	23.2	10.3	10.1	11.1	7.7	6.3	14.1	10.1
Automatic enrolment	26.6	37.0	26.8	27.6	31.8	26.7	30.8	25.0	23.8	26.9
Others	1.0	2.2	3.6	6.9	0.7	2.2	—	3.1	3.6	1.5

Table 3.3 Comparison of the methods of selecting union presidents in different types of enterprises (%)

	Types of ownership									Total
	SOEs/state-holding public-listed firms	Collective-owned enterprises	Private enterprises	Joint-venture cooperative firms	Limited-liability companies	Joint-venture companies limited	Hong Kong, Macao or Taiwan invested firms	Foreign-invested firms	Others	
Assigned by the organisation	25.1	20.7	19.3	21.9	19.6	16.1	21.4	9.7	24.9	23.3
Nominated by the organisation, and elected by representative assembly or general assembly	53.2	41.4	49.1	56.3	58.0	55.2	50.0	45.2	45.6	51.7
Directly elected by one of the two assemblies	15.9	36.2	24.6	18.8	21.0	25.3	28.6	32.3	22.4	19.6
After the test, elected by one of the two assemblies	3.4		1.8	3.1	1.4	2.3		3.2	1.4	2.6
Others	2.4	1.7	5.3			1.1	9.7	9.7	5.7	2.9

Emerging signs and practices of democracy within grassroots unions

Member representative assembly is becoming increasingly influential

The union member representative assembly is the decision-making body within enterprise trade unions. However, it is not explicated on the 2001 amendment draft of the Trade Union Law. This survey shows 83.8% of the enterprise unions have set up representative assemblies, but 16.2% still have not. Among enterprises with different types of ownership, SOEs are more likely to establish representative assemblies (see Table 3.4). The majority of medium and small-sized firms still haven't set up the assemblies.

Gradual completion of union institutions

Among all enterprises, around 23.4% of grassroots union committees set up standing committees, of which 48.5% have fewer than 5 members of standing committee, 36.9% 6–10 members and 14.6% more than 11 members. Importantly, enterprise trade union is a whole bureaucratic institution with full range of functional departments or committees, which are set up immediately after the union establishment (Table 3.5).

Selection of deputy chairpersons

In most of the cases, vice enterprise CPC branch director serves as chairperson of a grassroots union, so it is often the deputy who is actually responsible for doing the daily works.

Usually, each of the unions has only one deputy chairperson. The survey shows 81.1% of such cases, with 15.4% having two deputies and only 3.5% having more than three deputy union chairpersons. Concerning union committees, 53.6% of them have no more than 5 members, 29.9% have 6–10 and 16.5% no fewer than 11 members.

Of all, 57.3% of the deputies are nominated by the organisations, and then elected by representative assembly or general assembly; 20.1% are directly appointed by the organisation and 16.3% are elected through member representatives.

Professionalisation and socialisation of union chairpersons

In recent years, some local trade unions select union leadership through open recruitment. All qualified persons are registered in a talent database of professional trade union chairpersons. Then, these talents are ready to be detached, according to the needs of non-public enterprise unions. After a probation period, they may be officially installed through democratic election of the member assembly. The local trade union, rather than enterprise union, pays their wages and other welfare. Such reform is distinguished as 'professionalisation and socialisation of union chairpersons'. The survey tries to see the opinions of union chairpersons on this reform (see Table 3.6).

Table 3.4 Comparison of the establishment of trade union member representative assembly in different types of enterprises (%)

	Types of ownership									Total
	SOEs/state-holding public-listed firms	Collective-owned enterprises	Private enterprises	Joint-venture cooperative firms	Limited-liability companies	Joint-venture companies limited	Hong Kong, Macao or Taiwan invested firms	Foreign-invested firms	Others	
Established	89.5	84.3	58.9	60.7	82.9	81.8	66.7	73.3	74.4	83.8
Not yet	10.5	15.7	41.1	39.3	17.1	18.2	33.3	26.7	25.6	16.2

Table 3.5 Institutions in grassroots trade unions (%)

Titles of operational department/committee	Proportion of established	Titles of operational department/committee	Proportion of established
General office	36.4	Work of women workers	65.1
Organising	36.5	Labour protection	45.5
Propaganda	38.9	Support employees in need	41.5
Publicity	33.1	Protection of rights and benefits	32.1
Work of employees	33.4		

Table 3.6 Different opinions on professionalisation and socialisation of union chairpersons (%)

Ideas	Agree	Disagree
1. Favourable for reasonably delegating capable union leaders	91.8	8.2
2. Favourable for ensuring economic security of union leaders	90.5	9.5
3. Favourable for independently launching activities to protect employees' legal rights and benefits in assigned enterprises	87.7	12.3
4. Favourable for strengthening the connection between grassroots unions and upper-level unions to enhance the power of union as a whole	88.4	11.6
5. Unfavourable for further work, since delegated union leaders know little about the enterprise conditions	50.7	49.3
6. Even though it is good to set up a talent bank, not many people will actively apply	43.5	56.5
7. Delegated union presidents/leaders may easily have conflicts with other union leaders, which harms the solidarity within grassroots unions	40.8	59.2
8. The relations between delegated union presidents/leaders and party and administration organisations may be hard to coordinate, which is unfavourable for developing union activities and improving union status	45.5	54.5
9. This practice is worth to be promoted in all parts of the country	74.7	25.3

Consensus on alliance and representation system

Alliance and representation system is another key union institution, in which union leadership is composed of representatives from subordinate grassroots unions or lower-level unions, so that trade unions can be responsible for bottom-up alliance and representation.

Table 3.7 Different opinions on alliance and representation system (%)

Major points of view	Agree	Disagree
1. In favour of implementing the guidelines and decisions of the upper unions	95.9	4.1
2. In favour of reporting problems of grassroots union activities to the upper unions	94.9	5.1
3. To strengthen the organisational power of unions through improved leading system between upper and lower unions	93.7	6.3
4. Even participating in the assemblies of upper unions, it is still hard to influence on the decisions	45.0	55.0
5. Since each grassroots union is facing different problems, only the respective trade union itself can manage to handle them.	55.3	44.7
6. It is not favourable for a harmonious relationship among the party, administration and trade union at grassroots level, if the connection between grassroots unions and upper unions is too close.	20.6	79.4

This system was put forward in the Eleventh Trade Union Congress in 1998. Until now, it has been recorded into the constitution of the ACFTU. Table 3.7 demonstrates that the attitudes of grassroots union chairpersons are relatively consistent. Nevertheless, since this survey does not list 'to strengthen the internal democracy within trade unions' as one of the optional reasons for promoting the alliance and representation system, it is hard to illustrate what values grassroots union chairpersons hold towards this system.

Establishment of 'Warrant Fund for Trade Union Chairpersons'

In recent years, the establishment of 'Warrant Fund for Trade Union Chairpersons' or 'Special Fund for Trade Union Chairpersons' is an important protective measure for union chairpersons, who can be vulnerable in representing labour rights; 83.4% of union chairpersons think this fund is necessary. Among those supporters, 85.4% believe that 'although I have no experience of life difficulties as mentioned above, I think these measures are necessary to help myself keep my mind on union work'. Only 5.7% of them show the major reason as 'I have been through such kinds of hardship'.

Financial independence of grassroots trade unions

The financial condition is the basis for union independence. Trade Union Law has the stipulation that unions are able to apply for the court enforcement order if the enterprises or institutions refuse to allocate union membership dues, which is 2% of the aggregate enterprise wage.

In general, 80.5% of sampled unions have their own independent bank accounts, and the other 19.5% not (Table 3.8). In most enterprises, trade union activities rely on union funds collected in the respective enterprise, but in other

Table 3.8 Comparison of independent financial accounts of enterprise unions with different ownerships (%)

Types of ownership									Total
SOEs/state-holding public-listed firms	Collective-owned enterprises	Private enterprises	Joint-venture cooperative firms	Limited-liability companies	Joint-venture companies limited	Hong Kong, Macao or Taiwan invested firms	Foreign-invested firms	Others	
With such accounts 85.5	67.3	53.8	48.3	82.1	81.0	75.0	78.1	73.3	80.5
Without such accounts 14.2	32.7	46.2	51.7	17.9	19.0	25.0	21.9	26.9	19.5

Table 3.9 Comparison of whether corporate administrative approval is required in using union funds with different ownerships (%)

Types of ownership									Total
SOEs/state-holding public-listed firms	Collective-owned enterprises	Private enterprises	Joint-venture cooperative firms	Limited-liability companies	Joint-venture companies limited	Hong Kong, Macao or Taiwan invested firms	Foreign-invested firms	Others	
Yes 25.9	40.5	66.7	66.7	26.3	27.6	33.3	18.5	39.0	30.6
No 74.1	59.5	33.3	33.3	73.7	72.4	66.7	81.5	61.0	69.4

enterprises, unions may have other incomes from their own activities, while the union dues contributed by members account for a relatively smaller proportion in total union funds. When trade unions use the funds, 69.4% possess complete financial domination, and do not need any approval of administration in the employers (Table 3.9). However, the other 30.6% still need the ratification of corporate administrative leaders.

In recent years, the task of collecting grassroots union dues is entrusted to taxation bureaus of the local governments in some regions. Only 27.1% of union chairpersons support this practice, while 72.9% are not in favour of it. When we further asked whether they adopted such a method, 96.6% said no and only 3.4% answered yes. Among all unions having not adopted the method, only 14.4% indicate that they plan to use this method, and the other 85.6% clearly say they will not adopt it in future. The situation of whether expenditure of union fund is confused by enterprise administration with different ownership is shown in Table 3.10 and major arguments against entrustment to tax offices are listed in Table 3.11.

Union works

Protection of workers' rights and benefits has become the basic responsibility of enterprise unions. Safeguarding mechanisms such as collective bargaining, employees democratic participation and labour dispute settlement have been developing (Table 3.12).

According to Table 3.12, the top choice of union tasks includes: (1) collective negotiation and collective contract (68.9%), (3) to timely report to administration of members' opinions and work for a solution (12.5%) and (4) to promote democratic management and open-factory-affair activities (8.9%). Union activities which rank second are: (2) to mediate and arbitrate labour disputes (28.8%), (4) to promote democratic management and open-factory-affair activities (27.2%) and (3) to timely report to administration of members' opinions and work for a solution (19.0%). On the third position, union activities consist of: (4) to promote democratic management and open-factory-affair activities (22.1%), (3) to timely report to administration of members' opinions and work for a solution (15.3%), and (6) to help administration carry out labour protection measures and to administer them (15.1%). On the fourth position, activities are: (10) to organise activities such as occupational training and technological innovation (17.1%), (13) to defend the rights and benefits of women workers (13.4%), and (6) to help administration carry out labour protection measures and to administer them (12.7%). And on the fifth position, union tasks are: (14) to help members in life hardship through many activities (46.7%), (13) to defend the rights and benefits of women workers (12.9%) and (10) to organise activities such as occupational training and technological innovation (7.8%). We find that almost all top five popular choices are closely connected to protection of labour rights and benefits, which indicates a substantial enhancement of representation and safeguarding functions of trade unions. Besides, union presidents are highly unanimous in understanding this.

Let us take the example of collective negotiation and collective contract, which ranks at the top. Unions on behalf of members have signed collective contracts

Table 3.10 Comparison of whether expenditure of union fund is confused by enterprise administration with different ownerships (%)

	Types of ownership									Total
	SOEs/state-holding public-listed firms	Collective-owned enterprises	Private enterprises	Joint-venture cooperative firms	Limited-liability companies	Joint-venture companies limited	Hong Kong, Macao or Taiwan invested firms	Foreign-invested firms	Others	
Yes	24.6	16.4	36.7	37.9	22.2	25.6	100.0	13.8	24.8	24.4
No	75.4	83.6	63.3	62.1	77.8	74.4		86.2	75.2	75.6

Table 3.11 Reasons why union chairpersons are against the practice of collecting dues by taxation bureaus (%)

1. Distrust of tax offices on collecting dues	7.2
2. Collection of dues by tax offices may lead to the impression that union finance is subordinate to public finance, so it is unfavourable for union autonomy	40.5
3. Grassroots unions originally assume the responsibility of collecting dues. Giving up one part of its responsibility may act as a disincentive to grassroots unions	35.4
4. Grassroots unions originally assume the responsibility of collecting dues. Now the practice that local unions or tax offices start to collect dues by signing contracts may harm the solidarity between local unions and grassroots ones	29.5
5. Other causes	5.2

Table 3.12 Tasks of union work

1. To negotiate with corporate administration on working conditions, such as wage, bonus, working hours and welfare, and to sign collective contract
2. To mediate and arbitrate labour disputes
3. To listen to members, report their opinions to corporate administration and work for a solution
4. To promote democratic corporate management and open factory affairs, as the agency of employees' congress
5. To assist administration on handling social insurance and supervising it
6. To help administration carry out labour protection measures, including working hours, safety and health management, and to administer them
7. To educate members on labour rights and obligations
8. To register for new members, and manage files of members
9. To conduct ideological and political education for members, in cooperation with party committee and youth league committee
10. To organise activities such as occupational training and technological innovation
11. To elect advanced production workers and model workers
12. To know the life and thoughts of members from time to time
13. To defend the rights and benefits of women workers concerning physiological, maternal and parental leave, and to carry out family planning
14. To help members in life hardship through mutual helping funds, mutual insurance, and 'giving warmth' activities, as well as to organise cultural and sport activities

with enterprise administration in 72.6% of all investigated enterprises. In enterprises with different ownerships, SOEs have the highest rate of signing collective contracts, while this rate is the lowest in foreign-invested enterprises. Besides, in more market-oriented enterprises, the rate of signing collective contracts is lower (see Table 3.13). Among them, 82.1% of enterprises with collective contracts discuss and approve the draft of collective contract on employee congresses, while the other 17.9% do not (Table 3.14). Generally speaking, more drafts have been approved after discussion by employee congresses in public enterprises than in higher market-oriented enterprises. In fact, most private enterprises and

Table 3.13 Comparison of conclusion of collective contracts in enterprises with different ownerships

Types of ownership									Total
	SOEs/state-holding public-listed firms	Collective-owned enterprises	Private enterprises	Joint-venture cooperative firms	Limited-liability companies	Joint-venture companies limited	Hong Kong, Macao or Taiwan invested firms	Foreign-invested firms	Others	
Signed	79.5	71.1	69.1	70.4	77.8	71.3	64.3	51.7	48.0	72.6
Not yet signed	20.5	28.9	30.9	29.6	22.2	28.7	35.7	48.3	52.0	27.4

Table 3.14 Comparison of whether the draft of collective contracts should be passed by employee congress (%)

Types of ownership									Total
	SOEs/state-holding public-listed firms	Collective-owned enterprises	Private enterprises	Joint-venture cooperative firms	Limited-liability companies	Joint-venture companies limited	Hong Kong, Macao or Taiwan invested firms	Foreign-invested firms	Others	
Yes	88.8	89.1	54.2	56.5	84.6	80.3	70.0	53.3	62.1	82.1
No	11.2	10.9	45.8	43.5	15.4	19.7	30.0	46.7	37.9	17.9

foreign-invested enterprises do not even have institutions like employee congress. A majority of 84.1% collective contracts have been made public to all employees, but the other 15.9% have not been announced. Among enterprises which publicise collective contracts, 29.9% of them hold a special conference to announce the collective contracts, 20.3% distribute printed text of collective contracts to employees, 19.8% read out the text to all employees, 13.8% post up in the bulletin board and the other 4.0% use other methods to publish them. In addition, 55.3% of all enterprises with collective contracts even set up an inspection and supervision panel for collective contracts. In a word, if only looking at the procedures and forms, the framework of collective contract system has been constructed in China, and the concept of collective negotiation as the way of coordinating labour relations has also filtered into the minds of union presidents.

Regarding the mediation of labour disputes, 69.9% of all unions answered that they already set up the labour dispute mediation committee of enterprises, while the other 30.1% have not yet established such an organisation. Among different ownerships, SOEs have a higher percentage of setting up such committees than in collective-owned enterprises and private ones (see Table 3.15).

To inquire into the major causes of labour disputes, we devised ten options and asked union presidents to pick the most common three items (see Table 3.16).

From the statistical result, the top reasons for labour disputes are: (1) Signing labour contracts (32.1%); (2) Dismissal of employees (28.8%); (4) Payment of labour (25.6%). At the second rank, answers include: (4) Payment of labour (33.8%), (5) Insurance and welfare (18.3%) and (2) Dismissal of employees (14.5%). The third-ranked choices are: (8) Working hours/rest and vacation (26.0%), (5) Insurance and welfare (17.2%) and (6) Labour protection, safety and health (14.2%). We conclude that the top three popular choices are all closely linked to employment and working conditions of employees, among which employment and dismissal, wages and bonus, as well as insurance and welfare are the main causes of labour disputes.

New stage of social involvement of enterprise trade union to promote its status and strength

We investigated the relationship between grassroots unions and ordinary members. Of all union chairpersons, 12.6% believe ordinary members have highly positive impression about unions, 54.3% consider a relatively good impression, and the percentages of those answering 'not very good' or 'very bad' are 1.3% and 0.1%, respectively.

Meanwhile, we also find out the ways of unions to ask or to grasp the opinions and requests of ordinary members, which are family visit (35.7%), questionnaire survey (37.2%), special workshop (59.6%), publicising the reception telephone number of trade unions (20.2%), setting up reception days of union presidents (10.9%) and installing suggestion box on union work (20.9%).

Another topic concerned is how to deal with the relationship between grassroots union committees and upper-level unions. Regarding the job assistance for which

Table 3.15 Comparison of establishing labour dispute mediation committees in enterprise with different ownerships (%)

Types of ownership									Total
SOEs/state-holding public-listed firms	Collective-owned enterprises	Private enterprises	Joint-venture cooperative firms	Limited-liability companies	Joint-venture companies limited	Hong Kong, Macao or Taiwan invested firms	Foreign-invested firms	Others	
Established	77.1	44.2	46.3	63.0	76.2	72.3	57.1	64.3	52.2	69.9
Not yet established	22.9	55.8	53.7	37.0	23.8	27.7	42.9	35.7	47.8	30.1

Table 3.16 Major causes of labour disputes

1. Signing labour contracts
2. Dismissal of employees
3. Voluntary resignation of employees
4. Payment of labour
5. Insurance and welfare
6. Labour protection, safety and health
7. Occupational training
8. Working hours/rest and vacation
9. Safeguarding rights and benefits of women workers
10. Others

grassroots unions need most from upper-level unions, 45.7% of chairpersons select the task to better response on labour rights and employees' requirements, 34.8% believe in active participation in macro-level lawmaking or regulation-making, and another 18.5% hope to receive policy training and legal consultation for higher hierarchical unions.

Participation in the CPC activities is an important way for trade union to promote its own position. CPC organisations exist in 96.5% of all the sampled enterprises. Moreover, 68.9% of all union chairpersons are members of enterprise CPC committees, which also host 7.1% of deputy chairpersons and 8.2% of other union committee members.

The mutual relations between grassroots unions and enterprise administration also have direct impact on union status. Among all enterprises with directorates, 31.0% of union chairpersons engage in the company board of directors as employee representatives. It is the case for 3.5% of union deputy chairpersons, or 5.2% of other union committee members. During the process of selecting employee board directors, 57.6% are elected by employee congress and 11.5% by union committee, while the remaining 30.9% do not have any election.

With regard to the relationship with other social organisations, such as local Women's Federation, Communist Youth League Committee, Committee of Aged Personnel, etc., 67.2% of the sampled unions have set up cooperative mechanisms. For instance, in the year 2003, 24.7% of the unions provided labour force and material resources for community works, 38.6% held social and public activities in cooperation with local communities, 4.0% made all facilities open to local communities and 11.2% organised active members to undertake a variety of voluntary labour in spare time. However, 19.5% of all unions have still not participated in any community activities.

In recent years, grassroots unions pay more attention to media relations. About 26.2% of the unions published union newspapers or journals. Besides, unions also reached local newspapers or journals (19.3%), local radio or television (15.3%), ACFTU newspapers or journals (8.3%), national newspapers or magazines (4.8%), and national broadcast or television (2.1%).

During our survey, an evaluation from union chairpersons on certain organisations (as in Table 3.17) is also required. The question is the contact with which

Table 3.17 Organisations most influential on realising the opinions and requests of grassroots unions and their members

---

1. Corporate administration of the very unit
2. CPC organisation of the very unit
3. Local government
4. Local CPC committee
5. Local deputy to the People's Congress/Commissar of the People's Political Consultative Conference
6. Local trade union federation
7. Government at a higher level
8. CPC committee at a higher level
9. Deputy to the People's Congress/Commissar of the People's Political Consultative Conference at a higher level
10. Trade union federation at a higher level
11. Central government
12. Central CPC Committee
13. Deputy to the National People's Congress/Commissar of the Chinese People's Political Consultative Conference
14. ACFTU
15. Social organisations/scholars/democratic parties[5]
16. Local media
17. National media

---

organisations could most effectively solve problems regarding reporting members' opinions and realising their requirements. Each chairperson was required to choose three organisations by the order of importance.

As the result, the top choices include: (1) Corporate administration of the very unit (73.3%), (2) CPC organisation of the very unit (13.7%) and (6) Local trade union federation (2.6%). On the second place, the choices are: (2) CPC organisation of the very unit (55.8%), (1) Corporate administration of the very unit (10.3%) and (6) Local trade union federation (6.4%). The third rank is composed of: (10) Trade union federation at a higher level (33.9%), (6) Local trade union federation (17.0%) and (8) CPC committee at a higher level (9.8%).

We find that enterprise CPC organisation or corporate administration receives most credits, which indicate union chairpersons can be quite realistic or rational in analysing local problems. In addition, chairpersons usually have higher expectations on upper-level unions, which show a high expectation for ACFTU from the grassroots union practitioners.

What are the major factors that obstruct union work? Of the union chairpersons, 50.2% consider insufficient understanding of enterprise administration on the status and function of trade unions as the major factor, 44.4% believe the difficult financial situation is a major problem for trade unions, 40.3% think union leaders have no adequate knowledge and ability, 34.9% attribute the obstruction to lack of initiative of union leaders, 25.9% criticise insufficient comprehension of enterprise CPC committee on the status and function of trade union, 17.9% deem current union activities do not meet the needs of employees and 13.1% impute to the inadequate support from upper unions. It is fair to say the answers of most union chairpersons reflect both their perplexity and deliberation on how to develop union work during the transition to market economy.

Conclusion

It is necessary to notice that this survey focuses on the subjective cognition of enterprise trade union chairpersons so as to understand their opinions on the transformation of Chinese trade union as well as its relationship with CPC, government, firms and workers. One interesting finding is about their identification with the professionalisation and socialisation of union chairpersons, independence of unions from employers, their affirmation of union democratic innovations such as alliance and representation systems, and so forth.

The most recognised conclusion of this survey is that grassroots trade unions have strengthened their efforts in protecting the rights and benefits of union members and other employees, which have been fully embodied in many aspects, such as the establishment of safeguarding mechanism and the growing awareness of protection for union chairpersons. Nevertheless, these achievements are rather the outcome of CPC pressure for political stability on the labour side, than a result of member-driven change within the union hierarchy.

Although there are signs of internal democracy within grassroots unions, top-down appointments or domination still maintains and leads to sustainable characteristics of union bureaucracy. Also, the empowerment of industrial or craft unions is out of question under the current CPC and union work agenda. Thus, many safeguarding mechanisms such as collective negotiation and democratic participation remain on-paper campaigns.

Moreover, it is almost impossible to have union-led industrial actions like strike. At the end of 2006, the ACFTU proposed 'the Socialist Trade Union's Perspective on Safeguarding Workers' Rights with Chinese Characteristics', which indicates a lawful and scientific protection of labour rights. It puts forward that the concept of 'harmonious labour relations' that depend on unified labour–capital–state interests and a collaborative model of dispute resolution.

In this sense, it is not likely that China will ratify the right to strike in the near future, and the ACFTU hierarchy is not about to introduce confrontational tools to represent labour interests. Under this circumstance, realisation of labour rights relies heavily on state legislation or regulation. There is not much space for grassroots unions to initiate assertive tactics or strategies to stand for employee rights and interests, besides act as an enforcement institution of labour law.

For this reason, the ACFTU even revised its working guideline into 'Promoting enterprise development and safeguarding employees rights and interests', which creates a special combination of capital and labour interests for restructuring labour relations in the market economy.

As a result, the Chinese trade union is playing an extremely complicated role towards the party-state, firms and workers. The emphasis of trade union on labour right protection and representation is more vested in the function of maintaining political and social stability. The changes mentioned above on the survey are in the process, so it still demands further observation to see if they exercise a great influence on the transformation of union movement. This reminds us that trade union is not just the outcome of economic interest contradiction, but even more an instrument of political game. As Chinese workers are practising self or non-governmental organisations to pursue their interests, the union is under an awkward situation. The characteristics of the Chinese trade union can be clarified as a multiple representative organisation for both the state and market actors.

Endnotes

1   This chapter is based on the project 'Survey on Grassroots Trade Union Chairman', which is jointly conducted by the China Institute of Industrial Relations of the All China Federation of Trade Unions, Hosei University, and Meiji University of Japan.
2   The Labour Law of China was enacted in 1995. However, the Chinese labour legislation has two definitions, collective and individual labour relations. The current Labour Law acts as a de facto employment law, rather than a safeguard for collective labour rights.
3   Ten provinces are covered, including Liaoning, Beijing, Shanghai, Zhejiang, Guangdong, Gansu, Guizhou, Guangxi, Hebei and Henan.
4   Chinese educational system is composed of six-year primary schooling, three-year junior middle school, three-year senior middle school and four-year college education. Secondary technical school and occupational school recruit graduates from junior middle school, and take 3–4 years to finish the courses.
5   According to the Constitution of China, CPC is the leading party and there are eight so-called democratic parties, which participate in political consulting but cannot replace the ruling party.
6   They are nominated either by the upper-level unions or by the CPC branches.

References

Chen, Feng (2003), "Between the State and Labor: The Conflict of Chinese Trade Unions' Double Identity in Market Reform," *The China Quarterly*, vol. 176: 1006–1028.

Chen Lihua (2005), "Group Incidents are Testing China," no. 8: 54–56.

He, Luli (2005), "Report by The Standing Committee of The National People's Congress about Examination On Implementation of The Labour Law of China," National People's Congress of China.

Qiao, Jian and Jiang, Ying (2004), "*Shichanghua jincheng zhong de laodong zhengyi he laogong quntixingshijian fenxi*" (Analysis on Labor Disputes and Collective Labor Incidents in Market Reform), in Lu Xueyi and Li Peilin (eds), *Analysis and Forecast of Social Trends in China 2005*, Beijing: China Social Sciences Press, pp. 315.

Qiao, Jian (2007), "*Luelun woguo laodongguanxi de zhuanxing ji dangqian tezheng*" (Theory on Transformation of Labor Relations in China and Its Current Features), *Journal of China Institute of Industrial Relations*, vol. 2: 35.

Research Centre of the All China Federation of Trade Unions (2006), "Outline of New Socialist Labour Relations," *Study on Trade Union Movements*, vol. 5: 18.

Sun, Chunlan (2006), "Report on The Fourth Executive Committee Meeting at 14th ACFTU Congress," All China Federation of Trade Unions.

Sun, Zhongfan, An, Miao and Feng, Tongqing (eds) (1997), "*Xiang shehuizhuyi shichangjingji zhuanbian shiqi de gonghui lilun langyao yu shuping*" (Outline and Review of Trade Union Theory During The Transition To Socialist Market Economy), Beijing: People's Publishing House.

Wang, Shaoguang and He, Jianyu (2004), "*Zhongguo de shetuan geming*" (Mass Organization Revolution in China), *Zhejiang Academic Journal*, vol. 149, November: 67.

Yue, Ximing (2005), "*Woguo xianxing laodong tongji de wenti*" (Problems of Existing Labor Statistics in China), *Economic Research*, vol. 3: 46.

Zhang, Guimao and Zheng, Yongnian (eds) (2005), "*Liangan shehuiyundong fenxi*" (Analysis on Social Movements in Two Shores), Taipei: Taiwan Third Nature Publishing Co. Ltd.

Zhang, Zuhua (2007), "*Weiquan shidai de lailin*" (The Coming Epoch of Right Protection), *Citizen*, vol. 1: 12.

4 The morphogenesis of the CPC: Organizational issues

Masaharu Hishida

Introduction

In area studies on contemporary China, whether in the field of politics or economics or society, the Communist Party of China (CPC) is always at the heart of the matter. Even when research makes a certain degree of headway, the existence of the party remains as a final enigma. The CPC, whose party constitution stipulates that it is "the core of leadership," looms over everything.

The CPC has an extremely unique character. As the only legally established political party in China, it has held onto the reins of power for more than half a century, a rare example in the world, and it boasts the largest membership among political parties in the world. Not only that, this organization has a huge nationwide pyramid-shaped structure and taps the best and brightest human resources in the land.

Despite these facts, however, little is known about the CPC. One of the reasons is that in the pre-revolution period the CPC existed as an underground and illegal organization, and its closed and secretive character remained largely unchanged even after the party seized power in 1949. Indeed, during the Cold War period the party further intensified this traditional secretiveness with the aim of maintaining power, and a kind of esotericism became one of its characteristics.

In this chapter, I will look at the CPC as a political and social organization. Analyzing its characteristics from the point of view of organizational theory, and in particular the evolutionary theory of organizations and the theory of self-organization, I will attempt to illustrate the state of morphogenesis in the party (the process of transformation of an organization from confusion and chaos to a new order) in order to demonstrate this as a main background factor for various efforts of reforming trade unions discussed in the previous chapters.

An "organization," of course, is mainly a social system for controlling the exercise of "intimidation and coercion" among different entities.[1] However, if the aspect of the exercise of "persuasion and guidance" is also taken into consideration, then first and foremost the CCP can be understood as a network type of social system. Although the tendency toward centralization as described in classical bureaucratic theory can certainly be seen in the CPC, the characteristics of formulation (the performance of duties based on clear regulations and procedures) and impersonalization (weakened human relations) are not apparent. Indeed, it can be said conversely that personalized informality and individuality have traditionally been the principal characteristics of the CPC.

As a result of changes in the external environment surrounding the party (the weakening of ideology, the slackening of party cell functions, doubts about legitimacy, etc.), the *magnetic strength* and *magnetic field* that this party has maintained are declining.[2] Following on from this work, in this chapter I will consider changes in the internal conditions of the organization in terms of changes in shared objectives, the desire to contribute, communication, and membership structure, which are the factors of analysis in organizational theory. From the uncertainty of the external environment and the slackening of the internal structure, I will show that while still maintaining its role as "the core of leadership," this organization is pregnant with elements of chaos and confusion within.

For a start, why do people participate in this organization? What are their motives in joining the party? Are there any differences in the meaning of the organization and its image between party members (and potential members) and nonparty members ("the masses")?

Furthermore, how far do these motives for joining the party actually function in the real world, and are there really any practical merits in becoming a party member?

As a consequence of reforms since 1978, which have changed the social system in China as a whole to one focusing on personal gain, the tendency toward individualization within the party itself has become striking. In addition to the above-mentioned traditional characteristic of individuality that exists in the organization, this feature of personal gain casts a serious shadow over the legitimacy of the party's rhetoric about being "the core of leadership."

In response to this internal crisis, the CCP eventually adopted the theory of the "Three Represents." Will this theory save the organization from confusion, or will it bring about new chaos? Will the private entrepreneurs, the so-called *laoban* party members, really bring about the evolution of the organization as a mutation of the neo-contingency theory? I will consider the possibilities for the morphogenesis of the organization as it shifts from being an ideological "normative" organization to being a "utilitarian" organization (Etzioni 1964).

Organizational crisis

Stagnation of activities

If one looks at the CPC as an organization, one can see that it is indeed facing a crisis. That is to say, the external environment surrounding the party is undergoing major changes. Over a zigzag course of political changes since the founding of the present state in 1949, the socialist ideology that was the source of this organization's absorptive power has become less and less effective. This decline has reached a climax since China entered a period of reform and opening.

Another reflection of the crisis is the fact that the party cells that supported the organization in the past have become steadily looser. In the period of Mao Zedong, party branches existed within all organizations in China, such as plants and enterprises, but now the number of places without cells is rapidly increasing. Although the establishment of party organizations is being urged in private companies and foreign-affiliated companies that have emerged as new entities since implementation of the policy of reform and opening, it cannot be said that the building of party organizations is progressing in accordance with the initial goal. The state-run sector is just about maintaining the level of party cell organizations, but in corporate management real authority has shifted to the management side. The function of absolute guidance and surveillance that the party previously boasted is now already a thing of the past. What this means is that the party is losing the bases that in the past functioned as a *magnetic field* enabling it to wield its absorptive power. As a result of this slackening of the external environment surrounding the party and doubts about its legitimacy from an ideological point of view, it can be said that the magnetic force and magnetic field that the party maintained in the past are weakening.[3]

Accordingly, in this sense, it appears that the party is seeing a rapid decline in its coercive and normative characteristics as an organization.

Let us specifically examine the situation. Among village-level party organizations at the base of the nationwide pyramid-shaped organizational structure, "empty nests" are expanding and rural party members are becoming marginalized. Looking at such cases as Cixi and Shanghai, we can see that the decline in cohesive power is giving rise to a situation in which "party members cannot find party organizations even if they look" and, vice versa, "party organizations cannot find party members even if they look."

Organizational strength of the party

As shown in Figure 4.1, in response to the question "Who do you want to help you when you are facing difficulty?, in Cixi Village Ningbo City, Zhejiang Province more respondents cited the local party organization (38%) than friends (28%) or relatives (27%). However, asked about the level of cohesive power of the party organization over its members, while a total of 61% replied "strong" or "quite strong," 34% replied "so-so" (Figure 4.2). In view of the reality of questionnaire surveys conducted in present-day China, this reply of "so-so" deserves attention. It seems to suggest a negative rejection. Similarly, asked about the mutual absorptive power among party members, while a total of 53% answered "strong" or "quite strong," 38% of respondents gave this "so-so" reply (Figure 4.3).

This negative dissatisfaction becomes even clearer in the level of enthusiasm for participating in party organization activities. As shown in Figure 4.4, while a high ratio of 70% of respondents had a positive attitude and replied "actively participate," other respondents had the negative motive of participating out of consideration for the party's position, with 17% giving the ambivalent reply

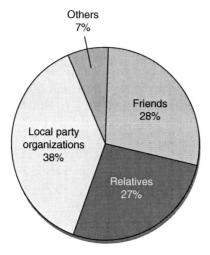

Figure 4.1 Who do you want to help you when you are facing difficulty?

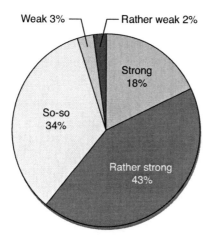

Figure 4.2 How do you evaluate cohesive power of the party organization over its members?

of "participate if interested, do not participate if not interested" and 13% saying "participate out of respect for the party organization." If a similar questionnaire had been conducted on rural party members in the past, for example, from immediately after the founding of the present-day Chinese state to the 1960s and the period of the Cultural Revolution, it can be easily guessed that expressing such an ambivalent attitude toward party activities – in other words, placing a certain distance between oneself and party activities – would have been impossible.

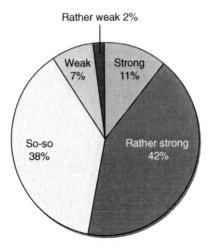

Figure 4.3 How do you evaluate the mutual absorptive power among party members?

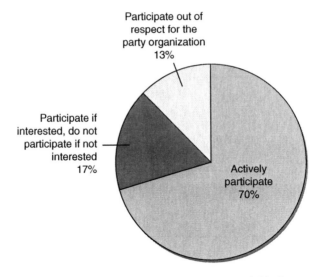

Figure 4.4 Do you actively participate in party organization activities?

Party dues

As a manifestation of the reality behind this enthusiasm to participate in party activities, let us take a look at the state of payment of party dues, which is a primary obligation of party members.

Members who have been officially allowed to join the CPC are obliged to pay party dues. These dues, which upon application are reduced or waived for people with no income or people in economic difficulty, amount to a fixed monthly sum of

Table 4.1 Payment of party dues

	Monthly wage in RMB¥ (after tax)	*Payment*
	<400	0.5%
	400–600	1.0%
Fixed rate	600–800	1.5%
	800–1,500	2.0%
	>1,500	3.0%
Fixed amount	Peasants	2 *jiao*
	Unemployed, etc.	2 *jiao*
Dues reduced or waived	People with no income, or in economic difficulty	Reduced or waived upon application

0.2 yuan plus an amount calculated according to the member's standard monthly wage (0.5–3.0%). So even for the highest income earners receiving over 1,500 yuan a month, the party dues are no more than 45 yuan a month (Table 4.1).[2]

Figure 4.5 shows the state of payment of party dues in the Cixi area. Exemplary party members who "pay myself when the payment period comes" account for 63% of respondents. However, 33% of respondents also replied that they "pay when reminded after the payment period has passed." In other words, the ratio of positive payment to negative payment is 2:1. Moreover, it is somewhat surprising to see that 3% of respondents "have not been paying for a long time" and 1% "do not know" about the basic obligation of party members to pay party dues.[4]

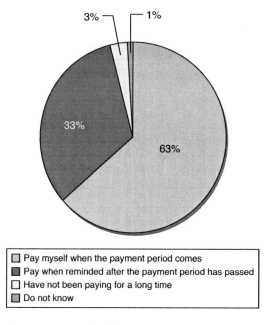

Figure 4.5 How do you pay party dues?

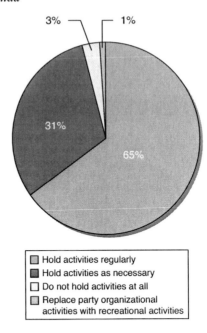

3%   ⌐   1%

31%

65%

Hold activities regularly
Hold activities as necessary
Do not hold activities at all
Replace party organizational
    activities with recreational activities

Figure 4.6 Party member organizational life system.

Party member organizational life system

As well as the payment of party dues, people who become party members are obliged to participate in the various activities carried out by the party organization. This is called the "party member organizational life *dang zuzhi shenghuo* system." As shown in Figure 4.6, members are required to participate in all kinds of activities, from regional party congresses to party study classes and so on. From the specific state of these activities, we can sense desperation on the organizing side and a low level of enthusiasm among participants.

First of all, regarding the state of holding of these activities, as shown in Figure 4.6, while almost all basic party organizations "hold activities regularly" (65%), 31% "hold activities as necessary" and, in extreme cases, 3% "do not hold activities at all" and 1% "replace party organizational activities with recreational activities."

Party study classes

At the core of these activities are party study classes. Outside observers might call them "political studies." According to the Organization Department of the CPC, party study classes "relating to central duties and matters of interest to party members shall be linked to practical work and developed in a planned manner." The objective of these party study classes is "to teach party members about party qualities, basic knowledge of the party, the party line, principles, and policies, and

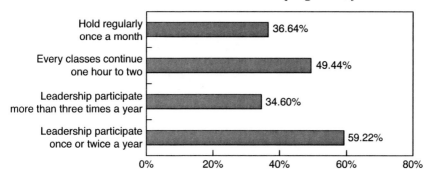

Figure 4.7 Party study classes.

other general educational topics and to increase its power of absorption." Although it is suggested that the main responsible officials in party branches should give lectures themselves in the classes, Figure 4.7 shows what actually happens in the case of Ningbo in Zhejiang Province.

It is obligatory to hold party study classes at least once a year. In almost one-third of cases, classes are held every month, which suggests a positive attitude. In practice, however, these classes last no more than a couple of hours at the most each time, and in the majority of cases the leadership (that is to say, the responsible officials in party branches and so on) participate only once or twice a year.

Regarding problems in the present state of implementation of party study classes, the party's Organization Department in Ningbo laments that first of all, with regard to ideological understanding, vague and erroneous ideas are increasing because of a lack of ideological awareness, and the grapevine is abuzz with gossip and doubts about the need for these classes.[5] It notes that in some quarters party study classes are confused with work reports and job-related studies, and that there are even cases of public health lectures and song and dance sessions being held in the guise of party study classes. Furthermore, with regard to the practical side of party study classes, the Ningbo party organization department recognizes that there are problems concerning the quality and effect of such classes, noting that they are "unplanned, inaccurate, patchwork, and lack creativity." It points out that some local secretaries emphasize "soft indicators" and that there is a big gap between the content of party study classes and the real needs of party members in terms of ideology. In particular, the Ningbo party organization department casts doubts on the practical effects of party study classes, saying that "there are few classes that touch on the hot topics, difficulties, and doubts" relating to the advance of reforms and opening in China in recent years. On top of that, the Ningbo party organization says that there is a big weakness in the actual state of implementation of party study classes and warns that party study classes in some rural areas and enterprises do not warrant optimism.[3] Specifically, as I shall explain later, educational management for party members in nonstate-run enterprises and floating party members is seen as an important issue.

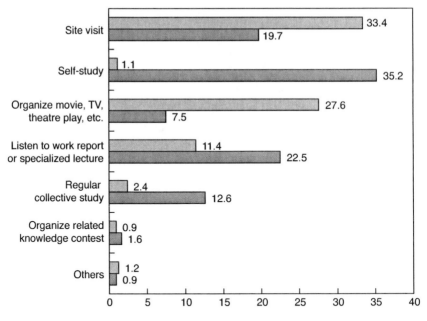

Figure 4.8 The desired form of party study classes.

In practice, a change in the attitudes of party members, the targets of these party study classes, is a major factor working in the background of their emasculation. As shown in Figure 4.8, visits for inspection and observation are cited as a desirable form of political theory study. However, it is probably no exaggeration to say that these visits, which are fully paid for by the party organization, are actually pleasure-seeking trips. If the first choice in the figure (self-study) is seen as a pro forma reply and the other choices, the second and the first and second combined, are seen as true intentions, then the top item in the first choice, "self-study," must be taken as pro forma "political theory study," and what party members really look forward to in this "political theory study" is not enlightenment on this subject but pleasure-seeking trips, watching movies, and going to the theater.

Accordingly, party organizations are employing formats for party study classes that are more in line with these genuine aspirations of the participants. For example, party organizations are proposing mini-classes, that is, talks by familiar people about familiar topics that, in consideration of the attention span of participants, last for only 10–20 minutes. They are also suggesting the invitation of well-known experts, professors, or leading exemplary cadres as outside lecturers or, conversely, visits by party members to revolutionary sites and vanguard regions to learn about traditional revolutionary education and advanced experiences. It has even been suggested that party study classes in the form of quizzes should be adopted. This emphasis on interest and recreation seems to reflect the desperate efforts of the organizers to cope with the situation.

Thus, it can be seen that the CPC, which unavoidably experienced a period of underground activity as an illegal organization before 1949 and was proud of its iron discipline, is losing its coercive force over rank-and-file members and, pressed to revise the content of its activities to suit the intentions of members, is also losing its normative role. Since the CPC is losing its coercive and normative qualities, the question is whether it is changing into a utilitarian organization. This is the issue that I will examine next.

Change in motives for party membership

So, to what extent can the transformation to a utilitarian organization be seen in the actual condition of CPC members? I would like to answer this question by examining the motives of people in joining the party in various areas.

Meaning of becoming a party member

First of all, what does it mean to become a party member? As a merit of becoming a party member, needless to say, the ideological value can be cited: the sense of belonging to an ideological organization that advocates socialism and communism, as well as the social honor that goes with becoming a party member and maybe a sense of self-realization. In view of the present situation in China, the party member label is no doubt a major political asset, and the consequent political protection might be a big merit. Furthermore, in view of the present situation in which the party undertakes the unified control of all information, no doubt the insider information that party members gain by being on the inside of this system is a considerable benefit.

On the other hand, demerits can also be assumed in becoming a party member. Being the center of attention all the time as a model citizen and having every little move scrutinized no doubt leads to serious mental stress, and the political study and organizational life mentioned above must take up a lot of time as well. Even though, except in the case of low-income earners, the obligatory party dues are not really a heavy burden, other expenses, including opportunity cost, are needed for organizational activities. When people compare the above-mentioned merits with these expenses, they might perhaps have doubts about the cost–performance ratio.

Social evaluation of party members

In relation to these assumed merits and demerits of becoming a party member, let us take a look at the image of party members and how they are evaluated by society.

As shown in Figure 4.9 on images of organization members, the CPC member image receives a higher level of prestige than the Communist Youth League or democratic parties member images. However, the CPC member image total of 49.1% for "high" and "very high" is actually surpassed by the corresponding Communist Youth League member image total of 53.2%, so it cannot be said that

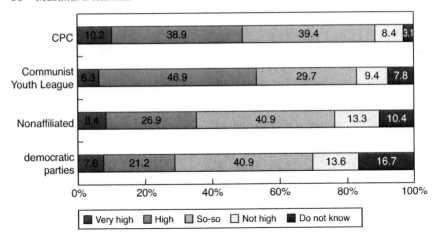

Figure 4.9 Membership prestige.

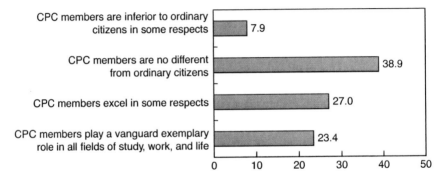

Figure 4.10 Image of CPC members.

the party member image is overwhelmingly prominent. Indeed, given the CPC's political rhetoric about being "the core of leadership" and having control over everything, it would not be strange at all if the party member image had a higher level of prestige.

As a specific evaluation of party members, one must ask whether people who become party members really do exist as outstanding human beings compared with ordinary citizens. A survey conducted in parallel with the above-mentioned one by the party Organization Department of the Shanghai Municipal Committee also examined the image of party members through a comparison between party members and nonparty members. The results, which are shown in Figure 4.10, show clearly that party members are certainly not viewed as "special citizens" in present-day Chinese society. That is to say, only 23.4%, or less than a quarter, of respondents thought that "CPC members play a vanguard exemplary role in all fields of study, work, and life." Another 27.0% gave a certain degree of positive evaluation, replying that "CPC members excel in some respects." But although this means that a half of the respondents gave a positive evaluation of CPC members, the highest ratio, 38.9%, said that "CPC members are no different from ordinary citizens." When you also consider that 7.9% of the respondents gave a negative evaluation, saying that "CPC members are inferior to ordinary citizens in some respects," it seems that the opinion that party members are not particularly special is spreading in present-day Chinese society.

Motive for party membership in Shanghai

What are the motives of people in Shanghai for joining the CPC? Is personal ideology, that is, a belief in communism, the main motive? Or is it a desire to join the leading organization, which just happens to be the CPC? Or, on a personal level, do people seek the privileges that go with becoming a party member for their own personal gain?

The survey results, which are shown in Figure 4.11, show that even among party members themselves, only about two-thirds of the respondents cited ideological or organizational motives. Interestingly, among nonaffiliated respondents (i.e. ordinary citizens), about 40% gave replies suggesting ideological or organizational motives for party membership, which is not far behind the figure of 57.9% for Communist Youth League members. But the most noteworthy feature is the distribution of the "individual promotion" motive: 22.2% of CPC members, 37.5% of Communist Youth League members, 46.1% of nonaffiliated respondents, and a majority of 56.1% of members of democratic parties said that people joined the CPC for personal gain. In particular, among members of democratic parties, rather than being an ideological organization, the CPC is considered to be a utilitarian organization driven by the motive of individual promotion.

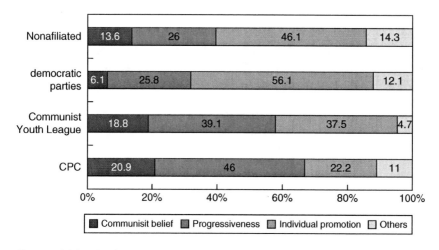

Figure 4.11 Motive for party membership.

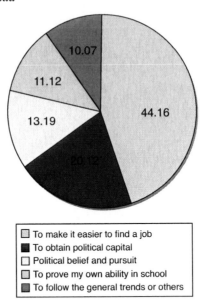

Figure 4.12 Motives for party membership (university students).

Motive for party membership among university students

This utilitarian aspect of the organization can be seen even more clearly in the motives for joining the party of university students. Figure 4.12 shows some of the results of a survey that asked 3,000 Chinese university students about their motives for joining the CPC. Of the 2,724 effective replies from the students, only about 10% answered that their motive was political belief.[6] The highest ratio by far, 44%, focused on immediate benefits and replied "to make it easier to find a job." Combined with the 20.1% of respondents who focused on long-term benefits and replied "to obtain political capital," about 65% of the respondents cited utilitarian motives.[4] Moreover, if the 10% of "weathercock" respondents who replied "to follow the general trend of others" are added to this category, the result shows that around 75% of student party members have been led to participate in the organization by utilitarian motives.

Furthermore, Figure 4.13 shows the results of a sample survey carried out at Dalian University of Technology, and almost the same tendency can be seen here. That is to say, the ratio of students who cited "belief in communism" as their motive for joining the party was only 4% of the total, and three-quarters of the students replied "to promote one's own advancement."

This tendency is particularly evident in the case of female students (Figure 4.14). Less than 10% of female students cited "belief in communism" as their motive for joining the party, which was just about the same as the overall trend in the student survey, but noticeably an overwhelming majority of about three-quarters of the female students answered "yes" to the frank motive of "to get a good job".[7]

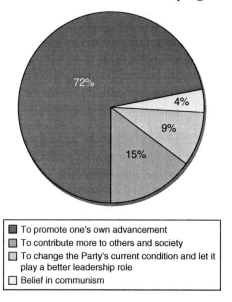

Figure 4.13 Motives for party membership (university students, Dalian).

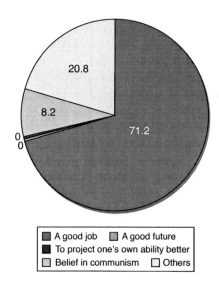

Figure 4.14 Motives for party membership (female students).

Can the traditions of the CPC that gave the organization sparkle in the past, such as the spirit of serving the people and selfless patriotic service or, going back to the origins, the objective of class struggle and the realization of communism, be seen in the students and other young people who are considering joining the party?

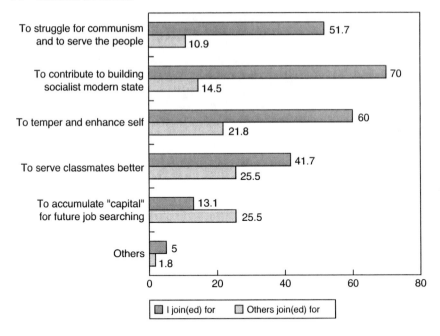

Figure 4.15 Double standards in motives for party membership.

To an extent, the answer seems to be "no they can't." Figure 4.15 shows the results of a survey in which the respondents were asked about their own motives in joining the party and what they perceived as the motives of others. Regarding their own motives, the top reply, cited by 70% of the respondents, was "to contribute to building a modern socialist state." This was followed by "to temper and enhance self" and "to struggle for communism and to serve the people." However, when they were asked about the motives of others in joining the party, a quarter of the respondents replied "to accumulate 'capital' for future job searching." Only 14.5% replied that others joined the party "to contribute to building a modern socialist state." What one can see from this survey is a double standard in which people say that they themselves joined the party for the lofty goals of "to contribute to building a modern socialist state" and "to struggle for communism and to serve the people" but think that others join for utilitarian purposes. One can also see here how the respondents themselves are conveniently separating their pro forma replies and their honest replies.

Incidentally, while these survey results concerned the motives of university students in joining the party, this tendency toward utilitarianism can be seen even more clearly among private entrepreneurs. As shown by Figure 4.16, utilitarianism and pragmatism are plainly evident in their motives for joining the party. This survey targeted entrepreneurs in 100 private companies in Guangdong Province. Asked why they joined the party, 45% of respondents, or nearly half, replied "advantages in developing business," followed by "improvement of social status" (20%) and "political security" (15%).

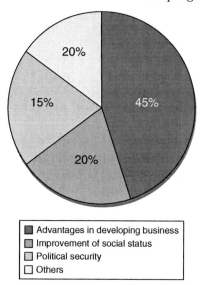

Figure 4.16 Motives for CPC membership (100 private business owners).

After achieving success in the risky business of setting up private enterprises, which in the past were regarded as the "tail of capitalism" in China, it can be presumed that established and well-known entrepreneurs next want to improve their social status and ensure political stability. In line with this assumption, the survey results do indeed show that private entrepreneurs wish to join the CPC as part of their efforts to build a safety net.

Avoidance of party membership

As explained in the previous sections, party membership has both merits and demerits. In consideration of this point, it should be possible to prove what we have been considering so far by examining the question of why people do not join the organization, that is, why they avoid party membership.

In her analysis of the apolitical attitude of well-educated young people in China, Wang Peiyuan asked such people why they had not joined the party. As shown in Figure 4.17, the main reason for not joining the party is the political apathy that is spreading among the ordinary people. The top reply of "no interest in politics" was cited by 71.4% of the respondents.[5] Well-educated young people see no advantages in joining the party and becoming politically committed. They also seem to have a strong pragmatic sense; 27.6% of the respondents replied that "it's just the same whether you join or don't join." In addition, almost the same ratio of respondents (27.0%) answered that they wanted to avoid the financial costs and other restraints that go with party membership, which I mentioned above as a demerit of party membership.

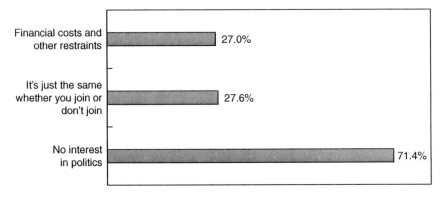

Figure 4.17 Avoidance of party membership.

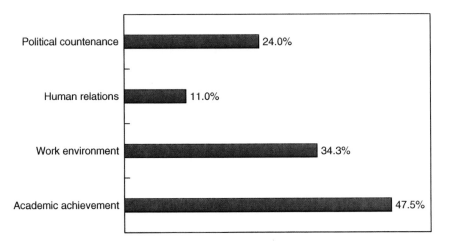

Figure 4.18 What is the most important of the various factors that influence the development of the individual?

In the background of this attitude toward party membership among well-educated young people is a kind of view of life underlying modern Chinese society. For example, asked "What is the most important of the various factors that influence the development of the individual?" most of the respondents (47.5%) cited "academic achievement," showing their awareness that "academic background determines your life" (Figure 4.18). This was followed by "work environment" (34.3%) and "human relations" (11.0%); only 24%, or less than a quarter, cited "political countenance" (i.e. being a member of the CPC, the Communist Youth League, the various democratic parties, or some other political organization). This shows that few well-educated young people have the view that "political standpoint determines your life." The idea that it is a political asset to be a party member, which I described above as a merit of becoming a party member, does not really seem to be functioning at all.

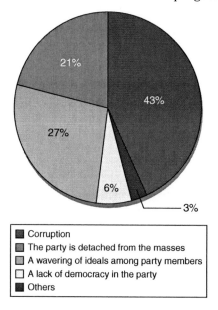

Figure 4.19 Difficulties facing the party organization.

Conclusion

Finally, what do people see as the difficulties facing the party organization? Figure 4.19 shows the replies to this question.

Since corruption has been rampant both inside and outside the party as the main hotbed of the greatest political crises since the founding of the present-day Chinese state, it is relatively easy to understand that the highest ratio of respondents (43%) cited corruption as "the biggest problem existing within the party." There is an extremely deep sense of crisis within the party leadership, which remembers that rule by the Kuomintang collapsed because of corruption within the party, but the elimination of corruption would require political reforms and in particular, since corruption extends to the core of party rule, the political determination to plunge the scalpel into its own body through incisive anticorruption policies. In terms of the merits of becoming a party member, that would lead to a self-negation of the utilitarian factor.

After this self-negation, would this organization be able to acquire new merits of party membership? Or are "ideological preparations" permeating throughout the party organization? In the above-mentioned survey, the reply about the problem of corruption was followed by "there is a wavering of ideals among party members" (27%), "the party is detached from the masses" (21%), and "there is a lack of democracy in the party" (6%). In view of this indication of the weakening of the party organization, it is hard to expect the organization to carry out *autopoiesis* (literally, self-production), the process by which an organization, prompted by some disturbance, noise, and so on, considers its self-transformation into something new. Because of the trend toward utilitarianism that I described earlier, this process itself is losing effect in the CPC.

So, from the standpoint of organizational theory, the only possibilities remaining for the CPC are *homeostasis* (maintenance of the status quo by transforming the disturbance back to the original order) or *morphogenesis* (transforming the disturbance into a new order).

Three possible scenarios can be imagined for morphogenesis: (1) permitting parties outside the CPC, (2) permitting factions within the CPC, or (3) morphogenesis of the CPC itself. The first scenario, permitting parties outside the CPC, would embrace resistance to the present regime, so, for exactly the same reasons as anticorruption policies, the possibility of its realization is extremely low. The second scenario, permitting factions within the CPC, would involve establishing a pseudo-multiparty system under one-party rule, rather like the model of the old Liberal Democratic Party in Japan. The concept of "intra-party democracy" that is being emphasized by Professor Wang Changjiang of the Party School of the Central Committee of the CPC and others can be included in this scenario. However, one wonders what factors would exist behind the formation of such intra-party groups. Would it be generation, or region, or background, or sector interest? Whatever the case, these factors all lack cohesive power as the driving force behind the formation of a faction and, it could be pointed out, might have a considerable reverse impact.

Thus, the only way remaining for the CPC to overcome the organizational crisis that I described earlier is through morphogenesis itself. In this process of morphogenesis, the role played by the new social class and in particular the new groups in Chinese society will most likely be a key factor. Will the bourgeois party members who are now allowed to exist in the party become a factor of mutation accelerating the process of morphogenesis? Similarly, will nonparty cabinet members like Minister of Science and Technology Wan Gang (vice-chairman of the China Zhi Gong Dang (Party for Public Interest)) and Minister of Health Chen Zhu (vice-president of the Chinese Academy of Sciences; unaffiliated) become a "Trojan horse" factor? We will have to watch the situation carefully.

Endnotes

1   Etzioni, Amitai. *A Comparative Analysis of Complex Organizations: On Power, Involvement, and their Correlates*, (Free Press, 1961).
2   For details, see my article "The Metamorphosis of the Communist Party of China" [in Japanese].
3   For details, see Masaharu Hishida, *Keizai hatten to shakai hendo* (Economic Growth and Social Change), University of Nagoya Press, 2005.
4   Other stipulations regarding criteria for the payment of party dues include the following: (1) in the case of annual salary schemes, etc., the dues are calculated from the average monthly sum; (2) the standard for households is the monthly net income in the previous fiscal year; (3) the standard for retired executives is their retirement expenses, and the standard for pension beneficiaries is their pension; (4) persons who for no justifiable reason fail to pay their party dues for six consecutive months are deemed to have given up their party membership; (5) party committees in each province, autonomous

region, directly controlled municipality, etc. shall give 5% of the total amount they receive from party dues every year to the center; and (6) local party committees related to the railways, airways, and finance industries shall give 10% of the total amount they receive from party dues every year to their regional party committee.

5   Interviews with anonymous officials from CPC Organization Department, Ningbo City, Zhejiang Province. (2007 summer)
6   See Wu and Guo 2007: 15–17; the number of effective survey samples was 2,724.
7   Wang Peiyuan, Gaozhishi Qingnian FeiZhengzhihua Xiansheng Fenxi (*Analysis of the Apolitical Phenomenon Among Well-Educated Young People*) Jiangxi People's Publisher, 2006.

Further Reading

Brodsgaard, Kjeld Erik and Zheng, Yongnian (2003) (eds) *Chinese Communist Party in Reform*, Eastern Universities Press.
Brodsgaard, Kjeld Erik and Zheng, Yongnian (2004) (eds) *Bringing the Party Back in. How China is Governed*, Eastern Universities Press.
Chan, Anita (1993) "Revolution or Corporatism? Workers and Trade Unions in Post-Mao China," *The Australian Journal of Chinese Affairs*, vol. 29, January, pp. 31–61.
Etzioni, Amitai (1961) *Complex Organizations: A Sociological Reader*, Holt, Rinehart and Winston.
Etzioni, Amitai (1964) *Modern Organizations*, Prentice-Hall.
Laliberte, Andre and Lanteigne, Marc (2007) *The Chinese Party-State in the 21st Century: Adaptation and the Reinvention of Legitimacy*, Routledge.
Liu, P. L. Alan (1966) *Mass Politics in the Peoples Republic: State and Society in Contemporary China*, Boulder, CO: Westview Press.
Oi, Jean (1999) *Rural China Take Off*, University of California Press.
Schmitter, P. C. and Lehmbruch, G. (1979) *Trends towards Corporatist Intermediation*, Sage Publication.
Shambaugh, David (2007) *China's Communist Party of China: Atrophy and Adaptation*, University of California Press.
White, Gordon (1995) *Chinese Trade Unions in the Transition from Socialism: The Emergence of Civil Society or the Road to Corporatism?* Institute of Development Studies.
Wu, X. and Guo, M. (2007) "Party Sponsorship and Political Incorporation under State Socialism: Communist Party Membership and Career Dynamics in Urban China," paper presented at the annual meeting of the American Sociological Association, TBA, New York, August 11, 2006.

No._____

Location: _____ Province _____City

Organization: _____

Date: _____, 2005

Appendix 1

China Institute of Industrial Relations: Questionnaire of primary trade union chairmen

Dear trade union chairman

With the development of the reforms of our primary enterprises and undertakings, workers and staff members extremely care about how trade unions could play more effectively their important roles in safeguarding the legitimate rights and interests of the workers and staff members, in coordinating labor relations, in promoting enterprises' development, etc. In order to summarize relevant experiences and explore avenues to solve the problems, and to submit relevant policy proposals to related Party/State departments and legislative organs, we organized this investigation into primary trade union chairmen. You do not need to put your name on this questionnaire. You can trust us to treat your answers confidentially according to relevant laws.

Please take notice of these, when you fill in this answer sheet:

(1) All answers have no 'right' or 'wrong', just reply truthfully;
(2) Please answer it by yourself. No replaces, no discussion;
(3) Please answer it one by one, make certain of answering all the questions;
(4) A single choice for each question, except for special explanations. Please check your answer or fill in the blank _____ with your answer.

Thank you for your cooperation and support!

China Institute of Industrial Relations
Research Group of "Basic-level Trade Union
Chairmen Investigation"
January, 2005.

First, please answer your personal background

(1) Sex: 1   Male

                  2   Female

(2) Age: _____ year-old;

(3) Educational background:

                  1   Junior High School;

                  2   High School, Vocational High School;

                  3   Vocational College;

                  4   University;

                  5   Master Course of graduate school;

                  6   Doctoral Course of graduate school

(4) Political appearance:

                  1   Chinese Communist Party member;

                  2   Democratic Party member;

                  3   Nonpartisan

Q1. When did you assume the current position of trade union chairman?

                                                      Year_____

Q2. What was your last position before being the trade union chairman?

_____

1	Middle class cadre Director, Section, Department	12	Workers and Staff
2	Factory manager, President	13	Financial Manager
3	Trade Unions Chairman	14	Labour and Security Supervisor
4	Teacher	15	Statistic Staff
5	CCP Secretary	16	Trade Union Cadre, Member of Committee
6	Township Cadre	17	Accountant
7	Township Governor	18	Lower Staff
8	Director of Department (Prefecture, Township	19	Female Cadre
9	Vice-Secretary of detached factory	20	Secretary of Chinese Communist Youth League
10	CCP Secretary of Administrative Affairs	21	Chief of Police Box
11	Chief of Security Department	22	Doctor
		23	Soldier
		24	Principal

Q3. How did you assume the responsibility of a trade union chairman

     1   Appointed by an organization;

     2   Elected by members' congress/members' assembly, following organization's recommendation;

     3   Elected by members' congress/members' assembly directly;

     4   Elected by members' congress/members' assembly, following open selective examinations;

     5   Others_____ (write in details)

Q4. (If you answered "Appointed by an organization" (1) in Q3) which organization appointed you?

    1   Party organization of work unit;

    2   Administrative organization of work unit;

    3   Higher-level trade union;

    4   Former primary trade union committee;

    5   Others _____ (write in details)

Q5. (If you answered "Elected" (2, 3, or 4) in Q3) what was the concrete way of
the election?

    1   Separate voting for chairman, vice-chairmen and other committees;

    2   Voting for chairman and vice-chairmen from elected committees;

    3   Others _____ (write in details)

Q6. (If you answered "Elected" (2, 3, or 4) in Q3) was it a single-candidate election or competitive election?

    1   Single-candidate election;

    2   Competitive election (including single-candidate election following com-
petitive preliminary election)

Q7. (If you answered you assumed the trade union chairman through democratic
election or through open selective examinations (2, 3, or 4) in Q3) what was
the reason for your taking part in the election or examinations? (Choose the
most appropriate one)

    1   Recommended by party organization of work unit;

    2   Recommended by administrative organization of work unit;

    3   Recommended by functionaries of workshop-level trade union;

    4   Self-recommended;

    5   Recommended by ordinary union members or trade union small groups;

    6   Others _____ (write in details)

Q8. Do you hold a concurrent post besides the trade union chairman?

    1   Hold;

    2   Not hold

Q9. (If you hold a concurrent post (1) in Q8) what are the specific posts? (multiple answers allowed)

    1   Secretary of the Party committee at the corresponding level;

    2   Vice-secretary of the Party committee at the corresponding level;

    3   Member of the Party committee at the corresponding level;

    4   CEO of the administrative organization at the corresponding level (e.g.
general manager);

    5   Vice-post of the administrative organization at the corresponding level;

    6   Others _____ (write in details)

Q10. Do you have any relatives who serve for the posts listed below in your enterprise? (multiple answers allowed)

1 Secretary of the Party committee at the corresponding level;
2 Vice-secretary of the Party committee at the corresponding level;
3 Member of the Party committee at the corresponding level;
4 CEO of the administrative organization at the corresponding level (ex. general manager);
5 Vice-post of the administrative organization at the corresponding level;
6 Others _____ (write in details)

Q11. Being as the trade union chairman, do you enjoy the same economic treatments as the vice post of the Party or administrative organization at the corresponding level?

Enjoy;
Not enjoy

Q12. Compared with the workload as a trade union chairman, are you satisfied with the current treatment?

1 Extremely satisfied;
2 Fundamentally satisfied;
3 Not very satisfied (compared with workload, treatment is not very good);
4 Dissatisfied (compared with workload, treatment is bad)

A1. Questions about your work unit

A1-1. Location of the trade union: _____ province _____
_____ city

A1-2. Ownership form of your enterprise:

1 State-owned/State-holding enterprise;
2 Collective-owned enterprise;
3 Private enterprise;
4 Cooperative enterprise;
5 Limited liability corporation;
6 Share Holding Corporation Ltd.;
7 Enterprise with funds from Hong Kong, Macao and Taiwan;
8 Foreign-funded enterprise;
9 Others _____

A1-3. Industry area of your enterprise:

1 Farming, Forestry, Animal Husbandry and Fishing
2 Mining and Quarrying;
3 Manufacturing;
4 Production and Supply of Electricity, Gas and Water;
5 Construction;

    6   Geological Prospecting and Water Conservancy;

    7   Transport, Storage, Post & Telecommunication Services;

    8   Wholesale and Retail Trade & Catering Services;

    9   Finance and Insurance;

   10   Real estate;

   11   Social services;

   12   Health Care, Sports & Social Welfare;

   13   Education, Culture and Arts, Radio, Film and Television;

   14   Scientific Research and Polytechnic Services;

   15   Government Agencies, Party Agencies and Social Organizations

A1-4. When was your enterprise established?

                    Year _____

A1-5. The total number of workers and staff members of your enterprise by the end of 2003 (including part-time workers and short-time contract workers): _____ people

     Of them, part-time/short-time contract workers: _____ people.

A2. Questions about the trade union

A2-1. When was the trade union established?

                    Year _____

A2-2. How was the trade union established?

    1   By Workers and Staff Members' voluntary request;

    2   By determination of Organization;

    3   Others _____

A2-3-1. Has the union obtained the status of a legal person as a public organization?

    1   Has obtained;

    2   Has not obtained, yet

A2-3-2 (If you answered "Has obtained" (1) in A2-3-1) the year of acquisition:

A2-4. The total number of members of the trade union by the end of 2003: _____ people; Of them, part-time/short-time contract workers: _____ people.

A2-5. According to your understanding, how do workers and staff members enter the trade union?

    1   Enter the trade union voluntarily;

    2   Apply for the entry by taking the advice of trade union functionaries;

    3   All workers join the trade union automatically;

    4   Others _____ (indicate)

A3. Questions about trade union members' congress/union members' assembly

A3-1. Has the members' congress been established?

1 Established;

2 Not established

A3-2. (If you answered "Established" (1) in A3-1) the total number of member representatives by the end of 2003:_____ people; Of them, the representatives under 35 year-old: people; the representatives of middle or lower level workers and staff members: _____ people

A3-3. In the past three years (April 2001–March 2004), how many times members' congress or members' assembly have been held?
Members' congress: ___ times; Members' assembly: ___ times

A4. Questions about the primary trade union

A4-1a. How many vice-chairmen are there in the union?: _____ people;

Of them, full-time vice-chairmen: ___ people;
Of them, males: ___ people;
Of them, Communist Party members: ___ people;
Of them, Democratic Party members: ___ people

A4-1b. How many committee members (except chairman and vice-chairmen) are there in the union?: _____ people;

Of them, full-time committee members: ___ people;
Of them, males: ___ people;
Of them, Communist Party members: ___ people;
Of them, Democratic Party members: ___ people

A4-2. Age and educational background of vice-chairmen and committee members (except chairman and vice-chairmen)

	Item	*Vice-chairmen*	*Committee members (except chairman and vice-chairmen)*
	39 and under	__ people	__ people
Age	40–49	__ people	__ people
	50–59	__ people	__ people
	60 and over	__ people	__ people
Educational background	Master course of graduate school and higher	__ people	__ people
	University	__ people	__ people
	Vocational college	__ people	__ people
	High school, vocational high school	__ people	__ people
	Junior high school and lower	__ people	__ people

A4-3. Has the standing committee been established in the primary trade union committee?

Established;

Not established

(If you answered "Established" (1) in A4-3) the number of the committee members: _____ people

A4-4. Has the department/committee below been established in your union? (multiple answers allowed, check in the corresponding ones)

Name of department/committee	Established or not	Name of department/committee	Established or not
Office		Female worker support	
Organization work		Labor protection work	
Propaganda work		Assistance of workers with financial difficulties	
Organization propagandizes		Rights and interests protection	
Mass production work		Other (write in details)	

A4-5. How many trade union branches and trade union small groups are there under your trade union?

Trade union branch:_____;

Trade union small group: _____

A4-6. How many times of conferences were held by your primary trade union committee in 2003?: _____ times

B1. How did the incumbent vice-chairman being responsible for the routine work (or the first vice-chairman) assume the office?

1   Appointed by an organization;
2   Elected at members' congress/members' assembly, following Organization recommendation;
3   Elected at members' congress/members' assembly directly;
4   Others _____ (write in details)

B1-1. (If you answered "Appointed by an organization" (1) in B1) which organization appointed him/her?

1   Party organization of work unit;
2   Administrative organization of work unit;
3   Higher-level trade union;
4   Former primary trade union committee;
5   Others _____ (write in details)

B1-2. (If you answered "Elected at members' congress/members' assembly, following Organization recommendation" (2) in B1) who/which organization recommended you?

    1   Party organization of work unit;
    2   Administrative organization of work unit;
    3   Functionaries of workshop-level trade union;
    4   Self-recommended;
    5   Ordinary union members or trade union small groups;
    6   Others _____ (write in details)

B1-3. (If you answered "Elected at members' congress/members' assembly directly" (3) in B1) what was the concrete way of the election?

    1   Separate voting for chairman, vice-chairmen and other committees;
    2   Voting for chairman and vice-chairmen from elected committees;
    3   Others _____ (write in details)

B2. Some local country-level unions select excellent persons for the leadership through public recruitment and examination, register the passers on Professional Trade Union Chairman Storehouse and dispatch them in the need of non-public ownership enterprises. After the probation period, they can be voted formally as the trade union chairman by the Union Members' Assembly. Their wage and benefits are provided by the local country-level union. Regarding this method, do you agree with the opinions below? (multiple answers allowed, check in the corresponding ones)

Related Opinions	*Agree*	*Disagree*
1 Advantageous for disposing competent trade union chairman and cadres		
2 Advantageous for assuring trade union cadres' security of income		
3 Advantageous for trade union cadres' safeguarding workers and staff members' legitimate rights and interests in the dispatched enterprise independently		
4 Benefits for strengthening the relationship between primary trade unions and higher-level trade unions, enhancing the trade union's organizational power		
5 Disadvantages in developing trade union activities because dispatched chairmen or cadres are not familiar with the inside details of the enterprise		
6 Few people would apply for the Professional Trade Union Chairman Storehouse		
7 Disadvantages in the unity of the primary trade union because dispatched chairman and cadres would create discord with other cadres		

Related Opinions	Agree	Disagree
8 Disadvantages in trade union activity developments and trade union status enhancement because dispatched chairman and cadres would create discord with party and administrative organizations within the enterprise		
9 This method is worth promoting nationwide		

B3. Questions about the trade union vice-chairman (If there are two or more vice-chairmen, answer about the situation of the vice-chairman responsible for the routine work or the first vice-chairman)

B3-1. Does he/she hold a concurrent post besides the trade union vice-chairman?

1   Hold;

2   Not hold

B3-1-1. (If you answered "hold"(1) in B3-1) what are the specific posts? (multiple answers allowed)

1   Secretary of the Party committee at the corresponding level;

2   Vice-secretary of the Party committee at the corresponding level;

3   Member of the Party committee at the corresponding level;

4   CEO of the administrative organization at the corresponding level (ex. general manager);

5   Vice-post of the administrative organization at the corresponding level;

6   Others _____ (write in details)

B3-2. Does he/she have any relatives who serve the posts below in your work unit? (multiple answers allowed)

1   Secretary of the Party committee at the corresponding level;

2   Vice-secretary of the Party committee at the corresponding level;

3   Member of the Party committee at the corresponding level;

4   CEO of the administrative organization at the corresponding level (ex. general manager);

5   Vice-post of the administrative organization at the corresponding level;

6   Others _____ (write in details)

B3-3. What was his/her last position before being the trade union vice-chairman? _____

1	Middle class cadre Director, Section, Department	12	Workers and Staff
2	Factory manager, President	13	Financial Manager
3	Trade Unions Chairman	14	Labour and Security Supervisor
4	Teacher	15	Statistic Staff
5	CCP Secretary	16	Trade Union Cadre, Member of Committee
6	Township Cadre	17	Accountant
7	Township Governor	18	Lower Staff
8	Director of Department (Prefecture, Township	19	Female Cadre
9	Vice-Secretary of detached factory	20	Secretary of Chinese Communist Youth League
10	CCP Secretary of Administrative Affairs	21	Chief of Police Box
11	Chief of Security Department	22	Doctor
		23	Soldier
		24	Principal

B4. Questions about the former union chairman

B4-1. Why did he/she resign as the trade union chairman?

His/Her tenure of office expired, no longer sought re-election;
Followed organizational personnel transfer;
Failed in the election;
Other _____ (write in details)

B4-2. Term of his/her office as trade union chairman:

From year of _____ to year of _____

B4-3. (If he/she is still on duty) what is his/her current duty? _____

1	Middle class cadre Director, Section, Department	12	Workers and Staff
2	Factory manager, President	13	Financial Manager
3	Trade Unions Chairman	14	Labour and Security Supervisor
4	Teacher	15	Statistic Staff
5	CCP Secretary	16	Trade Union Cadre, Member of Committee
6	Township Cadre	17	Accountant
7	Township Governor	18	Lower Staff
8	Director of Department (Prefecture, Township	19	Female Cadre
9	Vice-Secretary of detached factory	20	Secretary of Chinese Communist Youth League
10	CCP Secretary of Administrative Affairs	21	Chief of Police Box
11	Chief of Security Department	22	Doctor
		23	Soldier
		24	Principal

B5. Questions about federation and representation system

B5-1. Has your primary trade union ever sent delegates to the next higher-level congress of trade unions?

1   Has sent;
2   Has not sent

(If you answered "Has sent" (1) in B5-1) since when has it sent delegates?

B5-2. Do you agree with federation and representation system?

1   Agree;
2   Disagree

B5-3. Regarding federation and representation system, do you agree with the opinions below? (Check your answer in the blank)

Related Opinions	*Agree*	*Disagree*
1 Benefits for enforcing higher-level unions' policy lines and decisions at primary level		
2 Benefits for reporting the problems encountered by primary trade unions on a daily basis to the higher-level trade unions		
3 Benefits for strengthening the vertical leadership structure between higher and lower level trade unions, enhancing the trade union's organizational power		
4 Even if attended higher-level congress of trade unions, it would be difficult to make individual opinions be reflected into decisions		
5 Because each primary union faces different problems, solutions could only be found by each primary union itself		
6 If the primary trade union has excessively close relationships with higher-level trade unions, it could harm the Party–Administration–Union coordination at primary level		

B6. Questions about the treatment of the trade union chairman

B6-1. Some local federations of trade unions established 'Trade Union Chairman Fund' or 'Special Fund of Trade Union Chairman', for the purpose of supporting the primary trade union Chairmen and full-time vice-chairmen, who are mistreated for safeguarding legitimate rights and interests of workers and staff members, or with serious economic problems because of layoffs, bankrupts, natural disasters and diseases.

B6-1-1. Do you think this policy is necessary?

1   Necessary;
2   Not necessary

B6-1-2. (If you answered "Necessary" (1) in B6-1-1) choose your answer from the following reasons:

1 Have ever experienced living difficulties;
2 Although have never experienced similar living difficulties described above, this policy is necessary to be devoted to union activities without anxiety;
3 Other reasons _____

C1. Questions about the basic-level union's financial situation of previous fiscal year

C1-1. Does your trade union have its own account for managing fund independently?

1 Have;
2 Not have

C1-2. Of total revenue, how much percentage each item listed below accounts for?

1 Membership dues paid by union members _____%;
2 Contribution allocated by the enterprise, institution or government department where the trade union is established _____%;
3 Incomes derived from the trade union's own activities _____%;
4 Other incomes _____ % (write in details)

C1-3. In using the union funds, is it necessary to get the approval of administrative manager of work unit?

1 Necessary;
2 Not necessary

C1-4. Have you ever experienced the situation of nondistinctiveness of union expense and administrative expense?

1 Have experienced;
2 Have not experienced

C1-5. Do you face revenue shortfall in conducting union activities?

1 Revenue shortfall is serious
2 Face revenue shortfall
3 Not face revenue shortfall so much
4 Not face revenue shortfall at all

C2. Questions about the situation of payment of the membership dues

C2-1. By what means does your trade union collect the membership dues?

1 Deduction from the payroll;
2 Direct payment by union members;
3 Other means _____ (write in details)

C2-2. Is union members' non-payment of the membership dues serious?

1   Very serious;
2   Relatively serious;
3   The problem exists, but not very serious;
4   Not exist non-payment

C3. Questions about the situation of work units' contribution of the trade union expense

C3-1. Is the work units' non-payment of the contribution of the trade union expense serious? (a single choice)

1   Very serious;
2   Relatively serious;
3   The problem exists, but not very serious;
4   Not exist non-payment

C3-2. According to the revised Trade Union Law, when an enterprise or undertaking delays in allocating or refuses to allocate the contribution to the trade union, the trade unions may apply to the People's Court for an order for payment or compulsory enforcement. What do you think about this regulation?

1   Agree;
2   Disagree

C3-2-1. Have you ever exercised the right actually?

1   Have exercised;
2   Have not exercised

C3-2-2. In case non-payment or delay of payment is very serious, do you consider to exercise this right? (a single choice)

1   Want to exercise this right very much;
2   Do not want to exercise this right, but if there are no other way, have to exercise;
3   Do not want to exercise this right

C3-3. Recently, some local primary trade unions entrust the collection of the contribution to taxation affairs department. What do you think about this method?

1   Agree;
2   Disagree

C3-3-1. Have you ever used this way actually?

1   Have used;
2   Have not used

C3-3-2. (If you answered "Have not used" (2) in C3-3-1) are you going to use it in the future?

    1 Yes;

    2 No

C3-3-3. (If you answered "Disagree" (2) in C3-3) choose the reasons
of disagreement (multiple answers allowed)

    1 Collection by the taxation affairs department is
untrustworthy;

    2 Collection by the taxation affairs departments would
create the image of trade unions' funds belong to government finance, and disadvantage in the trade unions'
displaying its independency;

    3 Primary trade unions have taken their inherent responsi-
bility to collect the contribution for themselves. If they
renounce some certain parts of the responsibility, it might
be disadvantageous for mobilizing primary trade unions'
enthusiasm;

    4 Primary trade unions have taken their inherent respon-
sibility to collect the contribution for themselves. If the
collection is changed to be the contract matter between
local trade union and taxation affairs department, it
would be disadvantageous for the unity between local
trade union and primary trade unions;

    5 Other reasons _____ (write in details)

D. Questions about the activity contents of the trade union

D1. Choose five most important activities from the following:

The order of five most important activities: ( )( )( )( )( )

    1 Negotiate with the administration/management on the working
conditions including wages, bonus, working hour and benefits, sign
collective agreement;

    2 Participate in the mediation and arbitration of labor disputes;

    3 Solicit members' opinions, present them to the administration/man-
agement without delay, and request for the solutions;

    4 Promote the democratic management and disclosure of factory
management affairs as the working body of the congress of workers
and staff members;

    5 Assist and supervise the administration/management in properly
dealing with social insurance;

    6 Assist the administration/management to execute the labor protec-
tion measures including the measures on working hour, occupational safety and health;

7   Conduct education among members, encourage them to learn their rights and obligations;

8   Handle new members' entrance formalities, manage the personal records of members;

9   Cooperate with Party Committees and Communist Youth League Committees to carry out ideological and political education among members;

10   Organize members to launch activities for vocational training and technical innovation;

11   Appraise advanced workers and model workers;

12   Understand members' living conditions and their thoughts promptly;

13   Safeguard women workers' rights including menstruation leave, maternity leave and child-care leave. Implement Family Planning program;

14   Remove difficulties in members' living condition through mutual aid activities of mutual aid saving associations, mutual aid insurance, and Warmth Project. Organize members to enjoy culture and sports activities.

D2. Questions about the equal consultations and signing collective agreements

D2-1. Has your union, on behalf of the members, signed collective agreements with the administration of your work unit?

1   Has signed;
2   Has not signed

D2-1-1. (If you answered "Has signed" (1) in D2-1) was the draft of the collective agreement passed through the discussion at the congress of workers and staff members?

1   Passed though the discussion at the congress of workers and staff members;
2   Not passed through the discussion at the congress of workers and staff members

D2-1-2. (If you answered "Has signed" (1) in D2-1) was the content of the collective agreement announced to the entire workers?

1   Announced;
2   Not announced

D2-1-3. (If you answered "Announced" (1) in D2-1-2, please check the means of the announcement (multiple answers allowed)

1   Announced at a meeting;
2   Distributed the copies of the collective agreements to the workers and staff members;
3   Read out the collective agreements in front of the entire workers;
4   Displayed the collective agreements on a wall;
5   Others _____ (write in details)

D2-1-4. (If you answered "Has signed" (1) in D2-1) has the collective agreements Surveillance and Inspection Group been organized?

   1 Organized
   2 Not organized

D3. Questions about the work of mediation and arbitration of labor disputes

D3-1. Has the Labor Dispute Mediation Committee been established in your work unit?

   1 Established;
   2 Not established

D3-2. What are major causes of the labor disputes? Choose three causes that happen most frequently: (   ), (   ), (   )

   1 Conclusion of labor contracts;
   2 Dismissal of workers and staff members;
   3 Workers and staff members' voluntary resigning;
   4 Labor remuneration;
   5 Insurance and welfare;
   6 Labor protection, occupational safety and health;
   7 Vocational training;
   8 Working hours, rest and vacation;
   9 Protection of female workers' rights and interests;
   10 Other reasons _____ (write in details)

D3-3. In recent five years from 1999 to 2003, how many times of labor disputes have occurred in your work unit? _____ times

   D3-3-1. From the results of these labor disputes, what is the percentage of each situation below?

      1 Winning of the workers and staff members _____%;
      2 Winning of the employers _____%;
      3 Partly winning of both sides _____%

D4. Questions about Mutual Aid Supplementary Insurance

D4-1. Does your trade union provide mutual aid supplementary insurance for the union members?

   1 Provide;
   2 Not provide

D4-2. (If you answered "Provide" (1) in D4-1) what kinds of mutual aid supplementary insurances has the trade union provided for the members? (multiple answers allowed)

   1 Annuity mutual aid supplementary insurance;
   2 Medical mutual aid supplementary insurance;
   3 Death and mortuary mutual aid supplementary insurance;

4   Unemployment mutual aid supplementary insurance;
5   Industrial injury mutual aid supplementary insurance;
6   Unexpected calamity mutual aid supplementary insurance;
7   Other mutual aid supplementary insurance_____
_____ (write in details)

D4-3. Has your trade union built up a record for workers with living difficulties?

1   Built;
2   Not built

E1. Questions about the relationship between the primary trade union committee and the ordinary members

E1-1. According to your understandings, how is the image of the trade union among the members?

1   very good;
2   good;
3   fair;
4   bad;
5   very bad

E1-2. In order to understand the opinions and demands of the members, what kinds of methods has the union ever used? (multiple answers allowed)

1   home visits;
2   questionnaire survey;
3   round-table discussion on special topic;
4   telephone counseling;
5   reception day of trade union chairman;
6   opinion box;
7   Others _____(indicate)

E2. Questions about the relationship between the primary trade union committee and members' congress/members' assembly

E2-1. Are there any cases that delegations or over 10 representatives bring in a bill at members' congress/members' assembly?

1   There are;
2   There are not

E3. Questions about the relationship between the primary trade union committee and higher-level trade union organizations

E3-1. Choose one item from the following, as regards what you want the higher-level trade union organizations to do. (   )

1   Convey the interests and demands of workers and staff members more effectively;

2 Actively engage in establishing laws and regulations concerning vital interests of workers and staff members;

3 Provide basic-level trade unions with theoretical policies and legal consultations;

4 Others _____(write in details)

E4. Questions about the relationship between the primary committee and the Party organizations of the work unit

E4-1. Has your work unit established party organizations?

1 Established;

2 Not established

E4-1-1. (If you answered "Established" (1) in E4-1) are the following cadres the members of the party committee of work unit? (multiple answers allowed)

1 Trade union chairman;

2 Trade union vice-chairman;

3 Other committee members of the basic-level trade union committee

E4-2. Has your primary trade union committee established a party group or party branch in it?

1 Established;

2 Not established

E5. Questions about the relationship between the primary trade union committee and the administrative organizations of the work unit

E5-1. If a board of directors is set up in your work unit, have the following trade union cadres participated in it as the representatives of workers and staff members? (multiple answers allowed)

1 Trade union chairman;

2 Trade union vice-chairman;

3 Other committee members of the primary trade union committee

E5-1-1. (If you answered "has participated" as to 1–3 in E5-1) are the representatives elected by following organizations or not?

1 Elected by the congress of workers and staff members;

2 Elected by the trade union committee;

3 Not passed through the election

E5-2. If a board of supervisors is set up in your work unit, have the following trade union cadres participated in it as the representatives of workers and staff members? (multiple answers allowed)

1 Trade union chairman;

2 Trade union vice-chairman;

3 Other committee members of the primary trade union committee

E5-2-1. (If you answered "has participated" as to 1–3 in E5-2) are the representatives elected by following organizations or not?

    1   Elected by the congress of workers and staff members;

    2   Elected by the trade union committee;

    3   Not passed through the election

E6. Questions about the relationship between the primary trade union committee and other organizations in your work unit

E6-1. Is the primary trade union committee doing any activities jointly with other mass organizations such as the local Women's Federation, Communist Youth League or the Aging Committee?

    1   Doing activities jointly;

    2   Doing activities solely

E6-2. Which neighborhood activity below did your trade union participate actively in 2003? (choose one item)

    1   Provide human power and material resources for the utilities of the neighborhood community;

    2   Hold various social activities and public welfare activities of health promotion and enlightenment jointly with the neighborhood community;

    3   Open the trade union's facilities to the neighborhood community;

    4   Organize the trade union activists to do volunteer work in the leisure time;

    5   Others _____;

    6   Have never participated in any activities of neighborhood community

E7. Questions about the relationship between the trade union and Media, People's Congress and Political Consultative Conference

E7-1. In the past three years, has your trade union ever worked hard to be reported in the following media? (multiple answers allowed)

    1   Newspapers and magazines published by local trade unions;

    2   Local newspapers and magazines;

    3   Local radios and televisions;

    4   Newspapers and magazines published by All-China Federation of Trade Unions;

    5   National newspapers and magazines;

    6   National radios and televisions

E7-1-1. Among them, which media did a report on your trade union? (multiple answers allowed)

    1   Newspapers and magazines published by local trade unions;

    2   Local newspapers and magazines;

    3   Local radios and televisions;

      4   Newspapers and magazines published by All-China Federation of Trade Unions;

      5   National newspapers and magazines;

      6   National radios and televisions

E7-2. In conveying the opinions of primary trade unions and the members, and in meeting their demands, which organizations below do you think are worth contacting with to solve the problems effectively? Choose three of them in orders from high to low level: (   ), (   ), (   )

    1   Administrative organizations in the work unit;

    2   Party organizations in the work unit;

    3   Local government where the work unit locates;

    4   Party committee where the work unit locates;

    5   Deputies of the People's Congress/Commissars of the Political Consultative Conference where the work unit locates;

    6   Local federation of trade unions where the work unit locates;

    7   Higher-level government;

    8   Higher-level Party Committee;

    9   Deputies of the higher-level People's Congress/Commissars of the higher-level Political Consultative Conference;

   10 Higher-level federations of trade unions;

   11 Central government;

   12 Central Party Committee;

   13 Deputies of the National People's Congress/Commissars of the Chinese People's Political Consultative Conference;

   14 All-China Federation of Trade Unions;

   15 Public celebrities/scholars/Democratic parties;

   16 Local media;

   17 National media

E8. What do you think are the major impediments of the development of trade union work? (multiple answers allowed)

1   The trade union cadres' enthusiasm is not high;

2   The trade union cadres' knowledge and competence are not sufficient;

3   Activities do not meet the needs of workers and staff members;

4   Lack in the awareness of the position and roles of the trade union by the administration of the work unit;

5   Lack in the awareness of the position and roles of the trade union by the party organizations of the work unit;

6   Lack of support from higher-level trade unions;

7   Financial difficulties;

8   Others _____(write in details)

Please check the questionnaire again. We deeply appreciate your cooperation and support!

Appendix 2

Survey data

Part 1: Personal Background

(1) Sex

		Sum	State-owned/State-holding enterprise	Collective-owned enterprise	Private enterprise	Cooperative enterprise	Limited liability corporation	Share Holding Corporation Ltd	Enterprise with Funds from Hong Kong, Macao and Taiwan	Foreign funded enterprise	Others	NA
									Ownership form of your enterprise			
Male	Frequency	1204	690	32	37	17	101	54	8	26	161	78
	%		72.1	53.3	60.7	51.5	67.3	60.0	53.3	81.3	55.1	64.5
Female	Frequency	583	258	27	21	16	46	36	5	5	130	39
	%	32.2	27.0	45.0	34.4	48.5	30.7	40.0	33.3	15.6	44.5	32.2
NA	Frequency	24	9	1	3	0	3	0	2	1	1	4
	%	1.3	0.9	1.7	4.9	0.0	2.0	0.0	13.3	3.1	0.3	3.3

(2) Age

		Sum	State-owned/State-holding enterprise	Collective-owned enterprise	Private enterprise	Cooperative enterprise	Limited liability corporation	Share Holding Corporation Ltd	Enterprise with Funds from Hong Kong, Macao and Taiwan	Foreign funded enterprise	Others	NA
21–25	Frequency	16	1	0	4	2	0	2	0	2	2	3
	%	0.9	0.1	0.0	6.6	6.1	0.0	2.2	0.0	6.3	0.7	2.5
26–30	Frequency	49	19	3	2	1	5	3	3	1	10	2
	%	2.7	2.0	5.0	3.3	3.0	3.3	3.3	20.0	3.1	3.4	1.7
31–35	Frequency	97	54	0	10	2	15	1	2	1	9	3
	%	5.4	5.6	0.0	16.4	6.1	10.0	1.1	13.3	3.1	3.1	2.5
36–40	Frequency	236	119	5	10	9	23	13	1	8	34	14
	%	13.0	12.4	8.3	16.4	27.3	15.3	14.4	6.7	25.0	11.6	11.6
41–45	Frequency	329	188	8	8	7	19	20	1	6	51	21
	%	18.2	19.6	13.3	13.1	21.2	12.7	22.2	6.7	18.8	17.5	17.4
46–50	Frequency	559	294	23	10	7	43	26	6	5	111	34
	%	30.9	30.7	38.3	16.4	21.2	28.7	28.9	40.0	15.6	38.0	28.1

117

Ownership form of your enterprise

		Sum	State-owned/ State-holding enterprise	Collective-owned enterprise	Private enterprise	Cooperative enterprise	Limited liability corporation	Enterprise with Share Holding Corporation Ltd	Enterprise with Funds from Hong Kong, Macao and Taiwan	Foreign funded enterprise	Others	NA
51–55	Frequency	378	220	11	11	2	32	17	1	5	54	25
	%	20.9	23.0	18.3	18.0	6.1	21.3	18.9	6.7	15.6	18.5	20.7
56–60	Frequency	104	43	8	3	3	8	3	1	4	17	14
	%	5.7	4.5	13.3	4.9	9.1	5.3	3.3	6.7	12.5	5.8	11.6
61–65	Frequency	2	0	0	1	0	1	0	0	0	0	0
	%	0.1	0.0	0.0	1.6	0.0	0.7	0.0	0.0	0.0	0.0	0.0
Over 65	Frequency	1	0	0	0	0	0	1	0	0	0	0
	%	0.1	0.0	0.0	0.0	0.0	0.0	1.1	0.0	0.0	0.0	0.0
NA	Frequency	40	19	2	2	0	4	4	0	0	4	5
	%	2.2	2.0	3.3	3.3	0.0	2.7	4.4	0.0	0.0	1.4	4.1

(3) Educational background

		Sum	State-owned/ State-holding enterprise	Collective-owned enterprise	Private enterprise	Cooperative enterprise	Limited liability corporation	Enterprise with Share Holding Corporation Ltd	Enterprise with Funds from Hong Kong, Macao and Taiwan	Foreign funded enterprise	Others	NA
Junior high school	Frequency	61	16	4	9	4	9	5	0	1	4	9
	%	3.4	1.7	6.7	14.8	12.1	6.0	5.6	0.0	3.1	1.4	7.4
High school, Vocational high school	Frequency	348	121	18	23	16	31	20	6	8	80	25
	%	19.2	12.6	30.0	37.7	48.5	20.7	22.2	40.0	25.0	27.4	20.7
Vocational college	Frequency	753	426	29	22	9	68	37	7	11	103	41
	%	41.6	44.5	48.3	36.1	27.3	45.3	41.1	46.7	34.4	35.3	33.9
University	Frequency	564	338	8	5	4	39	23	1	11	94	41
	%	31.1	35.3	13.3	8.2	12.1	26.0	25.6	6.7	34.4	32.2	33.9

		Col1	Col2	Col3	Col4	Col5	Col6	Col7	Col8	Col9	Col10	Col11
Master course of graduate school	Frequency	67	49	1	1	0	1	4	1	0	9	1
	%	3.7	5.1	1.7	1.6	0.0	0.7	4.4	6.7	0.0	3.1	0.8
Doctoral course of graduate school	Frequency	1	0	0	0	0	0	0	0	0	1	0
	%	0.1	0.0	0.0	0.0	0.0	0.0	0.0	0.0	0.0	0.3	0
NA	Frequency	17	7	0	1	0	2	1	1	1	1	4
	%	0.9	0.7	0.0	1.6	0.0	1.3	1.1	3.1	3.1	0.3	3.3

(4) Political appearance

		Col1	Col2	Col3	Col4	Col5	Col6	Col7	Col8	Col9	Col10	Col11
Chinese Communist Party member	Frequency	1541	861	52	35	17	121	75	8	26	251	95
	%	85.1	90.0	86.7	57.4	51.5	80.7	83.3	53.3	81.3	86.3	78.5
Democratic party member	Frequency	6	1	0	1	0	0	1	0	0	1	2
	%	0.3	0.1	0.0	1.6	0.0	0.0	1.1	0.0	0.0	0.3	1.7
Nonpartisan	Frequency	159	52	7	19	10	23	10	5	2	20	11
	%	8.8	5.4	11.7	31.1	30.3	15.3	11.1	33.3	6.3	6.9	9.1
NA	Frequency	104	43	1	6	6	6	4	2	4	19	13
	%	5.7	4.5	1.7	9.8	18.2	4.0	4.4	13.3	12.5	6.5	10.7

Q1 The year of assumption of the current position of trade union chairman

		Col1	Col2	Col3	Col4	Col5	Col6	Col7	Col8	Col9	Col10	Col11
Before 1980	Frequency	8	2	0	0	0	2	0	0	0	3	1
	%	0.4	0.2	0.0	0.0	0.0	1.3	0.0	0.0	0.0	1.0	0.8
1980–1984	Frequency	7	3	1	0	1	0	0	0	0	2	0
	%	0.4	0.3	1.7	0.0	3.0	0.0	0.0	0.0	0.0	0.7	0
1985–1989	Frequency	31	16	0	0	2	1	1	1	1	8	2
	%	1.7	1.7	0.0	0.0	6.1	0.7	1.1	3.1	3.1	2.7	1.7
1990–1994	Frequency	61	32	2	1	2	5	3	0	0	10	6
	%	3.4	3.3	3.3	1.6	6.1	3.3	3.3	0.0	0.0	3.4	5.0
1995–1999	Frequency	242	120	16	5	7	21	13	3	1	40	16
	%	13.4	12.5	26.7	8.2	21.2	14.0	14.4	20.0	3.1	13.7	13.2

		Ownership form of your enterprise										
		Sum	State-owned/ State-holding enterprise	Collective-owned enterprise	Private enterprise	Cooperative enterprise	Limited liability corporation	Share Holding Corporation Ltd	Enterprise with Funds from Hong Kong, Macao and Taiwan	Foreign funded enterprise	Others	NA
2000–2004	Frequency	985	468	34	44	21	86	48	11	23	186	64
	%	54.4	48.9	56.7	72.1	63.6	57.3	53.3	73.3	71.9	63.7	52.9
2005	Frequency	12	9	1	0	0	0	0	0	0	2	0
	%	0.7	0.9	1.7	0.0	0.0	0.0	0.0	0.0	0.0	0.7	0.0
NA	Frequency	465	307	6	11	0	35	25	1	7	41	32
	%	25.7	32.1	10.0	18.0	0.0	23.3	27.8	6.7	21.9	14.0	26.4

Q2 The last position before being the trade union chairman

		Sum	State-owned/ State-holding enterprise	Collective-owned enterprise	Private enterprise	Cooperative enterprise	Limited liability corporation	Share Holding Corporation Ltd	Enterprise with Funds from Hong Kong, Macao and Taiwan	Foreign funded enterprise	Others	NA
Middle class cadre (Director, Section, Department)	Frequency	657	338	21	21	8	56	23	3	14	132	38
	%	36.3	35.3	35.0	34.4	24.2	37.3	25.6	20.0	43.8	45.2	31.4
Factory manager, President	Frequency	216	124	6	14	7	25	20	4	5	6	5
	%	11.9	13.0	10.0	23.0	21.2	16.7	22.2	26.7	15.6	2.1	4.1
Trade Unions Chairman	Frequency	105	52	3	1	1	5	3	2	2	29	7
	%	5.8	5.4	5.0	1.6	3.0	3.3	3.3	13.3	6.3	9.9	5.8
Teacher	Frequency	15	11	0	0	0	0	0	0	0	2	2
	%	0.8	1.1	0.0	0.0	0.0	0.0	0.0	0.0	0.0	0.7	1.7
CCP Secretary	Frequency	289	179	9	2	2	21	15	1	4	41	15
	%	16.0	18.7	15.0	3.3	6.1	14.0	16.7	6.7	12.5	14.0	12.4
Township Cadre	Frequency	2	1	0	0	0	0	0	0	0	1	0
	%	0.1	0.1	0.0	0.0	0.0	0.0	0.0	0.0	0.0	0.3	0.0
Township Governor	Frequency	1	0	0	0	0	0	0	0	0	0	1
	%	0.1	0.0	0.0	0.0	0.0	0.0	0.0	0.0	0.0	0.0	0.8

		1	2	3	4	5	6	7	8	9	10	11
Director of Department (Prefecture, Township)	Frequency	25	16	0	0	0	1	0	0	0	4	4
	%	1.4	1.7	0.0	0.0	0.0	0.7	0.0	0.0	0.0	1.4	3.3
Vice-Secretary of detached Factory	Frequency	1	1	0	0	0	0	0	0	0	0	0
	%	0.1	0.1	0.0	0.0	0.0	0.0	0.0	0.0	0.0	0.0	0.0
CCP secretary of Administrative Affairs	Frequency	28	16	1	0	1	2	2	0	1	4	1
	%	1.5	1.7	1.7	0.0	3.0	1.3	2.2	0.0	3.1	1.4	0.8
Chief of Security Department	Frequency	33	20	2	0	0	3	2	0	0	4	2
	%	1.8	2.1	3.3	0.0	0.0	2.0	2.2	0.0	0.0	1.4	1.7
Workers and Staff	Frequency	67	20	5	8	3	8	5	1	2	11	4
	%	3.7	2.1	8.3	13.1	9.1	5.3	5.6	6.7	6.3	3.8	3.3
Financial Manager	Frequency	5	1	0	1	0	2	0	1	0	0	0
	%	0.3	0.1	0.0	1.6	0.0	1.3	0.0	6.7	0.0	0.0	0.0
Labour and Security Supervisor	Frequency	4	3	0	0	0	1	0	0	0	0	0
	%	0.2	0.3	0.0	0.0	0.0	0.7	0.0	0.0	0.0	0.0	0.0
Statistic Staff	Frequency	5	2	0	0	1	1	0	0	0	1	0
	%	0.3	0.2	0.0	0.0	3.0	0.7	0.0	0.0	0.0	0.3	0.0
Trade Union Cadre Member of Committee	Frequency	27	16	2	0	0	3	1	1	0	3	1
	%	1.5	1.7	3.3	0.0	0.0	2.0	1.1	6.7	0.0	1.0	0.8
Accountant	Frequency	31	10	2	3	3	5	3	1	0	2	2
	%	1.7	1.7	3.3	4.9	9.1	3.3	3.3	6.7	0.0	0.7	1.7
Lower Staff	Frequency	40	14	2	2	1	2	7	0	1	8	3
	%	2.2	1.5	3.3	3.3	3.0	1.3	7.8	0.0	3.1	2.7	2.5
Female Cadre	Frequency	5	0	1	1	0	0	0	0	0	1	1
	%	0.3	0.0	1.7	1.6	0.0	0.0	0.0	0.0	0.0	0.3	0.8
Secretary of Chinese Communist Youth League	Frequency	19	12	0	0	1	3	1	0	0	3	0
	%	1.0	1.3	0.0	0.0	3.0	2.0	1.1	0.0	0.0	1.0	0.0
Chief of Police Box	Frequency	1	1	0	0	0	0	0	0	0	0	0
	%	0.1	0.1	0.0	0.0	0.0	0.0	0.0	0.0	0.0	0.0	0.0

Ownership form of your enterprise

		Sum	State-owned/ State-holding enterprise	Collective-owned enterprise	Private enterprise	Cooperative enterprise	Limited liability corporation	Share Holding Corporation Ltd	Enterprise with Funds from Hong Kong, Macao and Taiwan	Foreign funded enterprise	Others	NA
Doctor	Frequency	3	1	0	0	0	0	0	0	0	2	0
	%	0.2	0.1	0.0	0.0	0.0	0.0	0.0	0.0	0.0	0.7	0.0
Soldier	Frequency	4	2	0	0	0	0	0	0	0	2	0
	%	0.2	0.2	0.0	0.0	0.0	0.0	0.0	0.0	0.0	0.7	0.0
Principal	Frequency	14	4	0	0	0	0	0	0	0	6	4
	%	0.8	0.4	0.0	0.0	0.0	0.0	0.0	0.0	0.0	2.1	3.3
NA	Frequency	214	113	3	8	5	12	8	1	3	30	31
	%	11.8	11.8	5.0	13.1	15.2	8.0	8.9	6.7	9.4	10.3	25.6

Q3 Procedure to assume the post of trade union chairman

		Sum	State-owned/ State-holding enterprise	Collective-owned enterprise	Private enterprise	Cooperative enterprise	Limited liability corporation	Share Holding Corporation Ltd	Enterprise with Funds from Hong Kong, Macao and Taiwan	Foreign funded enterprise	Others	NA
1 Appointed by an organization	Frequency	390	216	12	11	7	28	14	3	3	70	26
	%	21.5	22.6	20.0	18.0	21.2	18.7	15.6	20.0	9.4	24.0	21.5
2 Elected by members' congress/members' assembly, following organization recommendation	Frequency	860	458	24	28	18	83	48	7	14	128	52
	%	47.5	47.9	40.0	45.9	54.5	55.3	53.3	46.7	43.8	43.8	43.0
3 Elected by members' congress/ members' assembly directly	Frequency	331	137	21	14	6	30	22	4	10	63	24
	%	18.3	14.3	35.0	23.0	18.2	20.0	24.4	26.7	31.3	21.6	19.8

4 Elected by members' congress/members' assembly, following open selective examinations	Frequency	42	29	0	1	1	2	2	0	1	4	2
	%	2.3	3.0	0.0	1.6	3.0	1.3	2.2	0.0	3.1	1.4	1.7
5 Others	Frequency	48	21	1	3	0	0	1	0	3	16	3
	%	2.7	2.2	1.7	4.9	0.0	0.0	1.1	0.0	9.4	5.5	2.5
NA	Frequency	140	96	2	4	1	7	3	1	1	11	14
	%	7.7	10.0	3.3	6.6	3.0	4.7	3.3	6.7	3.1	3.8	11.6

Q4 (If you chose 1 in Q3) the name of the organization

Party organization of work unit	Frequency	180	103	4	2	3	13	8	0	0	33	14
	%	46.2	47.7	33.3	18.2	42.9	46.4	57.1	0.0	0.0	47.1	53.8
Administrative organization of work unit	Frequency	30	8	3	6	1	5	0	2	1	1	3
	%	7.7	3.7	25.0	54.5	14.3	17.9	0.0	66.7	33.3	1.4	11.5
Higher-level trade union	Frequency	75	37	3	0	3	1	3	0	2	25	1
	%	19.2	17.1	25.0	0.0	42.9	3.6	21.4	0.0	66.7	35.7	3.8
Former primary trade union committee	Frequency	1	1	0	0	0	0	0	0	0	0	0
	%	0.3	0.5	0.0	0.0	0.0	0.0	0.0	0.0	0.0	0.0	0.0
Others	Frequency	88	61	2	0	0	6	3	1	0	9	6
	%	22.6	28.2	16.7	0.0	0.0	21.4	21.4	33.3	0.0	12.9	23.1
NA	Frequency	16	6	0	3	0	3	0	0	0	2	2
	%	4.1	2.8	0.0	27.3	0.0	10.7	0.0	0.0	0.0	2.9	7.7

Q5 (If you chose 2–4 in Q3) specific method of election

		Ownership form of your enterprise									
	Sum	State-owned/ State-holding enterprise	Collective-owned enterprise	Private enterprise	Cooperative enterprise	Limited liability corporation	Share Holding Corporation Ltd	Enterprise with Funds from Hong Kong, Macao and Taiwan	Foreign funded enterprise	Others	NA
Separate voting for chairman, vice-chairmen and other committees — Frequency	199	87	8	9	4	18	12	2	1	40	18
%	16.1	13.9	17.8	20.9	16.0	15.7	16.7	18.2	4.0	20.5	23.1
Voting for chairman and vice-chairmen from elected committees — Frequency	911	475	33	24	19	81	53	8	24	144	50
%	73.9	76.1	73.3	55.8	76.0	70.4	73.6	72.7	96.0	73.8	64.1
Others — Frequency	33	18	0	4	0	5	0	0	0	2	4
%	2.7	2.9	0.0	9.3	0.0	4.3	0.0	0.0	0.0	1.0	5.1
NA — Frequency	90	44	4	6	2	11	7	1	0	9	6
%	7.3	7.1	8.9	14.0	8.0	9.6	9.7	9.1	0.0	4.6	7.7

Q6 (If you chose 2–4 in Q3) single-candidate election or competitive election

	Sum	State-owned/ State-holding enterprise	Collective-owned enterprise	Private enterprise	Cooperative enterprise	Limited liability corporation	Share Holding Corporation Ltd	Enterprise with Funds from Hong Kong, Macao and Taiwan	Foreign funded enterprise	Others	NA
Single-candidate election — Frequency	310	155	12	11	4	33	17	1	3	52	22
%	25.1	24.8	26.7	25.6	16.0	28.7	23.6	9.1	12.0	26.7	28.2
Competitive election (including single-candidate election following competitive preliminary election) — Frequency	833	433	30	26	17	72	50	9	20	130	46
%	67.6	69.4	66.7	60.5	68.0	62.6	69.4	81.8	80.0	66.7	59.0
NA — Frequency	90	36	3	6	4	10	5	1	2	13	10
%	7.3	5.8	6.7	14.0	16.0	8.7	6.9	9.1	8.0	6.7	12.8

Q7 (If you chose 2–4 in Q3) the organizations or the persons you accepted recommendation

Recommended by party organization of work unit	Frequency	494	272	16	8	6	39	31	1	6	83	32
	%	40.1	43.6	35.6	18.6	24.0	33.9	43.1	9.1	24.0	42.6	41.0
Recommended by administrative organization of work unit	Frequency	104	40	6	11	5	11	3	1	1	18	8
	%	8.4	6.4	13.3	25.6	20.0	9.6	4.2	9.1	4.0	9.2	10.3
Recommended by functionaries of workshop-level trade union	Frequency	20	9	2	0	2	2	2	0	1	1	1
	%	1.6	1.4	4.4	0.0	8.0	1.7	2.8	0.0	4.0	0.5	1.3
Self-recommended	Frequency	37	26	1	0	0	4	1	1	0	4	0
	%	3.0	4.2	2.2	0.0	0.0	3.5	1.4	9.1	0.0	2.1	0.0
Recommended by ordinary union members or trade union small groups	Frequency	175	77	11	7	3	12	12	4	9	32	8
	%	14.2	12.3	24.4	16.3	12.0	10.4	16.7	36.4	36.0	16.4	10.3
Others	Frequency	22	9	0	2	0	3	2	0	0	6	0
	%	1.8	1.4	0.0	4.7	0.0	2.6	2.8	0.0	0.0	3.1	0.0
NA	Frequency	381	191	9	15	9	44	21	4	8	51	29
	%	30.9	30.6	20.0	34.9	36.0	38.3	29.2	36.4	32.0	26.2	37.2

Q8 Whether or not holding concurrent post other than trade union chairman

1 Hold	Frequency	1304	670	50	45	27	120	66	14	26	218	68
	%	72.0	70.0	83.3	73.8	81.8	80.0	73.3	93.3	81.3	74.7	56.2
2 Not hold	Frequency	348	192	7	10	6	21	19	1	6	56	30
	%	19.2	20.1	11.7	16.4	18.2	14.0	21.1	6.7	18.8	19.2	24.8
NA	Frequency	159	95	3	6	0	9	5	0	0	18	23
	%	8.8	9.9	5.0	9.8	0.0	6.0	5.6	0.0	0.0	6.2	19.0

Q9 (If you chose 1 in Q8) whether or not holding the following post concurrently

1. Secretary of CCP committee at the corresponding level

		Sum	State-owned/ State-holding enterprise	Collective-owned enterprise	Private enterprise	Cooperative enterprise	Limited liability corporation	Share Holding Corporation Ltd	Enterprise with Funds from Hong Kong, Macao and Taiwan	Foreign funded enterprise	Others	NA
Not Hold	Frequency	1202	610	47	43	23	114	58	14	23	203	67
	%	92.2	91.0	94.0	95.6	85.2	95.0	87.9	100.0	88.5	93.1	98.5
Hold	Frequency	102	60	3	2	4	6	8	0	3	15	1
	%	7.8	9.0	6.0	4.4	14.8	5.0	12.1	0.0	11.5	6.9	1.5

2. Vice-secretary of CCP committee at the corresponding level

Not Hold	Frequency	1064	516	35	41	23	101	58	14	22	197	57
	%	81.6	77.0	70.0	91.1	85.2	84.2	87.9	100.0	84.6	90.4	83.8
Hold	Frequency	240	154	15	4	4	19	8	0	4	21	11
	%	18.4	23.0	30.0	8.9	14.8	15.8	12.1	0.0	15.4	9.6	16.2

3. CCP committee member at the corresponding level

Not hold	Frequency	979	465	41	41	25	93	47	12	25	176	54
	%	75.1	69.4	82.0	91.1	92.6	77.5	71.2	85.7	96.2	80.7	79.4
Hold	Frequency	325	205	9	4	2	27	19	2	1	42	14
	%	24.9	30.6	18.0	8.9	7.4	22.5	28.8	14.3	3.8	19.3	20.6

4. Administrative manager in charge (president, etc.) at the corresponding level

Not hold	Frequency	1262	658	49	42	27	119	61	14	24	203	65
	%	96.8	98.2	98.0	93.3	100.0	99.2	92.4	100.0	92.3	93.1	95.6
Hold	Frequency	42	12	1	3	0	1	5	0	2	15	3
	%	3.2	1.8	2.0	6.7	0.0	0.8	7.6	0.0	7.7	6.9	4.4

5. Vice-post of administrative organization at the corresponding level

Not hold	Frequency	1012	517	41	32	16	97	57	9	24	167	52
	%	77.6	77.2	82.0	71.1	59.3	80.8	86.4	64.3	92.3	76.6	76.5
Hold	Frequency	292	153	9	13	11	23	9	5	2	51	16
	%	22.4	22.8	18.0	28.9	40.7	19.2	13.6	35.7	7.7	23.4	23.5

6. Any other posts

Not hold	Frequency	775	407	29	24	17	64	36	7	12	126	53
	%	59.4	60.7	58.0	53.3	63.0	53.3	54.5	50.0	46.2	57.8	77.9
Hold	Frequency	529	263	21	21	10	56	30	7	14	92	15
	%	40.6	39.3	42.0	46.7	37.0	46.7	45.5	50.0	53.8	42.2	22.1

Q10 Whether or not having relatives serving as the following
1. Secretary of CCP committee at the corresponding level

Not have	Frequency	1801	955	58	60	33	149	90	15	31	289	121
	%	99.4	99.8	96.7	98.4	100.0	99.3	100.0	100.0	96.9	99.0	100.0
Have	Frequency	9	2	1	1	0	1	0	0	1	3	0
	%	0.5	0.2	1.7	1.6	0.0	0.7	0.0	0.0	3.1	1.0	0.0
NA	Frequency	1	0	1	0	0	0	0	0	0	0	0
	%	0.1	0.0	1.7	0.0	0.0	0.0	0.0	0.0	0.0	0.0	0.0

2. Vice-secretary of CCP committee at the corresponding level

		Sum	State-owned/ State-holding enterprise	Collective-owned enterprise	Private enterprise	Cooperative enterprise	Limited liability corporation	Share Holding Corporation Ltd	Enterprise with Funds from Hong Kong, Macao and Taiwan	Foreign funded enterprise	Others	NA
											Ownership form of your enterprise	
Not have	Frequency	1790	947	53	60	33	149	90	15	31	291	121
	%	98.8	99.0	88.3	98.4	100.0	99.3	100.0	100.0	96.9	99.7	100.0
Have	Frequency	20	10	6	1	0	1	0	0	1	1	0
	%	1.1	1.0	10.0	1.6	0.0	0.7	0.0	0.0	3.1	0.3	0.0
NA	Frequency	1	0	1	0	0	0	0	0	0	0	0
	%	0.1	0.0	1.7	0.0	0.0	0.0	0.0	0.0	0.0	0.0	0.0

3. CCP committee member at the corresponding level

		Sum	State-owned/ State-holding enterprise	Collective-owned enterprise	Private enterprise	Cooperative enterprise	Limited liability corporation	Share Holding Corporation Ltd	Enterprise with Funds from Hong Kong, Macao and Taiwan	Foreign funded enterprise	Others	NA
Not have	Frequency	1772	934	57	60	31	147	87	15	31	290	120
	%	97.8	97.6	95.0	98.4	93.9	98.0	96.7	100.0	96.9	99.3	99.2
Have	Frequency	38	23	2	1	2	3	3	0	1	2	1
	%	2.1	2.4	3.3	1.6	6.1	2.0	3.3	0.0	3.1	0.7	0.8
NA	Frequency	1	0	1	0	0	0	0	0	0	0	0
	%	0.1	0.0	1.7	0.0	0.0	0.0	0.0	0.0	0.0	0.0	0.0

4. Administrative manager (president etc.) at the corresponding level

Not have	Frequency	1784	954	58	50	32	147	86	15	31	291	120
	%	98.5	99.7	96.7	82.0	97.0	98.0	95.6	100.0	96.9	99.7	99.2
Have	Frequency	26	3	1	11	1	3	4	0	1	1	1
	%	1.4	0.3	1.7	18.0	3.0	2.0	4.4	0.0	3.1	0.3	0.8
NA	Frequency	1	0	1	0	0	0	0	0	0	0	0
	%	0.1	0.0	1.7	0.0	0.0	0.0	0.0	0.0	0.0	0.0	0.0

5. Vice-post of the administrative organization at the corresponding level

Not have	Frequency	1775	939	55	58	32	148	90	15	31	286	121
	%	98.0	98.1	91.7	95.1	97.0	98.7	100.0	100.0	96.9	97.9	100.0
Have	Frequency	35	18	4	3	1	2	0	0	1	6	0
	%	1.9	1.9	6.7	4.9	3.0	1.3	0.0	0.0	3.1	2.1	0.0
NA	Frequency	1	0	1	0	0	0	0	0	0	0	0
	%	0.1	0.0	1.7	0.0	0.0	0.0	0.0	0.0	0.0	0.0	0.0

Q11 Whether or not enjoying the economic remuneration equivalent to that of the vice-post of the Party or administrative organization at the corresponding level

Enjoy	Frequency	1103	652	38	14	19	99	58	5	13	148	57
	%	60.9	68.1	63.3	23.0	57.6	66.0	64.4	33.3	40.6	50.7	47.1
Not enjoy	Frequency	441	149	17	37	11	38	28	8	18	99	36
	%	24.4	15.6	28.3	60.7	33.3	25.3	31.1	53.3	56.3	33.9	29.8
NA	Frequency	267	156	5	10	3	13	4	2	1	45	28
	%	14.7	16.3	8.3	16.4	9.1	8.7	4.4	13.3	3.1	15.4	23.1

Q12 Whether or not being satisfied with the current remuneration in consideration of the quantity of workload

		Ownership form of your enterprise									
	Sum	State-owned/State-holding enterprise	Collective-owned enterprise	Private enterprise	Cooperative enterprise	Limited liability corporation	Share Holding Corporation Ltd	Enterprise with Funds from Hong Kong, Macao and Taiwan	Foreign funded enterprise	Others	NA
Extremely satisfied Frequency	180	101	10	8	5	11	9	0	3	23	10
%	9.9	10.6	16.7	13.1	15.2	7.3	10.0	0.0	9.4	7.9	8.3
Fundamentally satisfied Frequency	1124	603	38	28	16	109	59	8	16	178	69
%	62.1	63.0	63.3	45.9	48.5	72.7	65.6	53.3	50.0	61.0	57.0
Not very satisfied (compared with workload, treatment is not very good) Frequency	210	99	6	15	6	16	9	4	6	35	14
%	11.6	10.3	10.0	24.6	18.2	10.7	10.0	26.7	18.8	12.0	11.6
Dissatisfied (compared with workload, treatment is bad) Frequency	90	39	3	4	2	3	7	1	4	21	6
%	5.0	4.1	5.0	6.6	6.1	2.0	7.8	6.7	12.5	7.2	5.0
NA Frequency	207	115	3	6	4	11	6	2	3	35	22
%	11.4	12.0	5.0	9.8	12.1	7.3	6.7	13.3	9.4	12.0	18.2

Part 2: Questions about work unit

A1-3 Field of industry of your work unit

Field of industry	Measure												
Farming, Forestry, Animal Husbandry and Fishing	Frequency	94	64	1	4	1	1	2	0	0	0	13	8
	%	5.2	6.7	1.7	6.6	3.0	0.7	2.2	0.0	0.0	0.0	4.5	6.6
Mining and Quarrying	Frequency	66	46	0	0	0	15	5	0	0	0	0	0
	%	3.6	4.8	0.0	0.0	0.0	10.0	5.6	0.0	0.0	0.0	0.0	0.0
Manufacturing	Frequency	397	187	13	34	20	48	41	11	26	3	11	6
	%	21.9	19.5	21.7	55.7	60.6	32.0	45.6	73.3	81.3	9.4	3.8	5.0
Production and Supply of Electricity, Gas and Water	Frequency	179	155	2	0	1	7	8	1	3	3	1	1
	%	9.9	16.2	3.3	0.0	3.0	4.7	8.9	6.7	9.4	9.4	0.3	0.8
Construction	Frequency	143	89	7	7	2	27	5	0	0	0	5	1
	%	7.9	9.3	11.7	11.5	6.1	18.0	5.6	0.0	0.0	0.0	1.7	0.8
Geological Prospecting and Water Conservancy	Frequency	30	16	1	0	0	1	0	0	0	0	6	6
	%	1.7	1.7	1.7	0.0	0.0	0.7	0.0	0.0	0.0	0.0	2.1	5.0
Transport, Storage, Post & Telecommunication Services	Frequency	257	190	3	1	1	16	6	1	3	3	29	7
	%	14.2	19.9	5.0	1.6	3.0	10.7	6.7	6.7	9.4	9.4	9.9	5.8
Wholesale and Retail Trade & Catering Services	Frequency	69	32	12	9	2	9	3	0	0	0	1	1
	%	3.8	3.3	20.0	14.8	6.1	6.0	3.3	0.0	0.0	0.0	0.3	0.8
Finance and Insurance	Frequency	38	20	4	0	1	2	8	0	0	0	3	0
	%	2.1	2.1	6.7	0.0	3.0	1.3	8.9	0.0	0.0	0.0	1.0	0.0
Real Estate	Frequency	32	15	3	1	0	5	2	0	0	0	6	0
	%	1.8	1.6	5.0	1.6	0.0	3.3	2.2	0.0	0.0	0.0	2.1	0.0
Social Services	Frequency	81	39	6	1	1	7	4	0	0	0	21	2
	%	4.5	4.1	10.0	1.6	3.0	4.7	4.4	0.0	0.0	0.0	7.2	1.7
Health Care, Sports & Social Welfare	Frequency	73	23	1	0	1	3	0	0	0	0	38	7
	%	4.0	2.4	1.7	0.0	3.0	2.0	0.0	0.0	0.0	0.0	13.0	5.8

			State-owned/ State-holding enterprise	Collective-owned enterprise	Private enterprise	Cooperative enterprise	Limited liability corporation	Share Holding Corporation Ltd	Enterprise with Funds from Hong Kong, Macao and Taiwan	Foreign funded enterprise	Others	NA
		Sum										
Education, Culture and Arts, Radio, Film and Television	Frequency	83	16	0	0	0	1	1	0	0	39	26
	%	4.6	1.7	0.0	0.0	0.0	0.7	1.1	0.0	0.0	13.4	21.5
Scientific Research and Polytechnic Services	Frequency	23	12	0	0	0	3	2	1	0	5	0
	%	1.3	1.3	0.0	0.0	0.0	2.0	2.2	6.7	0.0	1.7	0.0
Government Agencies, Party Agencies and Social Organizations	Frequency	149	24	1	1	0	1	0	1	0	90	31
	%	8.2	2.5	1.7	1.6	0.0	0.7	0.0	6.7	0.0	30.8	25.6
NA	Frequency	97	29	6	3	3	4	3	0	0	24	25
	%	5.4	3.0	10.0	4.9	9.1	2.7	3.3	0.0	0.0	8.2	20.7

Ownership form of your enterprise

A1-4 The year of establishment of work unit

		Sum	State-owned/ State-holding enterprise	Collective-owned enterprise	Private enterprise	Cooperative enterprise	Limited liability corporation	Share Holding Corporation Ltd	Enterprise with Funds from Hong Kong, Macao and Taiwan	Foreign funded enterprise	Others	NA
Before 1911	Frequency	8	8	0	0	0	0	0	0	0	0	0
	%	0.6	1.2	0.0	0.0	0.0	0.0	0.0	0.0	0.0	0.0	0.0
1911–1948	Frequency	24	15	0	0	1	0	1	0	0	5	2
	%	1.8	2.2	0.0	0.0	3.7	0.0	1.5	0.0	0.0	2.3	2.9
1949	Frequency	18	11	0	0	0	1	0	0	0	4	2
	%	1.4	1.6	0.0	0.0	0.0	0.8	0.0	0.0	0.0	1.8	2.9

Year		C1	C2	C3	C4	C5	C6	C7	C8	C9	C10	C11
1950	Frequency	2	6	0	0	0	0	0	0	0	7	15
	%	2.9	2.8	0.0	0.0	0.0	0.0	0.0	0.0	0.0	1.0	1.2
1951	Frequency	1	1	0	0	1	0	0	0	0	6	9
	%	1.5	0.5	0.0	0.0	0.8	0.0	0.0	0.0	0.0	0.9	0.7
1952	Frequency	1	4	0	0	1	0	0	0	1	26	32
	%	0.5	1.8	0.0	0.0	0.8	0.0	0.0	0.0	2.0	3.9	2.5
1953	Frequency	0	6	0	0	0	0	0	0	0	10	16
	%	0.0	2.8	0.0	0.0	0.0	0.0	0.0	0.0	0.0	1.5	1.2
1954	Frequency	0	2	0	0	2	0	0	0	1	9	14
	%	0.0	0.9	0.0	0.0	1.7	0.0	0.0	0.0	2.0	1.3	1.1
1955	Frequency	0	1	0	0	0	0	0	0	0	6	7
	%	0.0	0.5	0.0	0.0	0.0	0.0	0.0	0.0	0.0	0.9	0.5
1956	Frequency	1	4	0	1	0	1	0	0	5	19	31
	%	1.5	1.8	0.0	7.1	0.0	0.8	0.0	0.0	10.0	2.8	2.4
1957	Frequency	0	2	0	0	0	0	0	0	0	10	12
	%	0.0	0.9	0.0	0.0	0.0	0.0	0.0	0.0	0.0	1.5	0.9
1958	Frequency	1	7	0	0	0	9	0	0	1	26	46
	%	1.5	3.2	0.0	0.0	0.0	7.5	0.0	0.0	2.0	3.9	3.5
1959	Frequency	3	2	0	0	0	0	0	0	0	2	5
	%	4.4	0.9	0.0	0.0	0.0	0.0	0.0	0.0	0.0	0.3	0.4
1960	Frequency	1	2	0	0	0	1	0	0	2	4	9
	%	1.5	0.9	0.0	0.0	0.0	0.8	0.0	0.0	4.0	0.6	0.7
1961	Frequency	1	1	0	0	0	0	0	0	0	2	3
	%	0.0	0.5	0.0	0.0	0.0	0.0	0.0	0.0	0.0	0.3	0.2
1962	Frequency	1	5	0	0	0	0	0	0	0	4	10
	%	1.5	2.3	0.0	0.0	0.0	0.0	0.0	0.0	0.0	0.6	0.8
1963	Frequency	0	2	0	0	0	0	1	0	0	3	6
	%	0.0	0.9	0.0	0.0	0.0	0.0	1.5	0.0	0.0	0.4	0.5
1964	Frequency	0	1	0	0	0	0	0	1	2	6	9
	%	0.0	0.5	0.0	0.0	0.0	0.0	0.0	3.7	4.0	0.9	0.7
1965	Frequency	1	1	0	0	0	0	0	0	1	4	8
	%	1.5	0.5	0.0	0.0	0.0	0.0	0.0	0.0	2.0	0.6	0.6

Ownership form of your enterprise

Year		Sum	State-owned/ State-holding enterprise	Collective-owned enterprise	Private enterprise	Cooperative enterprise	Limited liability corporation	Share Holding Corporation Ltd	Enterprise with Funds from Hong Kong, Macao and Taiwan	Foreign funded enterprise	Others	NA
1966	Frequency	9	7	0	0	1	0	1	0	0	0	0
	%	0.7	1.0	0.0	0.0	3.7	0.0	1.5	0.0	0.0	0.0	0.0
1967	Frequency	2	2	0	0	0	0	0	0	0	0	0
	%	0.2	0.3	0.0	0.0	0.0	0.0	0.0	0.0	0.0	0.0	0.0
1968	Frequency	1	0	0	0	0	0	0	0	0	1	0
	%	0.1	0.0	0.0	0.0	0.0	0.0	0.0	0.0	0.0	0.5	0.0
1969	Frequency	4	2	0	0	0	1	1	0	0	0	0
	%	0.3	0.3	0.0	0.0	0.0	0.8	1.5	0.0	0.0	0.0	0.0
1970	Frequency	16	9	2	0	0	1	0	0	0	4	0
	%	1.2	1.3	4.0	0.0	0.0	0.8	0.0	0.0	0.0	1.8	0.0
1971	Frequency	3	1	0	0	0	1	0	0	1	0	0
	%	0.2	0.1	0.0	0.0	0.0	0.8	0.0	0.0	3.8	0.0	0.0
1972	Frequency	6	3	0	0	0	0	1	0	0	1	1
	%	0.5	0.4	0.0	0.0	0.0	0.0	1.5	0.0	0.0	0.5	1.5
1973	Frequency	9	6	0	0	0	1	1	0	0	1	0
	%	0.7	0.9	0.0	0.0	0.0	0.8	1.5	0.0	0.0	0.5	0.0
1974	Frequency	6	3	0	0	0	0	0	0	0	2	1
	%	0.5	0.4	0.0	0.0	0.0	0.0	0.0	0.0	0.0	0.9	1.5
1975	Frequency	5	2	1	0	0	0	0	0	1	1	0
	%	0.4	0.3	2.0	0.0	0.0	0.0	0.0	0.0	3.8	0.5	0.0
1976	Frequency	7	1	1	0	0	0	1	0	0	3	1
	%	0.5	0.1	2.0	0.0	0.0	0.0	1.5	0.0	0.0	1.4	1.5
1977	Frequency	2	0	0	0	0	0	0	0	0	1	1
	%	0.2	0.0	0.0	0.0	0.0	0.0	0.0	0.0	0.0	0.5	1.5

Year		1	2	3	4	5	6	7	8	9	10	11
1978	Frequency	23	10	1	1	0	2	0	0	0	8	1
	%	1.8	1.5	2.0	2.2	0.0	1.7	0.0	0.0	0.0	3.7	1.5
1979	Frequency	15	9	1	0	2	1	0	0	0	1	1
	%	1.2	1.3	2.0	0.0	7.4	0.8	0.0	0.0	0.0	0.5	1.5
1980	Frequency	19	8	1	0	0	0	1	0	0	5	3
	%	1.5	1.2	2.0	0.0	0.0	0.0	1.5	0.0	0.0	2.3	4.4
1981	Frequency	12	6	1	0	0	1	1	0	1	3	0
	%	0.9	0.9	2.0	0.0	0.0	0.8	1.5	0.0	3.8	1.4	0.0
1982	Frequency	11	4	0	1	1	0	1	0	0	2	2
	%	0.8	0.6	0.0	2.2	3.7	0.0	1.5	0.0	0.0	0.9	2.9
1983	Frequency	6	4	0	0	1	0	0	0	0	1	0
	%	0.5	0.6	0.0	0.0	3.7	0.0	0.0	0.0	0.0	0.5	0.0
1984	Frequency	20	7	4	0	0	4	0	0	0	3	2
	%	1.5	1.0	8.0	0.0	0.0	3.3	0.0	0.0	0.0	1.4	2.9
1985	Frequency	22	8	3	0	3	0	0	0	0	7	0
	%	1.7	1.2	6.0	0.0	11.1	0.0	0.0	0.0	0.0	3.2	0.0
1986	Frequency	16	11	1	0	0	2	1	0	0	1	1
	%	1.2	1.6	2.0	0.0	0.0	1.7	1.5	0.0	0.0	0.5	1.5
1987	Frequency	15	6	0	1	0	0	0	0	0	2	3
	%	1.2	0.9	0.0	2.2	0.0	0.0	0.0	0.0	0.0	0.9	4.4
1988	Frequency	23	9	0	1	0	2	2	0	1	7	3
	%	1.8	1.3	0.0	2.2	0.0	1.7	3.0	0.0	3.8	3.2	4.4
1989	Frequency	11	4	0	1	1	0	0	1	1	2	0
	%	0.8	0.6	0.0	2.2	3.7	0.0	0.0	7.1	3.8	0.9	0.0
1990	Frequency	9	4	1	0	0	2	2	0	0	2	0
	%	0.7	0.6	2.0	0.0	0.0	1.7	3.0	0.0	0.0	0.9	0.0
1991	Frequency	8	3	0	0	2	1	0	0	0	2	0
	%	0.6	0.4	0.0	0.0	7.4	0.8	0.0	0.0	0.0	0.9	0.0
1992	Frequency	38	18	3	3	1	4	1	3	0	5	0
	%	2.9	2.7	6.0	6.7	3.7	3.3	1.5	21.4	0.0	2.3	0.0
1993	Frequency	27	10	1	2	3	2	3	1	0	6	1
	%	2.1	1.5	2.0	4.4	3.7	1.7	4.5	7.1	0.0	2.8	1.5
1994	Frequency	37	13	1	3	3	4	1	0	3	9	0
	%	2.8	1.9	2.0	6.7	11.1	3.3	1.5	0.0	11.5	4.1	0.0

Ownership form of your enterprise

		Sum	State-owned/ State-holding enterprise	Collective-owned enterprise	Private enterprise	Cooperative enterprise	Limited liability corporation	Share Holding Corporation Ltd	Enterprise with Funds from Hong Kong, Macao and Taiwan	Foreign funded enterprise	Others	NA
1995	Frequency	20	3	1	4	0	5	0	1	1	3	2
	%	1.5	0.4	2.0	8.9	0.0	4.2	0.0	7.1	3.8	1.4	2.9
1996	Frequency	28	13	2	4	1	1	2	0	1	3	1
	%	2.1	1.9	4.0	8.9	3.7	0.8	3.0	0.0	3.8	1.4	1.5
1997	Frequency	23	8	1	4	1	2	2	1	1	3	0
	%	1.8	1.2	2.0	8.9	3.7	1.7	3.0	7.1	3.8	1.4	0.0
1998	Frequency	46	19	3	3	0	8	6	1	2	3	1
	%	3.5	2.8	6.0	6.7	0.0	6.7	9.1	7.1	7.7	1.4	1.5
1999	Frequency	32	9	0	1	2	6	4	0	3	6	1
	%	2.5	1.3	0.0	2.2	7.4	5.0	6.1	0.0	11.5	2.8	1.5
2000	Frequency	51	22	0	3	1	11	4	0	3	7	0
	%	3.9	3.3	0.0	6.7	3.7	9.2	6.1	0.0	11.5	3.2	0.0
2001	Frequency	37	16	0	4	0	6	2	1	2	6	0
	%	2.8	2.4	0.0	8.9	0.0	5.0	3.0	7.1	7.7	2.8	0.0
2002	Frequency	49	20	1	4	1	8	5	2	0	7	1
	%	3.8	3.0	2.0	8.9	3.7	6.7	7.6	14.3	0.0	3.2	1.5
2003	Frequency	30	15	0	1	0	1	5	1	0	6	1
	%	2.3	2.2	0.0	2.2	0.0	0.8	7.6	7.1	0.0	2.8	1.5
2004	Frequency	10	5	0	1	0	1	1	0	0	1	1
	%	0.8	0.7	0.0	2.2	0.0	0.8	1.5	0.0	0.0	0.5	1.5
NA	Frequency	314	192	7	3	3	26	15	1	5	37	25
	%	24.1	28.7	14.0	6.7	11.1	21.7	22.7	7.1	19.2	17.0	36.8

A1-5 Total number of workers and staff members (including part-time/short-time contract workers) by the end of 2003

Less than 200	Frequency	572	198	37	27	20	51	21	8	13	137	60
	%	31.6	20.7	61.7	44.3	60.6	34.0	23.3	53.3	40.6	46.9	49.6
200–999	Frequency	575	326	15	20	10	49	36	5	9	76	29
	%	31.8	34.1	25.0	32.8	30.3	32.7	40.0	33.3	28.1	26.0	24.0
1000–1999	Frequency	143	99	3	3	1	13	11	0	2	9	2
	%	7.9	10.3	5.0	4.9	3.0	8.7	12.2	0.0	6.3	3.1	1.7
2000–2999	Frequency	56	38	1	2	1	4	3	0	0	4	3
	%	3.1	4.0	1.7	3.3	3.0	2.7	3.3	0.0	0.0	1.4	2.5
3000–3999	Frequency	34	19	0	0	0	5	3	0	2	5	0
	%	1.9	2.0	0.0	0.0	0.0	3.3	3.3	0.0	6.3	1.7	0.0
4000–4999	Frequency	30	23	1	0	1	1	0	0	0	4	0
	%	1.7	2.4	1.7	0.0	3.0	0.7	0.0	0.0	0.0	1.4	0.0
5000–5999	Frequency	25	18	0	0	0	3	1	0	0	3	0
	%	1.4	1.9	0.0	0.0	0.0	2.0	1.1	0.0	0.0	1.0	0.0
6000–9999	Frequency	37	27	0	0	0	5	2	0	1	1	2
	%	2.0	2.8	0.0	0.0	0.0	3.3	2.2	0.0	3.1	0.3	1.7
More than 9999	Frequency	50	42	0	0	0	6	0	0	0	1	0
	%	2.8	4.4	0.0	0.0	0.0	4.0	0.0	0.0	0.0	0.3	0.0
NA	Frequency	289	167	3	9	0	13	13	2	5	52	25
	%	16.0	17.5	5.0	14.8	0.0	8.7	14.4	13.3	15.6	17.8	20.7

A1-5 Percentage of part-time/short-time contract workers in all employees

0	Frequency	531	255	26	14	3	48	20	2	9	106	48
	%	29.3	26.6	43.3	23.0	9.1	32.0	22.2	13.3	28.1	36.3	39.7
1–10	Frequency	247	125	8	6	3	19	10	0	5	51	20
	%	13.6	13.1	13.3	9.8	9.1	12.7	11.1	0.0	15.6	17.5	16.5
11–20	Frequency	135	72	4	3	4	10	3	2	1	27	9
	%	7.5	7.5	6.7	4.9	12.1	6.7	3.3	13.3	3.1	9.2	7.4
21–30	Frequency	95	54	3	2	1	9	4	1	0	15	6
	%	5.2	5.6	5.0	3.3	3.0	6.0	4.4	6.7	0.0	5.1	5.0

Ownership form of your enterprise

		Sum	State-owned/ State-holding enterprise	Collective-owned enterprise	Private enterprise	Cooperative enterprise	Limited liability corporation	Share Holding Corporation Ltd	Enterprise with Funds from Hong Kong, Macao and Taiwan	Foreign funded enterprise	Others	NA
31–40	Frequency	57	34	0	4	0	3	3	1	3	8	1
	%	3.1	3.6	0.0	6.6	0.0	2.0	3.3	6.7	9.4	2.7	0.8
41–50	Frequency	32	15	1	1	0	6	0	0	1	8	0
	%	1.8	1.6	1.7	1.6	0.0	4.0	0.0	0.0	3.1	2.7	0.0
51–60	Frequency	28	20	0	1	0	2	1	0	2	2	0
	%	1.5	2.1	0.0	1.6	0.0	1.3	1.1	0.0	6.3	0.7	0.0
61–70	Frequency	16	10	0	0	1	1	0	1	0	3	0
	%	0.9	1.0	0.0	0.0	3.0	0.7	0.0	6.7	0.0	1.0	0
71–80	Frequency	19	9	3	0	1	1	1	0	0	3	1
	%	1.0	0.9	5.0	0.0	3.0	0.7	1.1	0.0	0.0	1.0	0.8
81–90	Frequency	6	2	0	1	0	1	1	1	0	0	0
	%	0.3	0.2	0.0	1.6	0.0	0.7	1.1	6.7	0.0	0.0	0.0
91–100	Frequency	11	6	1	2	0	1	0	0	0	1	0
	%	0.6	0.6	1.7	3.3	0.0	0.7	0.0	0.0	0.0	0.3	0
NA	Frequency	634	355	14	27	20	49	47	7	11	68	36
	%	35.0	37.1	23.3	44.3	60.6	32.7	52.2	46.7	34.4	23.3	29.8

A2-1 The year of establishment of the trade union

		Sum	State-owned/ State-holding enterprise	Collective-owned enterprise	Private enterprise	Cooperative enterprise	Limited liability corporation	Share Holding Corporation Ltd	Enterprise with Funds from Hong Kong, Macao and Taiwan	Foreign funded enterprise	Others	NA
Before 1911	Frequency	3	2	0	0	0	0	0	0	0	1	0
	%	0.2	0.2	0.0	0.0	0.0	0.0	0.0	0.0	0.0	0.3	0.0
1911–1948	Frequency	2	1	0	0	0	0	0	0	0	1	0
	%	0.1	0.1	0.0	0.0	0.0	0.0	0.0	0.0	0.0	0.3	0.0
1949	Frequency	9	5	0	0	0	1	1	0	0	0	2
	%	0.5	0.5	0.0	0.0	0.0	0.7	1.1	0.0	0.0	0.0	1.7

Year	Measure	D1	D2	D3	D4	D5	D6	D7	D8	D9	D10	D11
1950	Frequency	19	10	0	0	0	1	0	0	0	3	5
	%	1.0	1.0	0.0	0.0	0.0	0.7	0.0	0.0	0.0	1.0	4.1
1951	Frequency	11	6	1	0	0	1	1	0	0	1	1
	%	0.6	0.6	1.7	0.0	0.0	0.7	1.1	0.0	0.0	0.3	0.8
1952	Frequency	14	12	0	0	0	1	0	0	0	1	0
	%	0.8	1.3	0.0	0.0	0.0	0.7	0.0	0.0	0.0	0.3	0.0
1953	Frequency	13	11	0	0	0	1	0	0	0	1	0
	%	0.7	1.1	0.0	0.0	0.0	0.7	0.0	0.0	0.0	0.3	0.0
1954	Frequency	14	10	1	0	0	0	1	0	0	2	0
	%	0.8	1.0	1.7	0.0	0.0	0.0	1.1	0.0	0.0	0.7	0.0
1955	Frequency	7	6	0	0	0	0	0	0	0	0	1
	%	0.4	0.6	0.0	0.0	0.0	0.0	0.0	0.0	0.0	0.0	0.8
1956	Frequency	31	22	2	0	0	1	0	2	0	2	2
	%	1.7	2.3	3.3	0.0	0.0	0.7	0.0	13.3	0.0	0.7	1.7
1957	Frequency	5	4	0	0	0	0	0	0	0	1	0
	%	0.3	0.4	0.0	0.0	0.0	0.0	0.0	0.0	0.0	0.3	0.0
1958	Frequency	34	24	1	0	0	3	2	0	0	2	2
	%	1.9	2.5	1.7	0.0	0.0	2.0	2.2	0.0	0.0	0.7	1.7
1959	Frequency	8	5	0	0	0	1	1	0	0	0	1
	%	0.4	0.5	0.0	0.0	0.0	0.7	1.1	0.0	0.0	0.0	0.8
1960	Frequency	13	12	0	0	0	1	0	0	0	0	0
	%	0.7	1.3	0.0	0.0	0.0	0.7	0.0	0.0	0.0	0.0	0.0
1962	Frequency	13	9	1	0	0	2	0	0	0	1	0
	%	0.7	0.9	1.7	0.0	0.0	1.3	0.0	0.0	0.0	0.3	0.0
1963	Frequency	5	4	0	0	0	0	0	0	0	1	0
	%	0.3	0.4	0.0	0.0	0.0	0.0	0.0	0.0	0.0	0.3	0.0
1964	Frequency	8	6	0	0	0	1	0	0	0	1	0
	%	0.4	0.6	0.0	0.0	0.0	0.7	0.0	0.0	0.0	0.3	0.0
1965	Frequency	9	8	1	0	0	0	0	0	0	0	0
	%	0.5	0.8	1.7	0.0	0.0	0.0	0.0	0.0	0.0	0.0	0.0
1966	Frequency	5	4	0	0	0	1	0	0	0	0	0
	%	0.3	0.4	0.0	0.0	0.0	0.7	0.0	0.0	0.0	0.0	0.0
1967	Frequency	1	1	0	0	0	0	0	0	0	0	0
	%	0.1	0.1	0.0	0.0	0.0	0.0	0.0	0.0	0.0	0.0	0.0

Ownership form of your enterprise

		Sum	State-owned/ State-holding enterprise	Collective-owned enterprise	Private enterprise	Cooperative enterprise	Limited liability corporation	Share Holding Corporation Ltd	Enterprise with Funds from Hong Kong, Macao and Taiwan	Foreign funded enterprise	Others	NA
1968	Frequency	4	2	0	0	0	2	0	0	0	0	0
	%	0.2	0.2	0.0	0.0	0.0	1.3	0.0	0.0	0.0	0.0	0.0
1969	Frequency	2	1	0	0	0	0	0	0	0	1	0
	%	0.1	0.1	0.0	0.0	0.0	0.0	0.0	0.0	0.0	0.3	0.0
1970	Frequency	16	8	1	0	0	1	1	0	0	3	2
	%	0.9	0.8	1.7	0.0	0.0	0.7	1.1	0.0	0.0	1.0	1.7
1971	Frequency	4	4	0	0	0	0	0	0	0	0	0
	%	0.2	0.4	0.0	0.0	0.0	0.0	0.0	0.0	0.0	0.0	0.0
1972	Frequency	8	5	0	0	0	1	1	0	0	1	0
	%	0.4	0.5	0.0	0.0	0.0	0.7	1.1	0.0	0.0	0.3	0.0
1973	Frequency	12	7	1	0	0	2	0	0	0	2	0
	%	0.7	0.7	1.7	0.0	0.0	1.3	0.0	0.0	0.0	0.7	0.0
1974	Frequency	5	4	0	0	0	1	0	0	0	0	0
	%	0.3	0.4	0.0	0.0	0.0	0.7	0.0	0.0	0.0	0.0	0.0
1975	Frequency	8	7	0	0	0	0	0	0	0	0	1
	%	0.4	0.7	0.0	0.0	0.0	0.0	0.0	0.0	0.0	0.0	0.8
1976	Frequency	9	7	0	0	0	0	1	0	0	1	0
	%	0.5	0.7	0.0	0.0	0.0	0.0	1.1	0.0	0.0	0.3	0.0
1977	Frequency	3	2	0	0	0	1	0	0	0	0	0
	%	0.2	0.2	0.0	0.0	0.0	0.7	0	0.0	0.0	0.0	0.0
1978	Frequency	27	10	0	0	1	2	2	0	0	9	3
	%	1.5	1.0	0.0	0.0	3.0	1.3	2.2	0.0	0.0	3.1	2.5
1979	Frequency	29	16	3	0	1	0	0	0	0	7	2
	%	1.6	1.7	5.0	0.0	3.0	0.0	0.0	0.0	0.0	2.4	1.7

Year	Measure	C1	C2	C3	C4	C5	C6	C7	C8	C9	C10	C11
1980	Frequency	38	16	5	0	0	2	1	0	1	10	3
	%	2.1	1.7	8.3	0.0	0.0	1.3	1.1	0.0	3.1	3.4	2.5
1981	Frequency	11	6	1	0	0	0	0	0	0	3	1
	%	0.6	0.6	1.7	0.0	0.0	0.0	0.0	0.0	0.0	1.0	0.8
1982	Frequency	23	11	0	0	1	2	2	0	2	4	1
	%	1.3	1.1	0.0	0.0	3.0	1.3	2.2	0.0	6.3	1.4	0.8
1983	Frequency	13	8	0	0	0	1	1	0	0	3	0
	%	0.7	0.8	0.0	0.0	0.0	0.7	1.1	0.0	0.0	1.0	0.0
1984	Frequency	35	20	3	0	1	3	0	0	0	7	1
	%	1.9	2.1	5.0	0.0	3.0	2.0	0.0	0.0	0.0	2.4	0.8
1985	Frequency	24	14	3	0	0	1	1	0	0	3	2
	%	1.3	1.5	5.0	0.0	0.0	0.7	1.1	0.0	0.0	1.0	1.7
1986	Frequency	27	16	1	0	1	1	1	0	0	4	3
	%	1.5	1.7	1.7	0.0	3.0	0.7	1.1	0.0	0.0	1.4	2.5
1987	Frequency	22	11	1	1	0	0	0	0	0	7	2
	%	1.2	1.1	1.7	1.6	0.0	0.0	0.0	0.0	0.0	2.4	1.7
1988	Frequency	28	11	1	0	1	0	1	0	1	6	7
	%	1.5	1.1	1.7	0.0	3.0	0.0	1.1	0.0	3.1	2.1	5.8
1989	Frequency	25	11	0	0	1	1	0	0	0	9	3
	%	1.4	1.1	0.0	0.0	3.0	0.7	0.0	0.0	0.0	3.1	2.5
1990	Frequency	20	11	2	0	0	2	0	0	0	3	2
	%	1.1	1.1	3.3	0.0	0.0	1.3	0.0	0.0	0.0	1.0	1.7
1991	Frequency	17	8	0	0	1	0	0	0	1	6	1
	%	0.9	0.8	0.0	0.0	3.0	0.0	0.0	0.0	3.1	2.1	0.8
1992	Frequency	22	10	2	1	0	2	1	1	0	2	3
	%	1.2	1.0	3.3	1.6	0.0	1.3	1.1	6.7	0.0	0.7	2.5
1993	Frequency	18	13	0	2	0	1	0	0	0	0	2
	%	1.0	1.4	0.0	3.3	0.0	0.7	0.0	0.0	0.0	0.0	1.7
1994	Frequency	30	15	0	3	0	2	2	1	1	4	2
	%	1.7	1.6	0.0	4.9	0.0	1.3	2.2	6.7	3.1	1.4	1.7
1995	Frequency	23	7	1	0	1	4	1	1	1	7	0
	%	1.3	0.7	1.7	0.0	3.0	2.7	1.1	6.7	3.1	2.4	0.0

Ownership form of your enterprise

		Sum	State-owned/ State-holding enterprise	Collective-owned enterprise	Private enterprise	Cooperative enterprise	Limited liability corporation	Share Holding Corporation Ltd	Enterprise with Funds from Hong Kong, Macao and Taiwan	Foreign funded enterprise	Others	NA
1996	Frequency	35	9	6	2	0	4	0	0	2	8	4
	%	1.9	0.9	10.0	3.3	0.0	2.7	0.0	0.0	6.3	2.7	3.3
1997	Frequency	35	14	2	1	4	4	2	2	0	5	1
	%	1.9	1.5	3.3	1.6	12.1	2.7	2.2	13.3	0.0	1.7	0.8
1998	Frequency	50	23	3	3	2	3	7	0	2	6	1
	%	2.8	2.4	5.0	4.9	6.1	2.0	7.8	0.0	6.3	2.1	0.8
1999	Frequency	40	15	0	6	0	4	4	1	2	7	2
	%	2.2	1.6	0.0	9.8	0.0	2.7	4.4	6.7	6.3	2.4	0.8
2000	Frequency	81	32	2	5	6	15	2	0	1	16	2
	%	4.5	3.3	3.3	8.2	18.2	10.0	2.2	0.0	3.1	5.5	1.7
2001	Frequency	73	26	1	8	2	12	4	0	1	17	2
	%	4.0	2.7	1.7	13.1	6.1	8.0	4.4	0.0	3.1	5.8	1.7
2002	Frequency	81	28	0	4	1	10	9	2	3	23	1
	%	4.5	2.9	0.0	6.6	3.0	6.7	10.0	13.3	9.4	7.9	0.8
2003	Frequency	83	27	2	4	1	9	11	0	4	14	11
	%	4.6	2.8	3.3	6.6	3.0	6.0	12.2	0.0	12.5	4.8	9.1
2004	Frequency	54	14	1	12	5	9	3	3	3	4	0
	%	3.0	1.5	1.7	19.7	15.2	6.0	3.3	20.0	9.4	1.4	0.0
2005	Frequency	1	1	0	0	0	0	0	0	0	0	0
	%	0.1	0.1	0.0	0.0	0.0	0.0	0.0	0.0	0.0	0.0	0.0
NA	Frequency	551	345	11	9	3	33	26	2	7	72	43
	%	30.4	36.1	18.3	14.8	9.1	22.0	28.9	13.3	21.9	24.7	35.5

A2-2 Procedure to establish the trade union

By workers and staff members' voluntary request	Frequency	240	118	11	3	3	29	13	3	9	35	16
	%	13.3	12.3	18.3	4.9	9.1	19.3	14.4	20.0	28.1	12.0	13.2
By determination of organization	Frequency	1363	731	44	45	26	114	67	11	22	219	84
	%	75.3	76.4	73.3	73.8	78.8	76.0	74.4	73.3	68.8	75.0	69.4
Others	Frequency	59	18	2	10	1	4	3	1	1	16	3
	%	3.3	1.9	3.3	16.4	3.0	2.7	3.3	6.7	3.1	5.5	2.5
NA	Frequency	149	90	3	3	3	3	7	0	0	22	18
	%	8.2	9.4	5.0	4.9	9.1	2.0	7.8	0.0	0.0	7.5	14.9

A2-3-1 Whether or not the trade union has obtained status of legal person as social corporation

1 Has obtained	Frequency	1097	651	39	25	13	89	52	5	17	146	60
	%	60.6	68.0	65.0	41.0	39.4	59.3	57.8	33.3	53.1	50.0	49.6
2 Has not obtained, yet	Frequency	535	221	17	27	17	45	32	6	12	115	43
	%	29.5	23.1	28.3	44.3	51.5	30.0	35.6	40.0	37.5	39.4	35.5
NA	Frequency	179	85	4	9	3	16	6	4	3	31	18
	%	9.9	8.9	6.7	14.8	9.1	10.7	6.7	26.7	9.4	10.6	14.9

A2-3-2 (If you chose 1 in A2-3-1) the year the trade union obtained the status

Before 1980	Frequency	24	8	1	0	1	1	1	0	0	9	4
	%	2.6	1.5	2.9	0.0	1.3	2.3	2.3	0.0	0.0	6.7	7.1
1980–1984	Frequency	19	11	1	0	0	1	1	0	0	6	0
	%	2.0	2.0	2.9	0.0	0.0	2.3	2.3	0.0	0.0	4.4	0
1985–1989	Frequency	24	16	1	0	1	1	1	0	0	3	2
	%	2.6	2.9	2.9	0.0	7.7	2.3	2.3	0.0	0.0	2.2	3.6
1990–1994	Frequency	50	35	2	1	4	4	0	0	1	3	4
	%	5.3	6.4	5.7	5.0	5.2	5.2	0.0	0.0	7.7	2.2	7.1

Ownership form of your enterprise

		Sum	State-owned/State-holding enterprise	Collective-owned enterprise	Private enterprise	Cooperative enterprise	Limited liability corporation	Share Holding Corporation Ltd	Enterprise with Funds from Hong Kong, Macao and Taiwan	Foreign funded enterprise	Others	NA
1995–1999	Frequency	133	78	17	2	1	8	3	1	6	12	5
	%	14.1	14.4	48.6	10.0	7.7	10.4	6.8	20.0	46.2	8.9	8.9
2000–2004	Frequency	266	120	6	10	9	38	18	0	3	47	15
	%	28.3	22.1	17.1	50.0	69.2	49.4	40.9	0.0	23.1	34.8	26.8
2005–	Frequency	2	2	0	0	0	0	0	0	0	0	0
	%	0.2	0.4	0.0	0.0	0.0	0.0	0.0	0.0	0.0	0.0	0.0
NA	Frequency	423	273	7	7	2	26	20	4	3	55	26
	%	44.9	50.3	20.0	35.0	15.4	33.8	45.5	80.0	23.1	40.7	46.4

A2-4 Total number of the trade union members by the end of 2003

		Sum	State-owned/State-holding enterprise	Collective-owned enterprise	Private enterprise	Cooperative enterprise	Limited liability corporation	Share Holding Corporation Ltd	Enterprise with Funds from Hong Kong, Macao and Taiwan	Foreign funded enterprise	Others	NA
Less than 100	Frequency	416	131	22	19	12	41	19	6	9	112	45
	%	24.4	14.8	37.9	32.2	36.4	29.5	23.2	40.0	31.0	38.8	38.5
100–199	Frequency	221	92	15	12	6	18	6	1	5	51	15
	%	13.0	10.4	25.9	20.3	18.2	12.9	7.3	6.7	17.2	17.6	12.8
200–399	Frequency	261	152	6	6	6	15	19	1	4	34	18
	%	15.3	17.2	10.3	10.2	18.2	10.8	23.2	6.7	13.8	11.8	15.4
400–599	Frequency	120	78	3	3	2	6	6	0	3	13	6
	%	7.0	8.8	5.2	5.1	6.1	4.3	7.3	0.0	10.3	4.5	5.1
600–799	Frequency	77	56	1	1	0	9	2	0	0	8	0
	%	4.5	6.3	1.7	1.7	0.0	6.5	2.4	0.0	0.0	2.8	0.0
800–999	Frequency	69	40	2	0	0	6	7	2	1	8	3
	%	4.0	4.5	3.4	0.0	0.0	4.3	8.5	13.3	3.4	2.8	2.6
1000–1999	Frequency	126	90	1	1	1	12	7	0	2	8	4
	%	7.4	10.2	1.7	1.7	3.0	8.6	8.5	0.0	6.9	2.8	3.4

2000–2999	Frequency	47	27	0	1	1	6	4	0	0	7	1
	%	2.8	3.1	0.0	1.7	3.0	4.3	4.9	0.0	0.0	2.4	0.9
3000–3999	Frequency	34	21	0	0	0	4	2	0	2	4	1
	%	2.0	2.4	0.0	0.0	0.0	2.9	2.4	0.0	6.9	1.4	0.9
4000–4999	Frequency	22	15	1	0	0	1	1	0	0	4	0
	%	1.3	1.7	1.7	0.0	0.0	0.7	1.2	0.0	0.0	1.4	0.0
5000–5999	Frequency	16	13	0	0	0	2	0	0	0	1	0
	%	0.9	1.5	0.0	0.0	0.0	1.4	0.0	0.0	0.0	0.3	0.0
6000–6999	Frequency	12	8	0	0	0	2	1	0	1	0	0
	%	0.7	0.9	0.0	0.0	0.0	1.4	1.2	0.0	3.4	0.0	0.0
7000–7999	Frequency	6	5	0	0	0	1	0	0	0	0	0
	%	0.4	0.6	0.0	0.0	0.0	0.7	0.0	0.0	0.0	0.0	0.0
8000–8999	Frequency	6	4	0	0	0	0	0	0	0	1	1
	%	0.4	0.5	0.0	0.0	0.0	0.0	0.0	0.0	0.0	0.3	0.9
9000–9999	Frequency	4	2	0	0	0	1	0	0	0	1	0
	%	0.2	0.2	0.0	0.0	0.0	0.7	0.0	0.0	0.0	0.3	0.0
over 9999	Frequency	40	33	0	0	0	3	1	0	0	0	3
	%	2.3	3.7	0.0	0.0	0.0	2.2	1.2	0.0	0.0	0.0	2.6
N.A.	Frequency	227	116	7	16	5	12	7	5	2	37	20
	%	13.3	13.1	12.1	27.1	15.2	8.6	8.5	33.3	6.9	12.8	17.1

A2-4. Percentage of part-time/short-time contract workers in all members

0	Frequency	11	7	0	0	0	0	0	0	0	4	0
	%	0.6	0.7	0.0	0.0	0.0	0.0	0.0	0.0	0.0	1.4	0.0
1–10	Frequency	121	60	5	3	1	7	5	2	2	26	10
	%	6.7	6.3	8.3	4.9	3.0	4.7	5.6	13.3	6.3	8.9	8.3
11–20	Frequency	59	32	0	2	1	7	2	3	3	8	4
	%	3.3	3.3	0.0	3.3	3.0	4.7	2.2	20.0	0.0	2.7	3.3
21–30	Frequency	25	12	0	0	0	2	3	0	0	6	2
	%	1.4	1.3	0.0	0.0	0.0	1.3	3.3	0.0	0.0	2.1	1.7
31–40	Frequency	18	12	1	0	1	1	0	1	0	1	1
	%	1.0	1.3	1.7	0.0	3.0	0.7	0.0	6.7	0.0	0.3	0.8

Ownership form of your enterprise

		Sum	State-owned/ State-holding enterprise	Collective-owned enterprise	Private enterprise	Cooperative enterprise	Limited liability corporation	Share Holding Corporation Ltd	Enterprise with Funds from Hong Kong, Macao and Taiwan	Foreign funded enterprise	Others	NA
41–50	Frequency	14	8	0	0	1	2	0	0	0	3	0
	%	0.8	0.8	0.0	0.0	3.0	1.3	0.0	0.0	0.0	1.0	0.0
51–60	Frequency	7	4	1	0	0	0	0	0	1	0	1
	%	0.4	0.4	1.7	0.0	0.0	0.0	0.0	0.0	3.1	0.0	0.8
61–70	Frequency	6	3	0	0	0	1	1	1	0	0	0
	%	0.3	0.3	0.0	0.0	0.0	0.7	1.1	6.7	0.0	0.0	0.0
71–80	Frequency	5	5	0	0	0	0	0	0	0	0	0
	%	0.3	0.3	0.0	0.0	0.0	0.0	0.0	0.0	0.0	0.0	0.0
81–90	Frequency	2	1	0	0	0	1	0	0	0	0	0
	%	0.1	0.1	0.0	0.0	0.0	0.7	0.0	0.0	0.0	0.0	0.0
91–100	Frequency	7	3	0	2	0	1	0	0	0	1	0
	%	0.4	0.3	0.0	3.3	0.0	0.7	0.0	0.0	0.0	0.3	0.0
NA	Frequency	1536	810	53	54	29	128	79	8	29	243	103
	%	84.8	84.6	88.3	88.5	87.9	85.3	87.8	53.3	90.6	83.2	85.1

A2-5 Procedure how workers and staff members entered the trade union

		Sum	State-owned/ State-holding enterprise	Collective-owned enterprise	Private enterprise	Cooperative enterprise	Limited liability corporation	Share Holding Corporation Ltd	Enterprise with Funds from Hong Kong, Macao and Taiwan	Foreign funded enterprise	Others	NA
Enter the trade union voluntarily	Frequency	1083	607	33	27	16	85	54	8	21	162	70
	%	59.8	63.4	55.0	44.3	48.5	56.7	60.0	53.3	65.6	55.5	57.9
Apply for the entry by taking the advice of trade union functionaries	Frequency	176	73	4	13	3	15	10	1	2	39	16
	%	9.7	7.6	6.7	21.3	9.1	10.0	11.1	6.7	6.3	13.4	13.2

All workers join the trade union automatically	Frequency	473	250	20	15	8	47	24	4	8	67	30
	%	26.1	26.1	33.3	24.6	24.2	31.3	26.7	26.7	25.0	22.9	24.8
Others	Frequency	28	9	1	2	2	1	2	0	1	10	0
	%	1.5	0.9	1.7	3.3	6.1	0.7	2.2	0.0	3.1	3.4	0.0
NA	Frequency	51	18	2	4	4	2	0	2	0	14	5
	%	2.8	1.9	3.3	6.6	12.1	1.3	0.0	13.3	0.0	4.8	4.1

A3-1 Whether or not the members' congress has been established

1 Established	Frequency	1427	831	43	33	17	116	72	8	22	202	83
	%	78.8	86.8	71.7	54.1	51.5	77.3	80.0	53.3	68.8	69.2	68.6
2 Not established	Frequency	289	97	11	23	11	24	16	4	8	69	26
	%	16.0	10.1	18.3	37.7	33.3	16.0	17.8	26.7	25.0	23.6	21.5
NA	Frequency	95	29	6	5	5	10	2	3	2	21	12
	%	5.2	3.0	10.0	8.2	15.2	6.7	2.2	20.0	6.3	7.2	9.9

A3-2 (If you chose 1 in A3-1) the total number of member representatives by the end of 2003

1–50	Frequency	465.	204	27	12	10	42	24	4	10	99	33
	%	32.6	24.5	62.8	36.4	58.8	36.2	33.3	50.0	45.5	49.0	39.8
51–100	Frequency	273	169	6	5	3	24	10	3	1	37	15
	%	19.1	20.3	14.0	15.2	17.6	20.7	13.9	37.5	4.5	18.3	18.1
101–200	Frequency	222	141	5	5	0	25	12	0	2	25	7
	%	15.6	17.0	11.6	15.2	0.0	21.6	16.7	0.0	9.1	12.4	8.4
201–300	Frequency	55	38	1	1	0	2	5	0	0	7	1
	%	3.9	4.6	2.3	3.0	0.0	1.7	6.9	0.0	0.0	3.5	1.2
301–400	Frequency	45	29	0	1	0	3	5	0	3	3	1
	%	3.2	3.5	0.0	3.0	0.0	2.6	6.9	0.0	13.6	1.5	1.2
401–500	Frequency	20	16	0	0	0	1	1	0	0	0	2
	%	1.4	1.9	0.0	0.0	0.0	0.9	1.4	0.0	0.0	0.0	2.4

Ownership form of your enterprise

		Sum	State-owned/State-holding enterprise	Collective-owned enterprise	Private enterprise	Cooperative enterprise	Limited liability corporation	Share Holding Corporation Ltd	Enterprise with Funds from Hong Kong, Macao and Taiwan	Foreign funded enterprise	Others	NA
More than 500	Frequency	77	55	1	0	0	8	4	0	0	4	5
	%	5.4	6.6	2.3	0.0	0.0	6.9	5.6	0.0	0.0	2.0	6.0
NA	Frequency	270	179	3	9	4	11	11	1	6	27	19
	%	18.9	21.5	7.0	27.3	23.5	9.5	15.3	12.5	27.3	13.4	22.9

A3-2 (If you chose 1) percentage of the representatives under 35 year old in all representatives

		Sum	State-owned/State-holding enterprise	Collective-owned enterprise	Private enterprise	Cooperative enterprise	Limited liability corporation	Share Holding Corporation Ltd	Enterprise with Funds from Hong Kong, Macao and Taiwan	Foreign funded enterprise	Others	NA
0	Frequency	0	0	0	0	0	0	0	0	0	0	0
	%	0.0	0.0	0.0	0.0	0.0	0.0	0.0	0.0	0.0	0.0	0.0
1–10	Frequency	63	35	5	2	1	7	1	0	1	9	2
	%	3.5	3.7	8.3	3.3	3.0	4.7	1.1	0.0	3.1	3.1	1.7
11–20	Frequency	139	84	10	1	1	14	6	0	1	18	4
	%	7.7	8.8	16.7	1.6	3.0	9.3	6.7	0.0	3.1	6.2	3.3
21–30	Frequency	109	64	4	2	2	10	2	0	1	20	4
	%	6.0	6.7	6.7	3.3	6.1	6.7	2.2	0.0	3.1	6.8	3.3
31–40	Frequency	126	73	3	2	1	9	8	4	0	20	6
	%	7.0	7.6	5.0	3.3	3.0	6.0	8.9	26.7	0.0	6.8	5.0
41–50	Frequency	107	60	2	2	0	11	8	0	2	15	7
	%	5.9	6.3	3.3	3.3	0.0	7.3	8.9	0.0	6.3	5.1	5.8
51–60	Frequency	84	41	3	1	2	7	5	0	3	17	5
	%	4.6	4.3	5.0	1.6	6.1	4.7	5.6	0.0	9.4	5.8	4.1
61–70	Frequency	69	39	1	0	0	5	3	0	3	13	5
	%	3.8	4.1	1.7	0.0	0.0	3.3	3.3	0.0	9.4	4.5	4.1
71–80	Frequency	70	31	3	4	1	12	2	2	3	9	3
	%	3.9	3.2	5.0	6.6	3.0	8.0	2.2	13.3	9.4	3.1	2.5

81–90	Frequency	30	10	1	5	1	1	6	0	0	3	3
	%	1.7	1.0	1.7	8.2	3.0	0.7	6.7	0.0	0.0	1.0	2.5
91–100	Frequency	32	15	0	1	1	3	1	1	1	7	2
	%	1.8	1.6	0.0	1.6	3.0	2.0	1.1	6.7	3.1	2.4	1.7
NA	Frequency	982	505	28	41	23	71	48	8	17	161	80
	%	54.2	52.8	46.7	67.2	69.7	47.3	53.3	53.3	53.1	55.1	66.1

A3-2 (If you chose 1) percentage of the representatives of middle or lower level workers and staff members in all representatives

		0	1–10	11–20	21–30	31–40	41–50	51–60	61–70	71–80	81–90	91–100
0	Frequency	0	0	0	0	0	0	0	0	0	0	0
	%	0.0	0.0	0.0	0.0	0.0	0.0	0.0	0.0	0.0	0.0	0.0
1–10	Frequency	33	19	1	1	1	2	1	0	1	8	1
	%	2.3	2.3	2.3	3.0	5.9	1.7	1.4	0.0	4.5	4.0	1.2
11–20	Frequency	56	32	3	0	1	7	4	0	1	9	0
	%	3.9	3.9	7.0	0.0	5.9	6.0	5.6	0.0	4.5	4.5	0.0
21–30	Frequency	50	31	2	0	0	10	5	0	1	5	1
	%	3.5	3.7	4.7	0.0	0.0	8.6	6.9	0.0	4.5	2.5	1.2
31–40	Frequency	60	35	2	0	0	4	0	0	1	12	1
	%	4.2	4.2	4.7	0.0	0.0	3.4	0.0	0.0	4.5	5.9	1.2
41–50	Frequency	80	44	4	1	2	8	2	1	1	11	5
	%	5.6	5.3	9.3	3.0	11.8	6.9	2.8	12.5	4.5	5.4	6.0
51–60	Frequency	75	48	3	1	0	8	5	0	1	6	3
	%	5.3	5.8	7.0	3.0	0.0	6.9	6.9	0.0	4.5	3.0	3.6
61–70	Frequency	108	63	3	5	1	7	5	1	2	11	10
	%	7.6	7.6	7.0	15.2	5.9	6.0	6.9	12.5	9.1	5.4	12.0
71–80	Frequency	129	68	10	4	2	12	8	3	2	14	6
	%	9.0	8.2	23.3	12.1	11.8	10.3	11.1	37.5	9.1	6.9	7.2
81–90	Frequency	88	48	2	3	1	9	6	0	3	11	5
	%	6.2	5.8	4.7	9.1	5.9	7.8	8.3	0.0	13.6	5.4	6.0
91–100	Frequency	66	34	0	3	1	5	4	1	0	13	3
	%	4.6	4.1	0.0	9.1	5.9	4.3	5.6	12.5	0.0	6.4	3.6
NA	Frequency	682	409	13	15	8	44	32	2	9	102	48
	%	47.8	49.2	30.2	45.5	47.1	37.9	44.4	25.0	40.9	50.5	57.8

A3-3 (If you chose 1) number of times of holding members' congress in the past 3 years (April 2001–March 2004)

		Ownership form of your enterprise									
	Sum	State-owned/State-holding enterprise	Collective-owned enterprise	Private enterprise	Cooperative enterprise	Limited liability corporation	Share Holding Corporation Ltd	Enterprise with Funds from Hong Kong, Macao and Taiwan	Foreign funded enterprise	Others	NA
0 Frequency	127	72	1	2	1	13	8	2	3	14	11
%	8.9	8.7	2.3	6.1	5.9	11.2	11.1	25.0	13.6	6.9	13.3
1–10 Frequency	1135	673	34	24	12	92	58	5	17	160	60
%	79.5	81.0	79.1	72.7	70.6	79.3	80.6	62.5	77.3	79.2	72.3
11–20 Frequency	38	23	3	0	0	2	2	0	1	6	1
%	2.7	2.8	7.0	0.0	0.0	1.7	2.8	0.0	4.5	3.0	1.2
21–30 Frequency	3	2	1	0	0	0	0	0	0	0	0
%	0.2	0.2	2.3	0.0	0.0	0.0	0.0	0.0	0.0	0.0	0.0
31–40 Frequency	3	1	0	0	0	0	0	0	0	2	0
%	0.2	0.1	0.0	0.0	0.0	0.0	0.0	0.0	0.0	1.0	0.0
over 40 Frequency	121	60	4	7	4	9	4	1	1	20	11
%	8.5	7.2	9.3	21.2	23.5	7.8	5.6	12.5	4.5	9.9	13.3

A3-3 Number of times of holding members' assembly in the past 3 years (April 2001–March 2004)

	Sum	State-owned/State-holding enterprise	Collective-owned enterprise	Private enterprise	Cooperative enterprise	Limited liability corporation	Share Holding Corporation Ltd	Enterprise with Funds from Hong Kong, Macao and Taiwan	Foreign funded enterprise	Others	NA
0 Frequency	553	301	13	11	3	48	28	1	12	91	45
%	30.5	31.5	21.7	18.0	9.1	32.0	31.1	6.7	37.5	31.2	37.2
1–10 Frequency	738	369	31	23	16	67	37	3	10	137	45
%	40.8	38.6	51.7	37.7	48.5	44.7	41.1	20.0	31.3	46.9	37.2
11–20 Frequency	34	15	2	0	2	2	4	0	0	6	3
%	1.9	1.6	3.3	0.0	6.1	1.3	4.4	0.0	0.0	2.1	2.5
21–30 Frequency	2	1	0	0	0	0	0	0	0	1	0
%	0.1	0.1	0.0	0.0	0.0	0.0	0.0	0.0	0.0	0.3	0.0

31–40	Frequency	3	0	0	0	0	0	0	0	0	0
	%	0.2	0.0	0.0	0.0	0.0	0.0	0.0	0.0	0.0	0.0
over 40	Frequency	481	268	14	27	12	33	21	11	10	57	28
	%	26.6	28.0	23.3	44.3	36.4	22.0	23.3	73.3	31.3	19.5	23.1

A4-1a Number of vice-chairmen in the trade union

1	Frequency	794	463	25	22	17	63	33	4	13	109	45
	%	43.8	48.4	41.7	36.1	51.5	42.0	36.7	26.7	40.6	37.3	37.2
2	Frequency	149	76	0	4	4	17	8	4	2	22	12
	%	8.2	7.9	0.0	6.6	12.1	11.3	8.9	26.7	6.3	7.5	9.9
3	Frequency	26	10	1	2	0	2	2	0	0	4	5
	%	1.4	1.0	1.7	3.3	0.0	1.3	2.2	0.0	0.0	1.4	4.1
4	Frequency	7	3	0	0	0	0	3	0	0	1	0
	%	0.4	0.3	0.0	0.0	0.0	0.0	3.3	0.0	0.0	0.3	0
5	Frequency	1	0	0	0	0	0	1	0	0	0	0
	%	0.1	0.0	0.0	0.0	0.0	0.0	1.1	0.0	0.0	0.0	0
6	Frequency	1	1	0	0	0	0	0	0	0	0	0
	%	0.1	0.1	0.0	0.0	0.0	0.0	0	0.0	0.0	0.0	0
7	Frequency	2	2	0	0	0	0	0	0	0	0	0
	%	0.1	0.2	0.0	0.0	0.0	0.0	0.0	0.0	0.0	0.0	0
8	Frequency	2	2	0	0	0	0	0	0	0	0	0
	%	0.1	0.2	0.0	0.0	0.0	0.0	0.0	0.0	0.0	0.0	0
9	Frequency	2	1	1	0	0	0	0	0	0	0	0
	%	0.1	0.1	1.7	0.0	0.0	0.0	0.0	0.0	0.0	0.0	0
10	Frequency	2	2	0	0	0	0	0	0	0	0	0
	%	0.1	0.2	0.0	0.0	0.0	0.0	0.0	0.0	0.0	0.0	0.0
over 10	Frequency	10	7	0	0	0	0	1	0	1	1	0
	%	1.0	0.7	0.0	0.0	0.0	0.0	1.1	0.0	3.1	0.3	0.0
NA	Frequency	815	390	33	33	12	68	42	7	16	155	59
	%	45.0	40.8	55.0	54.1	36.4	45.3	46.7	46.7	50.0	53.1	48.8

A4-1a Number of full-time vice-chairmen

		Sum	State-owned/State-holding enterprise	Collective-owned enterprise	Private enterprise	Cooperative enterprise	Limited liability corporation	Share Holding Corporation Ltd	Enterprise with Funds from Hong Kong, Macao and Taiwan	Foreign funded enterprise	Others	NA
									Ownership form of your enterprise			
1	Frequency	538	334	12	10	9	44	23	3	9	68	26
	%	29.7	34.9	20.0	16.4	27.3	29.3	25.6	20.0	28.1	23.3	21.5
2	Frequency	76	52	1	1	1	7	2	0	1	4	7
	%	4.2	5.4	1.7	1.6	3.0	4.7	2.2	0.0	3.1	1.4	5.8
3	Frequency	16	7	0	0	0	1	2	0	0	3	3
	%	0.9	0.7	0.0	0.0	0.0	0.7	2.2	0.0	0.0	1.0	2.5
4	Frequency	3	3	0	0	0	0	0	0	0	0	0
	%	0.2	0.3	0.0	0.0	0.0	0.0	0.0	0.0	0.0	0.0	0.0
5	Frequency	2	1	0	0	0	0	1	0	0	0	0
	%	0.1	0.1	0.0	0.0	0.0	0.0	1.1	0.0	0.0	0.0	0.0
6	Frequency	4	4	0	0	0	0	0	0	0	0	0
	%	0.2	0.4	0.0	0.0	0.0	0.0	0.0	0.0	0.0	0.0	0.0
7	Frequency	2	1	0	0	0	0	0	0	0	1	0
	%	0.1	0.1	0.0	0.0	0.0	0.0	0.0	0.0	0.0	0.3	0.0
8	Frequency	5	5	0	0	0	0	0	0	0	0	0
	%	0.3	0.5	0.0	0.0	0.0	0.0	0.0	0.0	0.0	0.0	0.0
NA	Frequency	1165	550	47	50	23	98	62	12	22	216	85
	%	64.3	57.5	78.3	82.0	69.7	65.3	68.9	80.0	68.8	74.0	70.2

A4-1a Percentage of male vice-chairmen in all vice-chairmen

0	Frequency	578	265	24	16	3	50	30	3	8	129	50
	%	31.9	27.7	40.0	26.2	9.1	33.3	33.3	20.0	25.0	44.2	41.3
1–10	Frequency	2	1	0	0	0	0	0	0	1	0	0
	%	0.1	0.1	0	0.0	0.0	0.0	0	0.0	3.1	0.0	0
11–20	Frequency	2	2	0	0	0	0	0	0	0	0	0
	%	0.1	0.2	0.0	0.0	0.0	0.0	0.0	0.0	0.0	0.0	0.0
21–30	Frequency	1	0	0	0	0	0	1	0	0	0	0
	%	0.1	0.0	0.0	0.0	0.0	0.0	1.1	0.0	0.0	0.0	0.0
31–40	Frequency	6	3	0	0	0	0	0	0	0	1	2
	%	0.3	0.3	0.0	0.0	0.0	0.0	0.0	0.0	0.0	0.3	1.7
41–50	Frequency	70	36	0	2	3	8	3	2	0	11	5
	%	3.9	3.8	0.0	3.3	9.1	5.3	3.3	13.3	0.0	3.8	4.1
51–60	Frequency	2	1	0	0	0	0	1	0	0	0	0
	%	0.1	0.1	0	0.0	0.0	0.0	1.1	0	0.0	0.0	0
61–70	Frequency	10	4	0	0	0	2	0	0	0	1	3
	%	0.6	0.4	0.0	0.0	0.0	1.3	0.0	0.0	0.0	0.3	2.5
71–80	Frequency	4	3	0	0	0	0	1	0	0	0	0
	%	0.2	0.3	0.0	0.0	0.0	0.0	1.1	0.0	0.0	0.0	0
81–90	Frequency	1	1	0	0	0	0	0	0	0	0	0
	%	0.1	0.1	0.0	0.0	0.0	0.0	0.0	0.0	0.0	0.0	0.0
91–100	Frequency	521	319	13	17	9	40	27	1	11	49	35
	%	28.8	33.3	21.7	27.9	27.3	26.7	30.0	6.7	34.4	16.8	28.9
NA	Frequency	614	322	23	26	18	50	27	9	12	101	26
	%	33.9	33.6	38.3	42.6	54.5	33.3	30.0	60.0	37.5	34.6	21.5

A4-1a Percentage of vice-chairmen who have the following political appearance

1. Chinese Communist Party member

		Ownership form of your enterprise						Enterprise with Funds from Hong Kong, Macao and Taiwan			
	Sum	State-owned/State-holding enterprise	Collective-owned enterprise	Private enterprise	Cooperative enterprise	Limited liability corporation	Share Holding Corporation Ltd		Foreign funded enterprise	Others	NA
0 Frequency	0	0	0	0	0	0	0	0	0	0	0
%	0.0	0.0	0.0	0.0	0.0	0.0	0.0	0.0	0.0	0.0	0.0
1–10 Frequency	2	1	0	0	0	0	0	0	1	0	0
%	0.1	0.1	0.0	0.0	0.0	0.0	0.0	0.0	3.1	0.0	0.0
11–20 Frequency	3	3	0	0	0	0	0	0	0	0	0
%	0.2	0.3	0.0	0.0	0.0	0.0	0.0	0.0	0	0.0	0.0
21–30 Frequency	1	0	0	0	0	0	1	0	0	0	0
%	0.1	0.0	0.0	0.0	0.0	0.0	1.1	0.0	0.0	0.0	0.0
31–40 Frequency	3	0	0	1	0	0	0	0	0	1	1
%	0.2	0.0	0.0	1.6	0.0	0.0	0.0	0.0	0.0	0.3	0.8
41–50 Frequency	30	12	0	1	4	2	2	0	0	5	4
%	1.7	1.3	0.0	1.6	12.1	1.3	2.2	0.0	0.0	1.7	3.3
51–60 Frequency	2	1	0	0	0	0	1	0	0	0	0
%	0.1	0.1	0.0	0.0	0.0	0.0	1.1	0.0	0.0	0.0	0.0
61–70 Frequency	3	0	0	0	0	0	1	0	0	1	2
%	0.2	0.0	0.0	0.0	0.0	0.0	1.1	0.0	0.0	0.3	1.7
71–80 Frequency	4	2	0	0	0	0	1	0	0	1	0
%	0.2	0.2	0.0	0.0	0.0	0.0	1.1	0.0	0.0	0.3	0.0
81–90 Frequency	1	1	0	0	0	0	0	0	0	0	0
%	0.1	0.1	0.0	0.0	0.0	0.0	0.0	0.0	0.0	0.0	0.0
91–100 Frequency	713	435	19	11	7	56	29	6	12	95	43
%	39.4	45.5	31.7	18.0	21.2	37.3	32.2	40.0	37.5	32.5	35.5
NA Frequency	1049	502	41	48	22	92	55	9	19	190	71
%	57.9	52.5	68.3	78.7	66.7	61.3	61.1	60.0	59.4	65.1	58.7

2. Democratic party member

0	Frequency	914	475	33	19	4	85	44	3	14	162	75
	%	50.5	49.6	55.0	31.1	12.1	56.7	48.9	20.0	43.8	55.5	62.0
1–10	Frequency	1	0	0	0	0	0	0	0	1	0	0
	%	0.1	0.0	0.0	0.0	0.0	0.0	0.0	0.0	3.1	0	0
11–20	Frequency	0	0	0	0	0	0	0	0	0	0	0
	%	0.0	0.0	0.0	0.0	0.0	0.0	0.0	0.0	0.0	0.0	0.0
21–30	Frequency	0	0	0	0	0	0	0	0	0	0	0
	%	0.0	0.0	0.0	0.0	0.0	0.0	0.0	0.0	0.0	0.0	0.0
31–40	Frequency	3	0	0	0	0	0	1	0	0	1	1
	%	0.2	0.0	0.0	0.0	0.0	0.0	1.1	0.0	0.0	0.3	1
41–50	Frequency	6	2	0	0	0	0	0	0	0	3	1
	%	0.3	0.2	0.0	0.0	0.0	0.0	0.0	0.0	0.0	1.0	0.8
51–60	Frequency	0	0	0	0	0	0	0	0	0	0	0
	%	0.0	0.0	0.0	0.0	0.0	0.0	0.0	0.0	0.0	0.0	0.0
61–70	Frequency	0	0	0	0	0	0	0	0	0	0	0
	%	0.0	0.0	0.0	0.0	0.0	0.0	0.0	0.0	0.0	0.0	0.0
71–80	Frequency	0	0	0	0	0	0	0	0	0	0	0
	%	0.0	0.0	0.0	0.0	0.0	0.0	0.0	0.0	0.0	0.0	0.0
81–90	Frequency	0	0	0	0	0	0	0	0	0	0	0
	%	0.0	0.0	0.0	0.0	0.0	0.0	0.0	0.0	0.0	0.0	0.0
91–100	Frequency	18	10	1	0	1	1	0	2	1	2	0
	%	1.0	1.0	1.7	0.0	3.0	0.7	0.0	13.3	3.1	0.7	0.0
NA	Frequency	869	470	26	42	28	64	45	10	16	124	44
	%	48.0	49.1	43.3	68.9	84.8	42.7	50.0	66.7	50.0	42.5	36.4

A4-1b Number of trade union committee members (except chairman and vice-chairmen)

		Sum	State-owned/ State-holding enterprise	Collective-owned enterprise	Private enterprise	Cooperative enterprise	Limited liability corporation	Share Holding Corporation Ltd	Enterprise with Funds from Hong Kong, Macao and Taiwan	Foreign funded enterprise	Others	NA
1	Frequency	45	24	0	2	2	3	2	3	3	4	2
	%	2.5	2.5	0.0	3.3	6.1	2.0	2.2	20.0	9.4	1.4	1.7
2	Frequency	145	65	7	8	5	13	8	3	5	25	6
	%	8.0	6.8	11.7	13.1	15.2	8.7	8.9	20.0	15.6	8.6	5.0
3	Frequency	174	62	9	8	7	23	6	1	5	40	13
	%	9.6	6.5	15.0	13.1	21.2	15.3	6.7	6.7	15.6	13.7	10.7
4	Frequency	222	110	4	9	3	24	16	3	4	42	7
	%	12.3	11.5	6.7	14.8	9.1	16.0	17.8	20.0	12.5	14.4	5.8
5	Frequency	194	102	11	8	4	14	8	2	1	32	12
	%	10.7	10.7	18.3	13.1	12.1	9.3	8.9	13.3	3.1	11.0	9.9
6	Frequency	139	77	6	1	0	12	11	0	3	22	7
	%	7.7	8.0	10.0	1.6	0.0	8.0	12.2	0.0	9.4	7.5	5.8
7	Frequency	153	93	4	2	1	12	6	1	2	24	8
	%	8.4	9.7	6.7	3.3	3.0	8.0	6.7	6.7	6.3	8.2	6.6
8	Frequency	67	44	1	3	1	6	2	0	0	5	5
	%	3.7	4.6	1.7	4.9	3.0	4.0	2.2	0.0	0.0	1.7	4.1
9	Frequency	0	0	0	0	0	0	0	0	0	0	0
	%	0.0	0.0	0.0	0.0	0.0	0.0	0.0	0.0	0.0	0.0	0.0
10	Frequency	27	17	0	0	0	1	1	1	0	5	2
	%	1.5	1.8	0.0	0.0	0.0	0.7	1.1	6.7	0.0	1.7	1.7
11	Frequency	20	14	1	2	0	1	0	0	0	1	1
	%	1.1	1.5	1.7	3.3	0.0	0.7	0.0	0.0	0.0	0.3	0.8

Ownership form of your enterprise

12	Frequency	25	18	0	0	0	0	4	0	0	1	2
	%	1.4	1.9	0.0	0.0	0.0	0.0	4.4	0.0	0.0	0.3	1.7
13	Frequency	38	26	0	1	0	3	1	0	1	4	2
	%	2.1	2.7	0.0	1.6	0.0	2.0	1.1	0.0	3.1	1.4	1.7
14	Frequency	11	8	0	1	0	0	1	0	0	1	0
	%	0.6	0.8	0.0	1.6	0.0	0.0	1.1	0.0	0.0	0.3	0.0
15	Frequency	39	23	0	1	1	4	3	0	2	5	0
	%	2.2	2.4	0.0	1.6	3.0	2.7	3.3	0.0	6.3	1.7	0.0
16	Frequency	7	7	0	0	0	0	0	0	0	0	0
	%	0.4	0.7	0.0	0.0	0.0	0.0	0.0	0.0	0.0	0.0	0.0
17	Frequency	8	5	0	0	1	0	2	0	0	0	0
	%	0.4	0.5	0.0	0.0	3.0	0.0	2.2	0.0	0.0	0.0	0.0
18	Frequency	7	3	0	0	0	0	0	0	0	2	2
	%	0.4	0.3	0.0	0.0	0.0	0.0	0.0	0.0	0.0	0.7	1.7
19	Frequency	15	10	0	0	0	3	0	0	0	2	0
	%	0.8	1.0	0.0	0.0	0.0	2.0	0.0	0.0	0.0	0.7	0.0
20	Frequency	6	4	0	0	0	1	1	0	0	0	0
	%	0.3	0.4	0.0	0.0	0.0	0.7	1.1	0.0	0.0	0.0	0.0
21–30	Frequency	35	25	2	0	0	2	0	0	2	1	3
	%	1.9	2.6	3.3	0.0	0.0	1.3	0.0	0.0	6.3	0.3	2.5
31–40	Frequency	14	12	0	0	0	0	0	0	0	1	1
	%	0.8	1.3	0.0	0.0	0.0	0.0	0.0	0.0	0.0	0.3	0.8
41–50	Frequency	3	1	0	0	0	1	1	0	0	0	0
	%	0.2	0.1	0.0	0.0	0.0	0.7	1.1	0.0	0.0	0.0	0.0
Over 50	Frequency	206	105	7	10	6	9	9	1	2	37	20
	%	11.4	11.0	11.7	16.4	18.2	6.0	10.0	6.7	6.3	12.7	16.5
NA	Frequency	211	102	8	5	2	18	8	0	2	38	28
	%	11.7	10.7	13.3	8.2	6.1	12.0	8.9	0.0	6.3	13.0	23.1

A4-1b Number of full-time trade union committee members

		Ownership form of your enterprise									
	Sum	State-owned/State-holding enterprise	Collective-owned enterprise	Private enterprise	Cooperative enterprise	Limited liability corporation	Share Holding Corporation Ltd	Enterprise with Funds from Hong Kong, Macao and Taiwan	Foreign funded enterprise	Others	NA
1 Frequency	218	148	3	2	5	18	11	0	3	23	5
%	12.0	15.5	5.0	3.3	15.2	12.0	12.2	0.0	9.4	7.9	4.1
2 Frequency	99	59	5	2	0	8	3	1	1	14	6
%	5.5	6.2	8.3	3.3	0.0	5.3	3.3	6.7	3.1	4.8	5.0
3 Frequency	69	46	2	2	0	4	3	0	2	6	4
%	3.8	4.8	3.3	3.3	0.0	2.7	3.3	0.0	6.3	2.1	3.3
4 Frequency	43	27	1	1	1	4	1	0	0	6	2
%	2.4	2.8	1.7	1.6	3.0	2.7	1.1	0.0	0.0	2.1	1.7
5 Frequency	38	17	0	0	1	6	4	0	2	3	5
%	2.1	1.8	0.0	0.0	3.0	4.0	4.4	0.0	6.3	1.0	4.1
6 Frequency	19	9	0	0	0	4	0	0	0	3	3
%	1.0	0.9	0.0	0.0	0.0	2.7	0.0	0.0	0.0	1.0	2.5
7 Frequency	16	9	0	1	0	0	0	0	1	4	1
%	0.9	0.9	0.0	1.6	0.0	0.0	0.0	0.0	3.1	1.4	0.8
8 Frequency	51	32	0	0	2	5	2	0	0	8	2
%	2.8	3.3	0.0	0.0	6.1	3.3	2.2	0.0	0.0	2.7	1.7
NA Frequency	1258	610	49	53	24	101	66	14	23	225	93
%	69.5	63.7	81.7	86.9	72.7	67.3	73.3	93.3	71.9	77.1	76.9

A4-1b Percentage of male committee members in all committee members

0	Frequency	252	134	6	6	1	21	7	2	4	50	21
	%	13.9	14.0	10.0	9.8	3.0	14.0	7.8	13.3	12.5	17.1	17.4
1–10	Frequency	14	10	0	0	0	2	2	0	0	0	0
	%	0.8	1.0	0.0	0.0	0.0	1.3	2.2	0.0	0.0	0.0	0.0
11–20	Frequency	39	26	0	0	1	6	0	0	0	5	1
	%	2.2	2.7	0.0	0.0	3.0	4.0	0.0	0.0	0.0	1.7	0.8
21–30	Frequency	47	19	0	1	0	6	3	0	1	13	4
	%	2.6	2.0	0.0	1.6	0.0	4.0	3.3	0.0	3.1	4.5	3.3
31–40	Frequency	90	40	8	4	1	6	5	0	2	16	8
	%	5.0	4.2	13.3	6.6	3.0	4.0	5.6	0.0	6.3	5.5	6.6
41–50	Frequency	158	82	8	5	4	12	10	1	3	29	4
	%	8.7	8.6	13.3	8.2	12.1	8.0	11.1	6.7	9.4	9.9	3.3
51–60	Frequency	83	51	1	3	0	4	4	1	3	13	3
	%	4.6	5.3	1.7	4.9	0.0	2.7	4.4	6.7	9.4	4.5	2.5
61–70	Frequency	139	77	3	5	2	14	9	1	3	19	6
	%	7.7	8.0	5.0	8.2	6.1	9.3	10.0	6.7	9.4	6.5	5.0
71–80	Frequency	164	96	2	7	3	11	9	1	2	28	5
	%	9.1	10.0	3.3	11.5	9.1	7.3	10.0	6.7	6.3	9.6	5.0
81–90	Frequency	65	40	2	3	0	4	3	0	0	8	5
	%	3.6	4.2	3.3	4.9	0.0	2.7	3.3	0.0	0.0	2.7	4.1
91–100	Frequency	117	54	6	6	3	15	8	1	6	10	8
	%	6.5	5.6	10.0	9.8	9.1	10.0	8.9	6.7	18.8	3.4	6.6
NA	Frequency	643	328	24	21	18	49	30	8	8	101	56
	%	35.5	34.3	40.0	34.4	54.5	32.7	33.3	53.3	25.0	34.6	46.3

A4-1b Percentage of committee members who have the following political appearance
1. Chinese Communist Party member

			Ownership form of your enterprise									
		Sum	State-owned/ State-holding enterprise	Collective-owned enterprise	Private enterprise	Cooperative enterprise	Limited liability corporation	Share Holding Corporation Ltd	Enterprise with Funds from Hong Kong, Macao and Taiwan	Foreign funded enterprise	Others	NA
0	Frequency	0	0	0	0	0	0	0	0	0	0	0
	%	0.0	0.0	0.0	0.0	0.0	0.0	0.0	0.0	0.0	0.0	0.0
1–10	Frequency	20	10	0	1	1	4	2	1	1	0	0
	%	1.1	1.0	0.0	1.6	3.0	2.7	2.2	6.7	3.1	0.0	0.0
11–20	Frequency	47	26	1	1	0	6	5	0	1	6	1
	%	2.6	2.7	1.7	1.6	0.0	4.0	5.6	0.0	3.1	2.1	0.8
21–30	Frequency	41	22	0	2	0	6	1	0	1	6	3
	%	2.3	2.3	0.0	3.3	0.0	4.0	1.1	0.0	3.1	2.1	2.5
31–40	Frequency	83	34	5	4	5	8	4	1	3	18	1
	%	4.6	3.6	8.3	6.6	15.2	5.3	4.4	6.7	9.4	6.2	0.8
41–50	Frequency	112	61	4	4	3	8	7	0	2	18	5
	%	6.2	6.4	6.7	6.6	9.1	5.3	7.8	0.0	6.3	6.2	4.1
51–60	Frequency	65	43	2	2	0	3	1	0	2	9	3
	%	3.6	4.5	3.3	3.3	0.0	2.0	1.1	0.0	6.3	3.1	2.5
61–70	Frequency	102	67	0	2	0	6	7	0	2	15	3
	%	5.6	7.0	0.0	3.3	0.0	4.0	7.8	0.0	6.3	5.1	2.5
71–80	Frequency	118	74	5	2	2	7	6	0	1	16	5
	%	6.5	7.7	8.3	3.3	6.1	4.7	6.7	0.0	3.1	5.5	4.1
81–90	Frequency	65	39	1	0	0	1	2	0	3	16	3
	%	3.6	4.1	1.7	0.0	0.0	0.7	2.2	0.0	9.4	5.5	2.5
91–100	Frequency	288	163	8	3	2	27	12	0	3	50	20
	%	15.9	17.0	13.3	4.9	6.1	18.0	13.3	0.0	9.4	17.1	16.5
NA	Frequency	870	418	34	40	20	74	43	13	13	138	77
	%	48.0	43.7	56.7	65.6	60.6	49.3	47.8	86.7	40.6	47.3	63.6

2. Democratic party member

0	Frequency	885	463	32	17	4	85	43	3	14	154	70
	%	48.9	48.4	53.3	27.9	12.1	56.7	47.8	20.0	43.8	52.7	57.9
1–10	Frequency	12	8	0	0	0	0	0	0	0	3	1
	%	0.7	0.8	0.0	0.0	0.0	0.0	0.0	0.0	0.0	1.0	0.8
11–20	Frequency	24	10	2	0	1	1	1	0	0	4	5
	%	1.3	1.0	3.3	0.0	3.0	0.7	1.1	0.0	0.0	1.4	4.1
21–30	Frequency	12	5	0	0	0	0	2	0	0	5	0
	%	0.7	0.5	0	0.0	0.0	0.0	2.2	0.0	0.0	1.7	0.0
31–40	Frequency	9	4	0	0	0	1	0	0	0	2	2
	%	0.5	0.4	0.0	0.0	0.0	0.7	0.0	0.0	0.0	0.7	1.7
41–50	Frequency	5	4	0	1	0	0	0	0	0	0	0
	%	0.3	0.4	0.0	1.6	0.0	0.0	0.0	0.0	0.0	0.0	0.0
51–60	Frequency	0	0	0	0	0	0	0	0	0	0	0
	%	0.0	0.0	0.0	0.0	0.0	0.0	0.0	0.0	0.0	0.0	0.0
61–70	Frequency	5	2	1	0	0	0	1	0	0	1	0
	%	0.3	0.2	1.7	0.0	0.0	0.0	1.1	0.0	0.0	0.3	0.0
71–80	Frequency	1	1	0	0	0	0	0	0	0	0	0
	%	0.1	0.1	0.0	0.0	0.0	0.0	0.0	0.0	0.0	0.0	0.0
81–90	Frequency	1	1	0	0	0	0	0	0	0	0	0
	%	0.1	0.1	0.0	0.0	0.0	0.0	0.0	0.0	0.0	0.0	0.0
91–100	Frequency	3	2	0	0	0	0	0	0	1	0	0
	%	0.2	0.2	0.0	0.0	0.0	0.0	0.0	0.0	3.1	0.0	0.0
NA	Frequency	854	457	25	43	28	63	43	12	17	123	43
	%	47.2	47.8	41.7	70.5	84.8	42.0	47.8	80.0	53.1	42.1	35.5

A4-3 Whether or not established the standing committee in the primary trade union

Established	Frequency	272	160	9	9	6	21	11	0	2	36	18
	%	15.0	16.7	15.0	14.8	18.2	14.0	12.2	0.0	6.3	12.3	14.9
Not established	Frequency	898	469	28	31	14	83	45	11	23	148	46
	%	49.6	49.0	46.7	50.8	42.4	55.3	50.0	73.3	71.9	50.7	38.0
NA	Frequency	641	328	23	21	13	46	34	4	7	108	57
	%	35.4	34.3	38.3	34.4	39.4	30.7	37.8	26.7	21.9	37.0	47.1

A4-4 Whether or not established the following department/committee in the trade union

1. Office

		Sum	State-owned/ State-holding enterprise	Collective-owned enterprise	Private enterprise	Cooperative enterprise	Limited liability corporation	Share Holding Corporation Ltd	Enterprise with Funds from Hong Kong, Macao and Taiwan	Foreign funded enterprise	Others	NA
Not established	Frequency	1152	550	47	45	20	92	54	12	24	225	83
	%	63.6	57.5	78.3	73.8	60.6	61.3	60.0	80.0	75.0	77.1	68.6
Established	Frequency	658	406	13	16	13	58	36	3	8	67	38
	%	36.3	42.4	21.7	26.2	39.4	38.7	40.0	20.0	25.0	22.9	31.4
NA	Frequency	1	1	0	0	0	0	0	0	0	0	0
	%	0.1	0.1	0.0	0.0	0.0	0.0	0.0	0.0	0.0	0.0	0.0

2. Organization work

		Sum	State-owned/ State-holding enterprise	Collective-owned enterprise	Private enterprise	Cooperative enterprise	Limited liability corporation	Share Holding Corporation Ltd	Enterprise with Funds from Hong Kong, Macao and Taiwan	Foreign funded enterprise	Others	NA
Not established	Frequency	1149	560	46	47	24	97	58	13	17	198	89
	%	63.4	58.5	76.7	77.0	72.7	64.7	64.4	86.7	53.1	67.8	73.6
Established	Frequency	660	395	14	14	9	53	32	2	15	94	32
	%	36.4	41.3	23.3	23.0	27.3	35.3	35.6	13.3	46.9	32.2	26.4
NA	Frequency	2	2	0	0	0	0	0	0	0	0	0
	%	0.1	0.2	0.0	0.0	0.0	0.0	0.0	0.0	0.0	0.0	0.0

Ownership form of your enterprise

3. Propaganda work

Not established	Frequency	86	185	20	14	59	94	23	42	48	535	1106
	%	71.1	63.4	62.5	93.3	65.6	62.7	69.7	68.9	80.0	55.9	61.1
Established	Frequency	35	107	12	1	31	56	10	19	12	420	703
	%	28.9	36.6	37.5	6.7	34.4	37.3	30.3	31.1	20.0	43.9	38.8
NA	Frequency	0	0	0	0	0	0	0	0	0	2	2
	%	0.0	0.0	0.0	0.0	0.0	0.0	0.0	0.0	0.0	0.2	0.1

4. Organization propagandizes

Not established	Frequency	94	208	22	15	55	103	22	50	45	596	1210
	%	77.7	71.2	68.8	100.0	61.1	68.7	66.7	82.0	75.0	62.3	66.8
Established	Frequency	27	84	10	0	35	47	11	11	15	360	600
	%	22.3	28.8	31.3	0.0	38.9	31.3	33.3	18.0	25.0	37.6	33.1
NA	Frequency	0	0	0	0	0	0	0	0	0	1	1
	%	0.0	0.0	0.0	0.0	0.0	0.0	0.0	0.0	0.0	0.1	0.1

5. Mass production work

Not established	Frequency	99	241	21	14	61	97	22	53	45	553	1206
	%	81.8	82.5	65.6	93.3	67.8	64.7	66.7	86.9	75.0	57.8	66.6
Established	Frequency	22	51	11	1	29	53	11	8	15	403	604
	%	18.2	17.5	34.4	6.7	32.2	35.3	33.3	13.1	25.0	42.1	33.4
NA	Frequency	0	0	0	0	0	0	0	0	0	1	1
	%	0.0	0.0	0.0	0.0	0.0	0.0	0.0	0.0	0.0	0.1	0.1

6. Female worker support

| | | Ownership form of your enterprise | | | | | | Enterprise with | | | |
	Sum	State-owned/ State-holding enterprise	Collective-owned enterprise	Private enterprise	Cooperative enterprise	Limited liability corporation	Share Holding Corporation Ltd	Funds from Hong Kong, Macao and Taiwan	Foreign funded enterprise	Others	NA
Not established Frequency	632	281	28	36	17	47	28	11	10	111	63
%	34.9	29.4	46.7	59.0	51.5	31.3	31.1	73.3	31.3	38.0	52.1
Established Frequency	1178	675	32	25	16	103	62	4	22	181	58
%	65.0	70.5	53.3	41.0	48.5	68.7	68.9	26.7	68.8	62.0	47.9
NA Frequency	1	1	0	0	0	0	0	0	0	0	0
%	0.1	0.1	0.0	0.0	0.0	0.0	0.0	0.0	0.0	0.0	0.0

7. Labor protection work

	Sum	State-owned/ State-holding enterprise	Collective-owned enterprise	Private enterprise	Cooperative enterprise	Limited liability corporation	Share Holding Corporation Ltd	Funds from Hong Kong, Macao and Taiwan	Foreign funded enterprise	Others	NA
Not established Frequency	986	461	34	38	20	82	52	11	14	182	92
%	54.4	48.2	56.7	62.3	60.6	54.7	57.8	73.3	43.8	62.3	76.0
Established Frequency	824	495	26	23	13	68	38	4	18	110	29
%	45.5	51.7	43.3	37.7	39.4	45.3	42.2	26.7	56.3	37.7	24.0
NA Frequency	1	1	0	0	0	0	0	0	0	0	0
%	0.1	0.1	0.0	0.0	0.0	0.0	0.0	0.0	0.0	0.0	0.0

8. Assistance of workers with financial difficulties

Not established	Frequency	1059	515	40	41	23	94	53	13	19	175	86
	%	58.5	53.8	66.7	67.2	69.7	62.7	58.9	86.7	59.4	59.9	71.1
Established	Frequency	750	440	20	20	10	56	37	2	13	117	35
	%	41.4	46.0	33.3	32.8	30.3	37.3	41.1	13.3	40.6	40.1	28.9
NA	Frequency	2	2	0	0	0	0	0	0	0	0	0
	%	0.1	0.2	0.0	0.0	0.0	0.0	0.0	0.0	0.0	0.0	0.0

9. Rights and interests protection

Not established	Frequency	1229	611	48	48	25	105	65	15	20	192	100
	%	67.9	63.8	80.0	78.7	75.8	70.0	72.2	100.0	62.5	65.8	82.6
Established	Frequency	580	344	12	13	8	45	25	0	12	100	21
	%	32.0	35.9	20.0	21.3	24.2	30.0	27.8	0.0	37.5	34.2	17.4
NA	Frequency	2	2	0	0	0	0	0	0	0	0	0
	%	0.1	0.2	0.0	0.0	0.0	0.0	0.0	0.0	0.0	0.0	0.0

A4-5 Number of trade union branches under the trade union

0	Frequency	0	0	0	0	0	0	0	0	0	0	0
	%	0.0	0.0	0.0	0.0	0.0	0.0	0.0	0.0	0.0	0.0	0.0
1–10	Frequency	710	383	32	15	7	68	34	6	9	111	45
	%	39.2	40.0	53.3	24.6	21.2	45.3	37.8	40.0	28.1	38.0	37.2
11–20	Frequency	253	162	2	4	2	18	12	0	3	34	16
	%	14.0	16.9	3.3	6.6	6.1	12.0	13.3	0.0	9.4	11.6	13.2
21–30	Frequency	98	60	1	0	0	6	5	0	4	18	4
	%	5.4	6.3	1.7	0.0	0.0	4.0	5.6	0.0	12.5	6.2	3.3
31–40	Frequency	47	41	0	0	0	2	3	0	0	1	0
	%	2.6	4.3	0.0	0.0	0.0	1.3	3.3	0.0	0.0	0.3	0.0
41–50	Frequency	31	24	1	0	0	3	1	0	0	2	0
	%	1.7	2.5	1.7	0.0	0.0	2.0	1.1	0.0	0.0	0.7	0.0
More than 50	Frequency	525	231	17	36	23	42	29	8	14	87	38
	%	29.0	24.1	28.3	59.0	69.7	28.0	32.2	53.3	43.8	29.8	31.4
NA	Frequency	147	56	7	6	1	11	6	1	2	39	18
	%	8.1	5.9	11.7	9.8	3.0	7.3	6.7	6.7	6.3	13.4	14.9

A4-5 Number of trade union small groups under the trade union

		Sum	State-owned/State-holding enterprise	Collective-owned enterprise	Private enterprise	Cooperative enterprise	Limited liability corporation	Share Holding Corporation Ltd	Enterprise with Funds from Hong Kong, Macao and Taiwan	Foreign funded enterprise	Others	NA
0	Frequency	0	0	0	0	0	0	0	0	0	0	0
	%	0.0	0.0	0.0	0.0	0.0	0.0	0.0	0.0	0.0	0.0	0.0
1–50	Frequency	972	493	39	21	20	91	47	6	15	176	64
	%	53.7	51.5	65.0	34.4	60.6	60.7	52.2	40.0	46.9	60.3	52.9
51–100	Frequency	131	92	3	2	1	9	10	2	1	9	2
	%	7.2	9.6	5.0	3.3	3.0	6.0	11.1	13.3	3.1	3.1	1.7
101–200	Frequency	83	61	0	2	0	7	4	0	0	5	4
	%	4.6	6.4	0.0	3.3	0.0	4.7	4.4	0.0	0.0	1.7	3.3
201–300	Frequency	45	28	1	0	0	5	3	0	3	2	3
	%	2.5	2.9	1.7	0.0	0.0	3.3	3.3	0.0	9.4	0.7	2.5
301–400	Frequency	14	14	0	0	0	0	0	0	0	0	0
	%	0.8	1.5	0.0	0.0	0.0	0.0	0.0	0.0	0.0	0.0	0.0
401–500	Frequency	8	7	0	0	0	0	0	0	0	1	0
	%	0.4	0.7	0.0	0.0	0.0	0.0	0.0	0.0	0.0	0.3	0.0
More than 500	Frequency	298	140	9	28	11	23	13	6	8	40	20
	%	16.5	14.6	15.0	45.9	33.3	15.3	14.4	40.0	25.0	13.7	16.5
NA	Frequency	260	122	8	8	1	15	13	1	5	59	28
	%	14.4	12.7	13.3	13.1	3.0	10.0	14.4	6.7	15.6	20.2	23.1

A4-6 Number of times the primary trade union held conferences in 2003

1	Frequency	93	32	1	1	12	4	1	1	20	15
	%	5.1	3.3	1.6	3.0	8.0	4.4	6.7	3.1	6.8	12.4
2	Frequency	254	112	7	8	30	13	0	6	47	18
	%	14.0	11.7	11.5	24.2	20.0	14.4	0.0	18.8	16.1	14.9
3	Frequency	184	92	4	4	8	10	2	1	43	13
	%	10.2	9.6	6.6	12.1	5.3	11.1	13.3	3.1	14.7	10.7
4	Frequency	220	127	8	3	13	7	0	3	36	18
	%	12.1	13.3	13.1	9.1	8.7	7.8	0.0	9.4	12.3	14.9
5	Frequency	125	63	4	2	14	11	1	4	14	8
	%	6.9	6.6	6.6	6.1	9.3	12.2	6.7	12.5	4.8	6.6
6	Frequency	110	65	1	2	5	10	1	4	17	2
	%	6.1	6.8	1.6	6.1	3.3	11.1	6.7	12.5	5.8	1.7
More than 6	Frequency	447	286	7	3	37	20	4	7	54	16
	%	24.7	29.9	11.5	9.1	24.7	22.2	26.7	21.9	18.5	13.2
NA	Frequency	378	180	29	10	31	15	6	6	61	31
	%	20.9	18.8	47.5	30.3	20.7	16.7	40.0	18.8	20.9	25.6

Part 3: Questions about personnel system

B1. Procedure to assume the post of trade union vice chairman

1 Appointed by an organization	Frequency	211	113	7	6	22	12	4	0	29	13
	%	11.7	11.8	11.5	18.2	14.7	13.3	26.7	0.0	9.9	10.7
2 Elected at members' congress/ members' assembly, following organization recommendation	Frequency	602	348	18	9	41	30	1	11	84	44
	%	33.2	36.4	29.5	27.3	27.3	33.3	6.7	34.4	28.8	36.4

167

| | | Ownership form of your enterprise | | | | | | | | | | |
		Sum	State-owned/ State-holding enterprise	Collective-owned enterprise	Private enterprise	Cooperative enterprise	Limited liability corporation	Share Holding Corporation Ltd	Enterprise with Funds from Hong Kong, Macao and Taiwan	Foreign funded enterprise	Others	NA
3 Elected at members' congress/members' assembly directly	Frequency	171	91	6	8	4	17	7	0	3	27	8
	%	9.4	9.5	10.0	13.1	12.1	11.3	7.8	0.0	9.4	9.2	6.6
4 Others	Frequency	67	35	2	2	1	3	5	0	3	12	4
	%	3.7	3.7	3.3	3.3	3.0	2.0	5.6	0.0	9.4	4.1	3.3
NA	Frequency	760	370	31	26	13	67	36	10	15	140	52
	%	42.0	38.7	51.7	42.6	39.4	44.7	40.0	66.7	46.9	47.9	43.0

B1-1 (If you chose 1 in B1) the name of the organization

		Sum	State-owned/ State-holding enterprise	Collective-owned enterprise	Private enterprise	Cooperative enterprise	Limited liability corporation	Share Holding Corporation Ltd	Enterprise with Funds from Hong Kong, Macao and Taiwan	Foreign funded enterprise	Others	NA
Party organization of work unit	Frequency	142	94	3	1	0	15	9	0	0	13	7
	%	67.3	83.2	60.0	14.3	0.0	68.2	75.0	0.0	0.0	44.8	53.8
Administrative organization of work unit	Frequency	35	7	1	6	4	3	2	3	0	4	5
	%	16.6	6.2	20.0	85.7	66.7	13.6	16.7	75.0	0.0	13.8	38.5
Higher-level trade union	Frequency	16	4	0	0	1	1	1	1	0	8	0
	%	7.6	3.5	0.0	0.0	16.7	4.5	8.3	25.0	0.0	27.6	0.0
Former primary trade union committee	Frequency	2	2	0	0	0	0	0	0	0	0	0
	%	0.9	1.8	0.0	0.0	0.0	0.0	0.0	0.0	0.0	0.0	0.0

Others	Frequency	3	2	0	0	0	0	0	0	0	1	0
	%	1.4	1.8	0.0	0.0	0.0	0.0	0.0	0.0	0.0	3.4	0.0
NA	Frequency	13	4	1	0	1	3	0	0	0	3	1
	%	6.2	3.5	20.0	0.0	16.7	13.6	0.0	0.0	0.0	10.3	7.7

B1-2 (If you chose 2 in B1) the organizations or the persons you accepted recommendation

Party organization of work unit	Frequency	448	281	6	7	4	25	20	0	8	64	33
	%	74.4	80.7	37.5	38.9	44.4	61.0	66.7	0.0	72.7	76.2	75.0
Administrative organization of work unit	Frequency	55	23	9	5	3	5	4	0	0	3	3
	%	9.1	6.6	56.3	27.8	33.3	12.2	13.3	0.0	0.0	3.6	6.8
Functionaries of workshop-level trade union	Frequency	6	2	0	0	1	0	0	0	1	1	0
	%	1.0	0.6	0.0	0.0	11.1	0.0	0.0	0.0	9.1	1.2	0.0
Self-recommended	Frequency	0	0	0	0	0	0	0	1	0	0	0
	%	0.0	0.0	0.0	0.0	0.0	0.0	0.0	100.0	0.0	0.0	0.0
Ordinary union members or trade union small groups	Frequency	40	15	1	4	1	4	5	0	1	7	2
	%	6.6	4.3	6.3	22.2	11.1	9.8	16.7	0.0	9.1	8.3	4.5
Others	Frequency	0	0	0	0	0	0	0	0	0	0	0
	%	0.0	0.0	0.0	0.0	0.0	0.0	0.0	0.0	0.0	0.0	0.0
NA	Frequency	53	27	0	2	0	7	1	0	1	9	6
	%	8.8	7.8	0.0	11.1	0.0	17.1	3.3	0.0	9.1	10.7	13.6

B1-3 (If you chose 3 in B1) the method of the election

			Ownership form of your enterprise								
		Sum	State-owned/ State-holding enterprise	Collective-owned enterprise	Private enterprise	Cooperative enterprise	Limited liability corporation	Share Holding Corporation Ltd	Enterprise with Funds from Hong Kong, Macao and Taiwan	Foreign funded enterprise	Others	NA
Separate voting for chairman, vice-chairmen and other committees	Frequency	32	16	1	4	1	3	0	0	0	5	2
	%	18.7	17.6	16.7	50.0	25.0	17.6	0.0	0.0	0.0	18.5	25.0
Voting for chairman and vice-chairmen from elected committees	Frequency	121	66	5	4	2	14	5	0	3	16	6
	%	70.8	72.5	83.3	50.0	50.0	82.4	71.4	0.0	100.0	59.3	75.0
Others	Frequency	2	0	0	0	0	0	0	0	0	2	0
	%	1.2	0.0	0.0	0.0	0.0	0.0	0.0	0.0	0.0	7.4	0.0
NA	Frequency	16	9	0	0	1	0	2	0	0	4	0
	%	9.4	9.9	0.0	0.0	25.0	0.0	28.6	0.0	0.0	14.8	0.0

B2 Questions about the construction of Professional Trade Union Chairman Storehouse system at county-level

Agree or disagree with the following opinions

1 Advantageous for disposing competent trade union chairman and cadres

Agree	Frequency	1173	626	36	38	21	110	56	12	21	195	58
	%	64.8	65.4	60.0	62.3	63.6	73.3	62.2	80.0	65.6	66.8	47.9
Disagree	Frequency	103	58	5	5	1	7	4	0	6	12	5
	%	5.7	6.1	8.3	8.2	3.0	4.7	4.4	0.0	18.8	4.1	4.1
NA	Frequency	535	273	19	18	11	33	30	3	5	85	58
	%	29.5	28.5	31.7	29.5	33.3	22.0	33.3	20.0	15.6	29.1	47.9

2 Advantageous for assuring trade union cadres' security of income

Agree	Frequency	1072	575	33	34	20	101	56	10	21	170	52
	%	59.2	60.1	55.0	55.7	60.6	67.3	62.2	66.7	65.6	58.2	43.0
Disagree	Frequency	112	59	5	8	3	9	4	0	4	14	6
	%	6.2	6.2	8.3	13.1	9.1	6.0	4.4	0.0	12.5	4.8	5.0
NA	Frequency	627	323	22	19	10	40	30	5	7	108	63
	%	34.6	33.8	36.7	31.1	30.3	26.7	33.3	33.3	21.9	37.0	52.1

3 Advantageous for trade union cadres' safeguarding workers and staff members' legitimate rights and interests in the dispatched enterprise independently

		Sum	Ownership form of your enterprise							Enterprise with Funds from Hong Kong, Macao and Taiwan	Foreign funded enterprise	Others	NA
			State-owned/State-holding enterprise	Collective-owned enterprise	Private enterprise	Cooperative enterprise	Limited liability corporation	Share Holding Corporation Ltd					
Agree	Frequency	1024	575	33	32	13	88	50	10	17	157	49
	%	56.5	60.1	55.0	52.5	39.4	58.7	55.6	66.7	53.1	53.8	40.5
Disagree	Frequency	146	65	4	7	3	18	7	0	7	23	12
	%	8.1	6.8	6.7	11.5	9.1	12.0	7.8	0.0	21.9	7.9	9.9
NA	Frequency	641	317	23	22	17	44	33	5	8	112	60
	%	35.4	33.1	38.3	36.1	51.5	29.3	36.7	33.3	25.0	38.4	49.6

4 Benefits for strengthening the relationship between primary trade unions and higher-level trade unions, enhancing the trade union's organizational power

		Sum	Ownership form of your enterprise							Enterprise with Funds from Hong Kong, Macao and Taiwan	Foreign funded enterprise	Others	NA
			State-owned/State-holding enterprise	Collective-owned enterprise	Private enterprise	Cooperative enterprise	Limited liability corporation	Share Holding Corporation Ltd					
Agree	Frequency	955	519	33	33	13	79	44	10	21	155	48
	%	52.7	54.2	55.0	54.1	39.4	52.7	48.9	66.7	65.6	53.1	39.7
Disagree	Frequency	125	64	2	3	1	18	8	1	3	15	10
	%	6.9	6.7	3.3	4.9	3.0	12.0	8.9	6.7	9.4	5.1	8.3
NA	Frequency	731	374	25	25	19	53	38	4	8	122	63
	%	40.4	39.1	41.7	41.0	57.6	35.3	42.2	26.7	25.0	41.8	52.1

5 Disadvantages in developing trade union activities because dispatched chairmen or cadres are not familiar with the inside details of the enterprise

Agree	Frequency	482	242	15	22	9	47	30	5	12	65	35
	%	26.6	25.3	25.0	36.1	27.3	31.3	33.3	33.3	37.5	22.3	28.9
Disagree	Frequency	468	251	17	12	7	37	20	5	12	82	25
	%	25.8	26.2	28.3	19.7	21.2	24.7	22.2	33.3	37.5	28.1	20.7
NA	Frequency	861	464	28	27	17	66	40	5	8	145	61
	%	47.5	48.5	46.7	44.3	51.5	44.0	44.4	33.3	25.0	49.7	50.4

6 Few people would apply for the Professional Trade Union Chairman Storehouse

Agree	Frequency	363	199	15	14	7	26	17	3	8	53	21
	%	20.0	20.8	25.0	23.0	21.2	17.3	18.9	20.0	25.0	18.2	17.4
Disagree	Frequency	468	251	15	14	6	42	25	7	10	72	26
	%	25.8	26.2	25.0	23.0	18.2	28.0	27.8	46.7	31.3	24.7	21.5
NA	Frequency	980	507	30	33	20	82	48	5	14	167	74
	%	54.1	53.0	50.0	54.1	60.6	54.7	53.3	33.3	43.8	57.2	61.2

7 Disadvantages in the unity of the primary trade union because dispatched chairman and cadres would create discord with other cadres

Agree	Frequency	366	194	15	16	4	31	20	4	10	50	22
	%	20.2	20.3	25.0	26.2	12.1	20.7	22.2	26.7	31.3	17.1	18.2
Disagree	Frequency	525	282	16	14	9	46	24	6	10	90	28
	%	29.0	29.5	26.7	23.0	27.3	30.7	26.7	40.0	31.3	30.8	23.1
NA	Frequency	920	481	29	31	20	73	46	5	12	152	71
	%	50.8	50.3	48.3	50.8	60.6	48.7	51.1	33.3	37.5	52.1	58.7

8 Disadvantages in trade union activity developments and trade union status enhancement because dispatched chairman and cadres would create discord with party and administrative organizations within the enterprise

		Sum	State-owned/State-holding enterprise	Collective-owned enterprise	Private enterprise	Cooperative enterprise	Limited liability corporation	Share Holding Corporation Ltd	Enterprise with Funds from Hong Kong, Macao and Taiwan	Foreign funded enterprise	Others	NA
Agree	Frequency	420	219	19	19	7	42	24	4	9	51	26
	%	23.2	22.9	31.7	31.1	21.2	28.0	26.7	26.7	28.1	17.5	21.5
Disagree	Frequency	498	272	12	12	8	35	27	6	13	89	24
	%	27.5	28.4	20.0	19.7	24.2	23.3	30.0	40.0	40.6	30.5	19.8
NA	Frequency	893	466	29	30	18	73	39	5	10	152	71
	%	49.3	48.7	48.3	49.2	54.5	48.7	43.3	33.3	31.3	52.1	58.7

9 This method is worth promoting nationwide

		Sum	State-owned/State-holding enterprise	Collective-owned enterprise	Private enterprise	Cooperative enterprise	Limited liability corporation	Share Holding Corporation Ltd	Enterprise with Funds from Hong Kong, Macao and Taiwan	Foreign funded enterprise	Others	NA
Agree	Frequency	742	378	26	28	18	58	41	10	17	123	43
	%	41.0	39.5	43.3	45.9	54.5	38.7	45.6	66.7	53.1	42.1	35.5
Disagree	Frequency	251	136	10	9	1	22	14	1	6	39	13
	%	13.9	14.2	16.7	14.8	3.0	14.7	15.6	6.7	18.8	13.4	10.7
NA	Frequency	818	443	24	24	14	70	35	4	9	130	65
	%	45.2	46.3	40.0	39.3	42.4	46.7	38.9	26.7	28.1	44.5	53.7

B-3 Questions about the first vice chairman

B3-1 Whether or not holding concurrent post other than trade union vice-chairman

1 Hold	Frequency	598	308	21	24	15	55	31	7	8	99	30
	%	33.0	32.2	35.0	39.3	45.5	36.7	34.4	46.7	25.0	33.9	24.8
2 Not hold	Frequency	359	226	6	6	4	20	17	1	11	43	25
	%	19.8	23.6	10.0	9.8	12.1	13.3	18.9	6.7	34.4	14.7	20.7
NA	Frequency	854	423	33	31	14	75	42	7	13	150	66
	%	47.2	44.2	55.0	50.8	42.4	50.0	46.7	46.7	40.6	51.4	54.5

B3-1-1 (If you chose 1 in B3-1) whether or not holding the following post concurrently

1 Secretary of CCP committee at the corresponding level

Hold	Frequency	17	5	0	2	0	1	2	1	0	5	1
	%	2.8	1.6	0.0	8.3	0.0	1.8	6.5	14.3	0.0	5.1	3.3
Not hold	Frequency	581	303	21	22	15	54	29	6	8	94	29
	%	97.2	98.4	100.0	91.7	100.0	98.2	93.5	85.7	100.0	94.9	96.7

2 Vice-secretary of CCP committee at the corresponding level

Hold	Frequency	29	19	1	0	0	2	1	0	0	4	2
	%	4.8	6.2	4.8	0.0	0.0	3.6	3.2	0.0	0.0	4.0	6.7
Not hold	Frequency	569	289	20	24	15	53	30	7	8	95	28
	%	95.2	93.8	95.2	100.0	100.0	96.4	96.8	100.0	100.0	96.0	93.3

3 CCP committee member at the corresponding level

		Ownership form of your enterprise									
	Sum	State-owned/State-holding enterprise	Collective-owned enterprise	Private enterprise	Cooperative enterprise	Limited liability corporation	Share Holding Corporation Ltd	Enterprise with Funds from Hong Kong, Macao and Taiwan	Foreign funded enterprise	Others	NA
Hold Frequency	67	39	0	3	2	8	3	0	0	8	4
%	11.2	12.7	0.0	12.5	13.3	14.5	9.7	0.0	0.0	8.1	13.3
Not hold Frequency	531	269	21	21	13	47	28	7	8	91	26
%	88.8	87.3	100.0	87.5	86.7	85.5	90.3	100.0	100.0	91.9	86.7

4 Administrative manager in charge (president, etc.) at the corresponding level

	Sum	State-owned/State-holding enterprise	Collective-owned enterprise	Private enterprise	Cooperative enterprise	Limited liability corporation	Share Holding Corporation Ltd	Enterprise with Funds from Hong Kong, Macao and Taiwan	Foreign funded enterprise	Others	NA
Hold Frequency	47	22	1	1	0	1	5	0	2	10	5
%	7.9	7.1	4.8	4.2	0.0	1.8	16.1	0.0	25.0	10.1	16.7
Not hold Frequency	551	286	20	23	15	54	26	7	6	89	25
%	92.1	92.9	95.2	95.8	100.0	98.2	83.9	100.0	75.0	89.9	83.3

5 Vice-post of administrative organization at the corresponding level

	Sum	State-owned/State-holding enterprise	Collective-owned enterprise	Private enterprise	Cooperative enterprise	Limited liability corporation	Share Holding Corporation Ltd	Enterprise with Funds from Hong Kong, Macao and Taiwan	Foreign funded enterprise	Others	NA
Hold Frequency	106	42	8	4	4	9	8	1	0	23	7
%	17.7	13.6	38.1	16.7	26.7	16.4	25.8	14.3	0.0	23.2	23.3
Not hold Frequency	492	266	13	20	11	46	23	6	8	76	23
%	82.3	86.4	61.9	83.3	73.3	83.6	74.2	85.7	100.0	76.8	76.7

B3-2 Whether or not having relatives serving as the following post

1 Secretary of CCP committee at the corresponding level

Has	Frequency	4	2	0	1	0	0	0	0	0	1	0
	%	0.7	0.6	0.0	4.2	0.0	0.0	0.0	0.0	0.0	1.0	0.0
Not have	Frequency	594	306	21	23	15	55	31	7	8	98	30
	%	99.3	99.4	100.0	95.8	100.0	100.0	100.0	100.0	100.0	99.0	100.0

2 Vice-secretary of CCP committee at the corresponding level

Has	Frequency	3	3	0	0	0	0	0	0	0	0	0
	%	0.5	1.0	0.0	0.0	0.0	0.0	0.0	0.0	0.0	0.0	0.0
Not have	Frequency	595	305	21	24	15	55	31	7	8	99	30
	%	99.5	99.0	100.0	100.0	100.0	100.0	100.0	100.0	100.0	100.0	100.0

3 CCP committee member at the corresponding level

Has	Frequency	6	5	0	0	0	0	0	0	0	1	0
	%	1.0	1.6	0.0	0.0	0.0	0.0	0.0	0.0	0.0	1.0	0.0
Not have	Frequency	592	303	21	24	15	55	31	7	8	98	30
	%	99.0	98.4	100.0	100.0	100.0	100.0	100.0	100.0	100.0	99.0	100.0

4 Administrative manager in charge (president, etc.) at the corresponding level

Has	Frequency	4	2	0	0	1	0	0	0	0	1	0
	%	0.7	0.6	0.0	0.0	6.7	0.0	0.0	0.0	0.0	1.0	0.0
Not have	Frequency	594	306	21	24	14	55	31	7	8	98	30
	%	99.3	99.4	100.0	100.0	93.3	100.0	100.0	100.0	100.0	99.0	100.0

5 Vice-post of administrative organization at the corresponding level

| | | Ownership form of your enterprise | | | | | | | Enterprise with | | | |
			State-owned/ State-holding enterprise	Collective-owned enterprise	Private enterprise	Cooperative enterprise	Limited liability corporation	Share Holding Corporation Ltd	Funds from Hong Kong, Macao and Taiwan	Foreign funded enterprise	Others	NA
		Sum										
Has	Frequency	18	8	1	1	1	2	2	0	0	3	0
	%	3.0	2.6	4.8	4.2	6.7	3.6	6.5	0.0	0.0	3.0	0.0
Not have	Frequency	580	300	20	23	14	53	29	7	8	96	30
	%	97.0	97.4	95.2	95.8	93.3	96.4	93.5	100.0	100.0	97.0	100.0

B3-3 The last position before being the trade union vice-chairman

		Sum	State-owned/ State-holding enterprise	Collective-owned enterprise	Private enterprise	Cooperative enterprise	Limited liability corporation	Share Holding Corporation Ltd	Funds from Hong Kong, Macao and Taiwan	Foreign funded enterprise	Others	NA
Middle class cadre (Director, Section, Department)	Frequency	318	166	8	4	5	32	13	4	7	60	19
	%	17.6	17.3	13.3	6.6	15.2	21.3	14.4	26.7	21.9	20.5	15.7
Factory manager, President	Frequency	55	37	2	1	2	4	4	0	1	1	3
	%	3.0	3.9	3.3	1.6	6.1	2.7	4.4	0.0	3.1	0.3	2.5
Trade Unions Chairman	Frequency	22	17	0	1	0	2	0	0	0	2	0
	%	1.2	1.8	0	1.6	0.0	1.3	0	0.0	0.0	0.7	0
Teacher	Frequency	5	3	0	0	0	0	0	0	0	2	2
	%	0.3	0.3	0.0	0.0	0.0	0.0	0.0	0.0	0.0	0.0	1.7
CCP Secretary	Frequency	58	42	0	2	1	4	1	0	1	5	2
	%	3.2	4.4	0.0	3.3	3.0	2.7	1.1	0.0	3.1	1.7	1.7
Township Cadre	Frequency	1	0	0	0	0	0	0	0	0	1	0
	%	0.1	0.0	0.0	0.0	0.0	0.0	0.0	0.0	0.0	0.3	0.0
Township Governor	Frequency	0	0	0	0	0	0	0	0	0	0	0
	%	0.0	0.0	0.0	0.0	0.0	0.0	0.0	0.0	0.0	0.0	0.0

Position		C1	C2	C3	C4	C5	C6	C7	C8	C9	C10	C11
Director of Department (prefecture, township)	Frequency	6	4	0	0	0	1	0	0	0	1	0
	%	0.3	0.4	0.0	0.0	0.0	0.7	0.0	0.0	0.0	0.3	0.0
Vice secretary of detached factory	Frequency	1	0	0	0	0	0	0	0	1	0	0
	%	0.1	0.0	0.0	0.0	0.0	0.0	0.0	0.0	3.1	0.0	0.0
CCP Secretary of Administrative Affairs	Frequency	15	13	0	0	0	1	0	0	0	1	1
	%	0.8	1.4	0.0	0.0	0.0	0.7	0.0	0.0	0.0	0.3	0.8
Chief of Security Department	Frequency	11	9	0	0	0	1	1	0	0	0	0
	%	0.6	0.9	0.0	0.0	0.0	0.7	1.1	0.0	0.0	0.0	0.0
Workers and Staffs	Frequency	24	5	1	4	4	2	3	0	1	3	1
	%	1.3	0.5	1.7	6.6	12.1	1.3	3.3	0.0	3.1	1.0	1
Financial Manager	Frequency	3	1	0	0	0	0	0	1	0	1	0
	%	0.2	0.1	0.0	0.0	0.0	0.0	0.0	6.7	0.0	0.3	0
Labour and Security Supervisor	Frequency	0	0	0	0	0	0	0	0	0	0	0
	%	0.0	0.0	0.0	0.0	0.0	0.0	0.0	0.0	0.0	0.0	0.0
Statistic Staff	Frequency	1	1	0	0	0	0	0	0	0	0	0
	%	0.1	0.1	0.0	0.0	0.0	0.0	0.0	0.0	0.0	0.0	0.0
Trade union Cadre, Member of Committee	Frequency	17	12	0	0	1	0	1	0	0	3	0
	%	0.9	1.3	0.0	0.0	3.0	0.0	1.1	0.0	0.0	1.0	0.0
Accountant	Frequency	8	4	0	0	1	2	0	0	0	1	0
	%	0.4	0.4	0.0	0.0	3.0	1.3	0.0	0.0	0.0	0.3	0.0
Lower Staff	Frequency	12	2	0	1	2	0	2	3	1	0	1
	%	0.7	0.2	0.0	1.6	6.1	0.0	2.2	20.0	3.1	0.0	1
Female Cadre	Frequency	2	1	0	0	0	0	0	0	0	0	1
	%	0.1	0.1	0.0	0.0	0.0	0.0	0.0	0.0	0.0	0.0	0.8
Secretary of Chinese Communist Youth League	Frequency	18	9	0	2	0	3	1	0	0	2	1
	%	1.0	0.9	0.0	3.3	0.0	2.0	1.1	0.0	0.0	0.7	0.8

Ownership form of your enterprise

		Sum	State-owned/ State-holding enterprise	Collective-owned enterprise	Private enterprise	Cooperative enterprise	Limited liability corporation	Share Holding Corporation Ltd	Enterprise with Funds from Hong Kong, Macao and Taiwan	Foreign funded enterprise	Others	NA
Chief of Police box	Frequency	0	0	0	0	0	0	0	0	0	0	0
	%	0.0	0.0	0.0	0.0	0.0	0.0	0.0	0.0	0.0	0.0	0.0
Doctor	Frequency	6	2	0	0	0	0	0	0	0	2	2
	%	0.3	0.2	0.0	0.0	0.0	0.0	0.0	0.0	0.0	0.7	1.7
Soldier	Frequency	1	0	1	0	0	0	0	0	0	0	0
	%	0.1	0.0	1.7	0.0	0.0	0.0	0.0	0.0	0.0	0.0	0.0
Principal	Frequency	5	1	0	0	0	0	0	0	1	2	1
	%	0.3	0.1	0.0	0.0	0.0	0.0	0.0	0.0	3.1	0.7	0.8
NA	Frequency	1222	628	48	46	17	98	64	7	19	207	88
	%	67.5	65.6	80.0	75.4	51.5	65.3	71.1	46.7	59.4	70.9	72.7

B4 Questions about the former union chairman 3.2

B4-1 The reason why the former union chairman resigned as the post

		Sum	State-owned/ State-holding enterprise	Collective-owned enterprise	Private enterprise	Cooperative enterprise	Limited liability corporation	Share Holding Corporation Ltd	Enterprise with Funds from Hong Kong, Macao and Taiwan	Foreign funded enterprise	Others	NA
His/Her tenure of office expired, no longer sought re-election	Frequency	271	152	11	4	5	14	10	1	6	48	20
	%	15.0	15.9	18.3	6.6	15.2	9.3	11.1	6.7	18.8	16.4	16.5
Followed organizational personnel transfer	Frequency	663	383	22	13	13	47	29	4	7	102	43
	%	36.6	40.0	36.7	21.3	39.4	31.3	32.2	26.7	21.9	34.9	35.5
Failed in the election	Frequency	38	24	0	1	1	4	2	0	1	4	1
	%	2.1	2.5	0.0	1.6	3.0	2.7	2.2	0.0	3.1	1.4	0.8

	420	213	15	17	8	39	24	4	9	64	27
Other Frequency	420	213	15	17	8	39	24	4	9	64	27
%	23.2	22.3	25.0	27.9	24.2	26.0	26.7	26.7	28.1	21.9	22.3
NA Frequency	419	185	12	26	6	46	25	6	9	74	30
%	23.1	19.3	20.0	42.6	18.2	30.7	27.8	40.0	28.1	25.3	24.8

B4-2 The length of his/her tenure of office as trade union chairman

	420	213	15	17	8	39	24	4	9	64	27
Shorter than 1 year Frequency	790	384	22	45	19	67	42	7	16	129	59
%	43.6	40.1	36.7	73.8	57.6	44.7	46.7	46.7	50.0	44.2	48.8
1 Frequency	52	25	2	2	1	8	2	2	0	9	1
%	2.9	2.6	3.3	3.3	3.0	5.3	2.2	13.3	0.0	3.1	0.8
2 Frequency	104	59	2	3	1	8	8	0	0	20	3
%	5.7	6.2	3.3	4.9	3.0	5.3	8.9	0.0	0.0	6.8	2.5
3 Frequency	160	71	9	4	8	9	3	2	3	40	11
%	8.8	7.4	15.0	6.6	24.2	6.0	3.3	13.3	9.4	13.7	11
4 Frequency	112	58	6	1	1	8	9	1	4	18	6
%	6.2	6.1	10.0	1.6	3.0	5.3	10.0	6.7	12.5	6.2	5.0
5 Frequency	86	45	2	0	0	9	4	0	2	12	12
%	4.7	4.7	3.3	0.0	0.0	6.0	4.4	0.0	6.3	4.1	9.9
6 Frequency	49	28	2	1	1	4	0	1	1	8	3
%	2.7	2.9	3.3	1.6	3.0	2.7	0.0	6.7	3.1	2.7	2.5
7 Frequency	42	21	1	0	1	5	2	0	1	6	5
%	2.3	2.2	1.7	0.0	3.0	3.3	2.2	0.0	3.1	2.1	4.1
8 Frequency	29	19	0	0	0	1	1	0	0	6	2
%	1.6	2.0	0.0	0.0	0.0	0.7	1.1	0.0	0.0	2.1	1.7
9 Frequency	24	15	1	1	0	2	0	0	0	5	0
%	1.3	1.6	1.7	1.6	0.0	1.3	0.0	0.0	0.0	1.7	0.0
10 Frequency	24	16	1	0	0	2	1	2	0	2	0
%	1.3	1.7	1.7	0.0	0.0	1.3	1.1	13.3	0.0	0.7	0.0
11 Frequency	18	10	1	0	0	1	1	0	0	4	1
%	1.0	1.0	1.7	0.0	0.0	0.7	1.1	0.0	0.0	1.4	0.8
12 Frequency	19	11	0	0	0	1	1	0	0	3	3
%	1.0	1.1	0.0	0.0	0.0	0.7	1.1	0.0	0.0	1.0	2.5

Ownership form of your enterprise

		Sum	State-owned/ State-holding enterprise	Collective-owned enterprise	Private enterprise	Cooperative enterprise	Limited liability corporation	Share Holding Corporation Ltd	Enterprise with Funds from Hong Kong, Macao and Taiwan	Foreign funded enterprise	Others	NA
13	Frequency	9	5	0	0	0	1	0	0	1	0	2
	%	0.5	0.5	0.0	0.0	0.0	0.7	0.0	0.0	3.1	0.0	1.7
14	Frequency	8	6	0	0	0	0	0	0	0	2	0
	%	0.4	0.6	0.0	0.0	0.0	0.0	0.0	0.0	0.0	0.7	0.0
15	Frequency	3	2	0	0	0	0	0	0	0	1	0
	%	0.2	0.2	0.0	0.0	0.0	0.0	0.0	0.0	0.0	0.3	0.0
longer than 15	Frequency	23	11	4	0	0	1	0	0	0	6	1
	%	1.5	1.1	6.8	0.0	0.0	0.7	0.0	0.0	0.0	1.9	0.8
NA	Frequency	259	171	7	4	1	23	16	0	4	21	12
	%	14.3	17.9	11.7	6.6	3.0	15.3	17.8	0.0	12.5	7.2	9.9

B4-3 His/her current duty

		Sum	State-owned/ State-holding enterprise	Collective-owned enterprise	Private enterprise	Cooperative enterprise	Limited liability corporation	Share Holding Corporation Ltd	Enterprise with Funds from Hong Kong, Macao and Taiwan	Foreign funded enterprise	Others	NA
Middle class cadre (Director, Section, Department)	Frequency	159	80	4	4	2	13	6	2	0	39	9
	%	8.8	8.4	6.7	6.6	6.1	8.7	6.7	13.3	0.0	13.4	7.4
Factory manager, President	Frequency	98	61	4	2	4	8	5	1	0	9	4
	%	5.4	6.4	6.7	3.3	12.1	5.3	5.6	6.7	0.0	3.1	3.3
Trade Unions Chairman,	Frequency	69	39	3	3	0	4	8	0	0	10	2
	%	3.8	4.1	5.0	4.9	0.0	2.7	8.9	0.0	0.0	3.4	1.7
Teacher	Frequency	2	2	0	0	0	0	0	0	0	0	0
	%	0.1	0.2	0.0	0.0	0.0	0.0	0.0	0.0	0.0	0.0	0.0
CCP Secretary	Frequency	133	80	7	2	0	9	5	2	2	18	8
	%	7.3	8.4	11.7	3.3	0.0	6.0	5.6	13.3	6.3	6.2	6.6
Township Cadre	Frequency	0	0	0	0	0	0	0	0	0	0	0
	%	0.0	0.0	0.0	0.0	0.0	0.0	0.0	0.0	0.0	0.0	0.0

Township Governor	Frequency	1	0	0	0	0	0	0	0	0	1	0
	%	0.1	0.0	0.0	0.0	0.0	0.0	0.0	0.0	0.0	0.3	0.0
Director of Department (prefecture, township)	Frequency	13	8	0	0	0	0	0	0	0	5	0
	%	0.7	0.8	0.0	0.0	0.0	0.0	0.0	0.0	0.0	1.7	0.0
Vice-secretary of detached factory	Frequency	0	0	0	0	0	0	0	0	0	0	0
	%	0.0	0.0	0.0	0.0	0.0	0.0	0.0	0.0	0.0	0.0	0.0
CCP Secretary of Administrative Affairs	Frequency	4	2	0	0	0	0	0	0	0	2	0
	%	0.2	0.2	0.0	0.0	0.0	0.0	0.0	0.0	0.0	0.7	0.0
Chief of Security Department	Frequency	11	7	0	0	1	1	0	0	1	1	1
	%	0.6	0.7	0.0	0.0	0.7	1.1	0.0	0.0	0.0	0.3	0.8
Workers and Staffs	Frequency	9	2	0	1	0	1	1	0	1	3	1
	%	0.5	0.2	0.0	3.0	0.0	1.1	6.7	0.0	0.0	1.0	0.8
Financial Manager	Frequency	0	0	0	0	0	0	0	0	0	0	0
	%	0.0	0.0	0.0	0.0	0.0	0.0	0.0	0.0	0.0	0.0	0.0
Labour and Security Supervisor	Frequency	0	0	0	0	0	0	0	0	0	0	0
	%	0.0	0.0	0.0	0.0	0.0	0.0	0.0	0.0	0.0	0.0	0.0
Statistic Staff	Frequency	1	0	0	0	1	0	0	0	0	0	0
	%	0.1	0.0	0.0	0.0	0.7	0.0	0.0	0.0	0.0	0.0	0.0
Trade Union Cadre, Member of Committee	Frequency	3	3	0	0	0	0	0	0	0	0	0
	%	0.2	0.3	0.0	0.0	0.0	0.0	0.0	0.0	0.0	0.0	0.0
Accountant	Frequency	1	0	0	1	0	0	0	0	0	0	0
	%	0.1	0.0	0.0	3.0	0.0	0.0	0.0	0.0	0.0	0.0	0.0
Lower Staff	Frequency	11	5	0	0	1	2	0	0	0	1	0
	%	0.6	0.5	0.0	0.0	0.7	2.2	0.0	0.0	0.0	0.3	0.0
Female Cadre	Frequency	1	0	2	0	0	0	0	0	0	1	0
	%	0.1	0.0	3.3	0.0	0.0	0.0	0.0	0.0	0.0	0.3	0.0
Secretary of Chinese Communist Youth League	Frequency	1	0	0	0	0	0	0	0	0	0	1
	%	0.1	0.0	0.0	0.0	0.0	0.0	0.0	0.0	0.0	0.0	0.8

Ownership form of your enterprise

	Sum	State-owned/ State-holding enterprise	Collective-owned enterprise	Private enterprise	Cooperative enterprise	Limited liability corporation	Share Holding Corporation Ltd	Enterprise with Funds from Hong Kong, Macao and Taiwan	Foreign funded enterprise	Others	NA
Chief of Police box Frequency	0	0	0	0	0	0	0	0	0	0	0
%	0.0	0.0	0.0	0.0	0.0	0.0	0.0	0.0	0.0	0.0	0.0
Doctor Frequency	1	0	0	0	0	0	0	0	0	1	0
%	0.1	0.0	0.0	0.0	0.0	0.0	0.0	0.0	0.0	0.3	0.0
Soldier Frequency	0	0	0	0	0	0	0	0	0	0	0
%	0.0	0.0	0.0	0.0	0.0	0.0	0.0	0.0	0.0	0.0	0.0
Principal Frequency	5	1	0	0	0	0	0	0	0	3	1
%	0.3	0.1	0.0	0.0	0.0	0.0	0.0	0.0	0.0	1.0	0.8
NA Frequency	1288	667	42	48	25	113	62	9	30	198	94
%	71.1	69.7	70.0	78.7	75.8	75.3	68.9	60.0	93.8	67.8	77.7

B5 Questions about federation and representation system

B5-1 Whether or not having ever sent delegates in the next higher-level congress of trade unions

	Sum	State-owned/ State-holding enterprise	Collective-owned enterprise	Private enterprise	Cooperative enterprise	Limited liability corporation	Share Holding Corporation Ltd	Enterprise with Funds from Hong Kong, Macao and Taiwan	Foreign funded enterprise	Others	NA
1 Has sent Frequency	1120	648	35	25	16	102	59	8	19	146	62
%	61.8	67.7	58.3	41.0	48.5	68.0	65.6	53.3	59.4	50.0	51.2
2 Has not sent Frequency	346	154	14	21	9	27	17	5	7	66	26
%	19.1	16.1	23.3	34.4	27.3	18.0	18.9	33.3	21.9	22.6	21.5
NA Frequency	345	155	11	15	8	21	14	2	6	80	33
%	19.1	16.2	18.3	24.6	24.2	14.0	15.6	13.3	18.8	27.4	27.3

(If you chose 1 in B5-1) the year when the delegates began to be sent

	Sum	State-owned/ State-holding enterprise	Collective-owned enterprise	Private enterprise	Cooperative enterprise	Limited liability corporation	Share Holding Corporation Ltd	Enterprise with Funds from Hong Kong, Macao and Taiwan	Foreign funded enterprise	Others	NA
1949 Frequency	1	0	0	0	0	1	0	0	0	0	0
%	0.1	0.0	0.0	0.0	0.0	1.0	0.0	0.0	0.0	0.0	0.0
1950–1959 Frequency	8	6	0	0	0	1	1	0	0	0	0
%	0.7	0.9	0.0	0.0	0.0	1.0	1.7	0.0	0.0	0.0	0.0

Year		C1	C2	C3	C4	C5	C6	C7	C8	C9	C10
1960–1969	Frequency	5	3	1	0	1	0	0	0	0	0
	%	0.4	0.5	2.9	0.0	1.0	0.0	0.0	0.0	0.0	0.0
1970–1979	Frequency	17	10	1	0	4	1	0	0	1	0
	%	1.5	1.5	2.9	0.0	3.9	1.7	0.0	0.0	0.7	0.0
1980–1989	Frequency	74	50	6	0	4	0	0	1	12	1
	%	6.6	7.7	17.1	0.0	3.9	0.0	0.0	5.3	8.2	1.6
1990	Frequency	12	2	1	0	2	1	0	0	3	3
	%	1.1	0.3	2.9	0.0	2.0	1.7	0.0	0.0	2.1	4.8
1991	Frequency	13	9	0	0	1	0	0	1	1	1
	%	1.2	1.4	0.0	0.0	1.0	0.0	0.0	5.3	0.7	1.6
1992	Frequency	15	8	1	0	2	0	0	0	3	0
	%	1.3	1.2	2.9	0.0	2.0	0.0	0.0	0.0	2.1	0.0
1993	Frequency	11	8	0	1	1	1	0	0	0	1
	%	1.0	1.2	0.0	6.3	1.0	1.7	0.0	0.0	0.0	1.6
1994	Frequency	7	6	0	0	0	0	0	0	0	0
	%	0.6	0.9	0.0	0.0	0.0	0.0	0.0	0.0	0.0	0.0
1995	Frequency	6	3	0	0	0	0	0	0	1	0
	%	0.5	0.5	0.0	1	0.0	0.0	0.0	0.0	0.7	0.0
1996	Frequency	19	10	0	1	5	0	0	1	0	3
	%	1.7	1.5	0.0	6.3	4.9	0.0	0.0	5.3	0.0	4.8
1997	Frequency	19	14	0	0	0	0	0	0	2	3
	%	1.7	2.2	0.0	0.0	0.0	0.0	0.0	0.0	1.4	3
1998	Frequency	30	12	3	0	3	3	0	1	6	2
	%	2.7	1.9	8.6	0.0	2.9	5.1	0.0	5.3	4.1	3.2
1999	Frequency	28	10	1	2	5	6	1	0	1	2
	%	2.5	1.5	2.9	12.5	4.9	10.2	12.5	0.0	0.7	3.2
2000	Frequency	56	23	1	1	6	2	0	1	16	5
	%	5.0	3.5	2.9	6.3	5.9	3.4	0.0	5.3	11.0	8.1
2001	Frequency	52	24	1	1	8	3	0	0	11	3
	%	4.6	3.7	2.9	6.3	7.8	5.1	0.0	0.0	7.5	4.8
2002	Frequency	77	32	4	1	11	6	2	1	16	2
	%	6.9	4.9	11.4	6.3	10.8	10.2	25.0	5.3	11.0	3.2
2003	Frequency	110	46	1	3	7	10	0	5	19	11
	%	9.8	7.1	2.9	18.8	6.9	16.9	0.0	26.3	13.0	17.7

Ownership form of your enterprise

	Sum	State-owned/State-holding enterprise	Collective-owned enterprise	Private enterprise	Cooperative enterprise	Limited liability corporation	Share Holding Corporation Ltd	Enterprise with Funds from Hong Kong, Macao and Taiwan	Foreign funded enterprise	Others	NA
2004 Frequency	33	19	1	2	1	3	1	1	0	2	3
%	2.9	2.9	2.9	8.0	6.3	2.9	1.7	12.5	0.0	1.4	4.8
NA Frequency	527	353	13	9	5	37	24	4	8	52	22
%	47.1	54.5	37.1	36.0	31.3	36.3	40.7	50.0	42.1	35.6	35.5

B5-2 Agree or disagree with federation and representation system

	Sum	State-owned/State-holding enterprise	Collective-owned enterprise	Private enterprise	Cooperative enterprise	Limited liability corporation	Share Holding Corporation Ltd	Enterprise with Funds from Hong Kong, Macao and Taiwan	Foreign funded enterprise	Others	NA
Agree Frequency	1076	582	36	34	24	90	53	7	20	168	62
%	59.4	60.8	60.0	55.7	72.7	60.0	58.9	46.7	62.5	57.7	51.2
Disagree Frequency	129	62	5	7	0	10	9	2	2	23	9
%	7.1	6.5	8.3	11.5	0.0	6.7	10.0	13.3	6.3	7.9	7.4
NA Frequency	606	313	19	20	9	50	28	6	10	101	50
%	33.5	32.7	31.7	32.8	27.3	33.3	31.1	40.0	31.3	34.6	41.3

B5-3 Agree or disagree with the following opinions
1 Benefits for enforcing higher-level unions' policy lines and decisions at primary level

	Sum	State-owned/State-holding enterprise	Collective-owned enterprise	Private enterprise	Cooperative enterprise	Limited liability corporation	Share Holding Corporation Ltd	Enterprise with Funds from Hong Kong, Macao and Taiwan	Foreign funded enterprise	Others	NA
Agree Frequency	1150	612	45	37	23	100	57	11	20	180	65
%	63.5	63.9	75.0	60.7	69.7	66.7	63.3	73.3	62.5	61.6	53.7
Disagree Frequency	49	22	1	2	0	5	6	0	1	8	4
%	2.7	2.3	1.7	3.3	0.0	3.3	6.7	0.0	3.1	2.7	3.3
NA Frequency	612	323	14	22	10	45	27	4	11	104	52
%	33.8	33.8	23.3	36.1	30.3	30.0	30.0	26.7	34.4	35.6	43.0

2 Benefits for reporting the problems encountered by primary trade unions on a daily basis to the higher-level trade unions

Agree	Frequency	1088	588	41	33	20	90	53	12	20	172	59
	%	60.1	61.4	68.3	54.1	60.6	60.0	58.9	80.0	62.5	58.9	48.8
Disagree	Frequency	58	24	1	3	1	6	7	0	1	9	6
	%	3.2	2.5	1.7	4.9	3.0	4.0	7.8	0.0	3.1	3.1	5.0
NA	Frequency	665	345	18	25	12	54	30	3	11	111	56
	%	36.7	36.1	30.0	41.0	36.4	36.0	33.3	20.0	34.4	38.0	46.3

3 Benefits for strengthening the vertical leadership structure between higher- and lower-level trade unions, enhancing the trade union's organizational power

Agree	Frequency	1053	569	39	31	22	88	54	12	19	165	54
	%	58.1	59.5	65.0	50.8	66.7	58.7	60.0	80.0	59.4	56.5	44.6
Disagree	Frequency	70	34	3	1	0	5	6	0	2	12	7
	%	3.9	3.6	5.0	1.6	0.0	3.3	6.7	0.0	6.3	4.1	5.8
NA	Frequency	688	354	18	29	11	57	30	3	11	115	60
	%	38.0	37.0	30.0	47.5	33.3	38.0	33.3	20.0	34.4	39.4	49.6

4 Even if attended higher-level congress of trade unions, it would be difficult to make individual opinions be reflected into decisions

Agree	Frequency	419	220	18	17	8	39	20	5	10	59	23
	%	23.1	23.0	30.0	27.9	24.2	26.0	22.2	33.3	31.3	20.2	19.0
Disagree	Frequency	514	279	16	12	10	39	30	6	10	81	31
	%	28.4	29.2	26.7	19.7	30.3	26.0	33.3	40.0	31.3	27.7	25.6
NA	Frequency	878	458	26	32	15	72	40	4	12	152	67
	%	48.5	47.9	43.3	52.5	45.5	48.0	44.4	26.7	37.5	52.1	55.4

5 Because each primary union faces different problems, solutions could only be found by each primary union itself

Ownership form of your enterprise

		Sum	State-owned/ State-holding enterprise	Collective-owned enterprise	Private enterprise	Cooperative enterprise	Limited liability corporation	Share Holding Corporation Ltd	Enterprise with Funds from Hong Kong, Macao and Taiwan	Foreign funded enterprise	Others	NA
Agree	Frequency	533	271	23	17	6	50	27	4	9	85	41
	%	29.4	28.3	38.3	27.9	18.2	33.3	30.0	26.7	28.1	29.1	33.9
Disagree	Frequency	434	238	12	10	13	31	27	7	10	67	19
	%	24.0	24.9	20.0	16.4	39.4	20.7	30.0	46.7	31.3	22.9	15.7
NA	Frequency	844	448	25	34	14	69	36	4	13	140	61
	%	46.6	46.8	41.7	55.7	42.4	46.0	40.0	26.7	40.6	47.9	50.4

6 If the primary trade union has excessively close relationships with higher-level trade unions, it could harm the Party-Administration-Union coordination at primary level

		Sum	State-owned/ State-holding enterprise	Collective-owned enterprise	Private enterprise	Cooperative enterprise	Limited liability corporation	Share Holding Corporation Ltd	Enterprise with Funds from Hong Kong, Macao and Taiwan	Foreign funded enterprise	Others	NA
Agree	Frequency	188	102	14	9	3	13	6	4	5	24	8
	%	10.4	10.7	23.3	14.8	9.1	8.7	6.7	26.7	15.6	8.2	6.6
Disagree	Frequency	725	386	19	20	14	61	42	7	13	119	44
	%	40.0	40.3	31.7	32.8	42.4	40.7	46.7	46.7	40.6	40.8	36.4
NA	Frequency	898	469	27	32	16	76	42	4	14	149	69
	%	49.6	49.0	45.0	52.5	48.5	50.7	46.7	26.7	43.8	51.0	57.0

B6-1 Questions about the treatment of the trade union chairman necessary or not necessary 'Trade Union Chairman Fund' or 'Special Fund of Trade Union Chairman'

1 Necessary	Frequency	1341	725	38	41	27	110	68	12	24	217	79
	%	74.0	75.8	63.3	67.2	81.8	73.3	75.6	80.0	75.0	74.3	65.3
2 Not necessary	Frequency	275	137	14	14	2	26	17	1	4	39	21
	%	15.2	14.3	23.3	23.0	6.1	17.3	18.9	6.7	12.5	13.4	17.4
NA	Frequency	195	95	8	6	4	14	5	2	4	36	21
	%	10.8	9.9	13.3	9.8	12.1	9.3	5.6	13.3	12.5	12.3	17.4

B6-1-2 (If you chose 1 in B6-1-1) the reason

Have ever experienced living difficulties	Frequency	66	31	0	2	0	3	4	3	1	10	12
	%	4.9	4.3	0.0	4.9	0.0	2.7	5.9	25.0	4.2	4.6	15.2
Although have never experienced similar living difficulties described above, this policy is necessary to be devoted to union activities without anxiety	Frequency	1085	584	31	33	23	95	56	9	22	177	55
	%	80.9	80.6	81.6	80.5	85.2	86.4	82.4	75.0	91.7	81.6	69.6
Other reasons	Frequency	101	52	5	4	4	7	3	0	1	21	4
	%	7.5	7.2	13.2	9.8	14.8	6.4	4.4	0.0	4.2	9.7	5.1
NA	Frequency	89	58	2	2	0	5	5	0	0	9	8
	%	6.6	8.0	5.3	4.9	0.0	4.5	7.4	0.0	0.0	4.1	10.1

Part 4: Questions about the financial situation of previous fiscal year

C1-1 Whether or not having the trade union's own account for managing fund independently

| | | Ownership form of your enterprise | | | | | | | Enterprise with Funds from Hong Kong, Macao and Taiwan | Foreign funded enterprise | Others | NA |
		Sum	State-owned/ State-holding enterprise	Collective-owned enterprise	Private enterprise	Cooperative enterprise	Limited liability corporation	Share Holding Corporation Ltd				
Have	Frequency	1355	775	43	29	14	115	68	9	25	199	78
	%	74.8	81.0	71.7	47.5	42.4	76.7	75.6	60.0	78.1	68.2	64.5
Not have	Frequency	334	128	12	24	15	25	16	3	7	72	32
	%	18.4	13.4	20.0	39.3	45.5	16.7	17.8	20.0	21.9	24.7	26.4
NA	Frequency	122	54	5	8	4	10	6	3	0	21	11
	%	6.7	5.6	8.3	13.1	12.1	6.7	6.7	20.0	0.0	7.2	9.1

C1-2 Percentage of the following items in total revenue

1. Membership dues paid by union members

		Sum	State-owned/ State-holding enterprise	Collective-owned enterprise	Private enterprise	Cooperative enterprise	Limited liability corporation	Share Holding Corporation Ltd	Enterprise with Funds from Hong Kong, Macao and Taiwan	Foreign funded enterprise	Others	NA
0	Frequency	433	216	15	9	2	46	17	2	5	84	37
	%	23.9	22.6	25.0	14.8	6.1	30.7	18.9	13.3	15.6	28.8	30.6
1–10	Frequency	580	329	26	9	8	49	34	5	12	81	27
	%	32.0	34.4	43.3	14.8	24.2	32.7	37.8	33.3	37.5	27.7	22.3
11–20	Frequency	148	80	2	7	3	10	8	1	3	28	6
	%	8.2	8.4	3.3	11.5	9.1	6.7	8.9	6.7	9.4	9.6	5.0
21–30	Frequency	65	31	0	1	1	6	4	0	1	14	7
	%	3.6	3.2	0.0	1.6	3.0	4.0	4.4	0.0	3.1	4.8	5.8
31–40	Frequency	24	12	1	0	0	2	2	0	0	4	3
	%	1.3	1.3	1.7	0.0	0.0	1.3	2.2	0.0	0.0	1.4	2.5
41–50	Frequency	19	7	2	0	0	2	2	1	0	4	1
	%	1.0	0.7	3.3	0.0	0.0	1.3	2.2	6.7	0.0	1.4	0.8

51–60	Frequency	4	1	0	1	0	0	0	0	0	1	1
	%	0.2	0.1	0.0	1.6	0.0	0.0	0.0	0.0	0.0	0.3	0.8
61–70	Frequency	6	3	0	0	0	1	0	0	0	1	1
	%	0.3	0.3	0.0	0.0	0.0	0.7	0.0	0.0	0.0	0.3	1
71–80	Frequency	10	6	2	0	0	0	0	0	0	2	1
	%	0.6	0.6	3.3	0.0	0.0	0.0	0.0	0.0	0.0	0.7	0.8
81–90	Frequency	4	3	0	0	0	0	1	0	0	0	0
	%	0.2	0.3	0.0	0.0	0.0	0.0	1.1	0.0	0.0	0.0	0.0
91–100	Frequency	67	30	2	2	1	5	5	0	1	11	10
	%	3.7	3.1	3.3	3.3	3.0	3.3	5.6	0.0	3.1	3.8	8.3
NA	Frequency	451	239	10	32	18	29	17	6	10	62	28
	%	24.9	25.0	16.7	52.5	54.5	19.3	18.9	40.0	31.3	21.2	23.1

2. Contribution allocated by the enterprise, institution or government department where the trade union is established

0	Frequency	410	201	14	7	1	41	18	2	5	78	43
	%	22.6	21.0	23.3	11.5	3.0	27.3	20.0	13.3	15.6	26.7	35.5
1–10	Frequency	195	104	9	4	2	19	10	2	1	31	13
	%	10.8	10.9	15.0	6.6	6.1	12.7	11.1	13.3	3.1	10.6	10.7
11–20	Frequency	27	12	2	1	2	1	0	0	1	7	1
	%	1.5	1.3	3.3	1.6	6.1	0.7	0.0	0.0	3.1	2.4	0.8
21–30	Frequency	15	10	0	0	0	1	0	1	0	2	1
	%	0.8	1.0	0.0	0.0	0.0	0.7	0.0	6.7	0.0	0.7	0.8
31–40	Frequency	50	23	2	1	1	2	4	1	3	7	6
	%	2.8	2.4	3.3	1.6	3.0	1.3	4.4	6.7	9.4	2.4	5.0
41–50	Frequency	31	12	2	0	0	6	3	0	0	5	3
	%	1.7	1.3	3.3	0.0	0.0	4.0	3.3	0.0	0.0	1.7	2.5
51–60	Frequency	35	15	1	1	3	3	3	1	0	6	2
	%	1.9	1.6	1.7	1.6	9.1	2.0	3.3	6.7	0.0	2.1	1.7
61–70	Frequency	71	38	1	1	0	4	3	0	1	16	7
	%	3.9	4.0	1.7	1.6	0.0	2.7	3.3	0.0	3.1	5.5	5.8
71–80	Frequency	100	52	2	6	2	7	5	0	2	17	7
	%	5.5	5.4	3.3	9.8	6.1	4.7	5.6	0.0	6.3	5.8	5.8
81–90	Frequency	181	104	4	3	2	18	12	2	6	27	3
	%	10.0	10.9	6.7	4.9	6.1	12.0	13.3	13.3	18.8	9.2	2.5

Ownership form of your enterprise

		State-owned/ State-holding enterprise	Collective-owned enterprise	Private enterprise	Cooperative enterprise	Limited liability corporation	Share Holding Corporation Ltd	Enterprise with Funds from Hong Kong, Macao and Taiwan	Foreign funded enterprise	Others	NA
	Sum										
91–100	Frequency	134	13	6	3	16	14	0	2	30	6
	224										
%	12.4	14.0	21.7	9.8	9.1	10.7	15.6	0.0	6.3	10.3	5.0
NA	Frequency	252	10	31	17	32	18	6	11	66	29
	472										
%	26.1	26.3	16.7	50.8	51.5	21.3	20.0	40.0	34.4	22.6	24.0

3. Incomes derived from the trade union's own activities

		State-owned/ State-holding enterprise	Collective-owned enterprise	Private enterprise	Cooperative enterprise	Limited liability corporation	Share Holding Corporation Ltd	Enterprise with Funds from Hong Kong, Macao and Taiwan	Foreign funded enterprise	Others	NA
0	Frequency	441	36	19	4	81	40	2	12	152	70
	857										
%	47.3	46.1	60.0	31.1	12.1	54.0	44.4	13.3	37.5	52.1	57.9
1–10	Frequency	44	2	0	1	1	3	2	3	12	9
	77										
%	4.3	4.6	3.3	0.0	3.0	0.7	3.3	13.3	9.4	4.1	7.4
11–20	Frequency	9	0	0	0	2	0	1	0	3	2
	17										
%	0.9	0.9	0.0	0.0	0.0	1.3	0.0	6.7	0.0	1.0	1.7
21–30	Frequency	8	0	0	0	1	1	0	0	2	1
	13										
%	0.7	0.8	0.0	0.0	0.0	0.7	1.1	0.0	0.0	0.7	0.8
31–40	Frequency	4	1	0	1	1	1	0	0	0	1
	9										
%	0.5	0.4	1.7	0.0	3.0	0.7	1.1	0.0	0.0	0.0	0.8
41–50	Frequency	3	1	0	1	0	0	0	0	2	0
	7										
%	0.4	0.3	1.7	0.0	3.0	0.0	0.0	0.0	0.0	0.7	0.0
51–60	Frequency	6	0	0	0	1	0	0	1	5	0
	13										
%	0.7	0.6	0.0	0.0	0.0	0.7	0.0	0.0	3.1	1.7	0.0
61–70	Frequency	1	0	0	0	0	0	0	0	1	0
	2										
%	0.1	0.1	0.0	0.0	0.0	0.0	0.0	0.0	0.0	0.3	0.0
71–80	Frequency	4	0	0	0	0	3	0	0	1	1
	9										
%	0.5	0.4	0.0	0.0	0.0	0.0	3.3	0.0	0.0	0.3	0.8

81–90	Frequency	0	0	0	0	0	0	0	0	0	0	0
	%	0.0	0.0	0.0	0.0	0.0	0.0	0.0	0.0	0.0	0.0	0.0
91–100	Frequency	7	3	0	0	1	0	0	0	0	2	1
	%	0.4	0.3	0.0	0.0	3.0	0.0	0.0	0.0	0.0	0.7	0.8
NA	Frequency	800	434	20	42	25	63	42	10	16	112	36
	%	44.2	45.4	33.3	68.9	75.8	42.0	46.7	66.7	50.0	38.4	29.8

4. Other incomes

0	Frequency	857	446	36	18	5	80	39	3	13	146	71
	%	47.3	46.6	60.0	29.5	15.2	53.3	43.3	20.0	40.6	50.0	58.7
1–10	Frequency	74	37	0	1	0	6	5	0	2	19	4
	%	4.1	3.9	0.0	1.6	0.0	4.0	5.6	0.0	6.3	6.5	3.3
11–20	Frequency	17	9	2	0	0	1	2	1	0	2	0
	%	0.9	0.9	3.3	0.0	0.0	0.7	2.2	6.7	0.0	0.7	0.0
21–30	Frequency	11	5	0	1	0	1	1	0	0	2	1
	%	0.6	0.5	0.0	1.6	0.0	0.7	1.1	0.0	0.0	0.7	0.8
31–40	Frequency	10	2	1	0	0	2	0	1	0	3	1
	%	0.6	0.2	1.7	0.0	0.0	1.3	0.0	6.7	0.0	1.0	0.8
41–50	Frequency	12	3	1	0	0	2	3	0	0	1	2
	%	0.7	0.3	1.7	0.0	0.0	1.3	3.3	0.0	0.0	0.3	1.7
51–60	Frequency	6	3	0	0	0	0	0	0	0	0	3
	%	0.3	0.3	0.0	0.0	0.0	0.0	0.0	0.0	0.0	0.0	2.5
61–70	Frequency	5	2	0	0	0	1	0	0	0	1	1
	%	0.3	0.2	0.0	0.0	0.0	0.7	0.0	0.0	0.0	0.3	0.8
71–80	Frequency	8	4	0	0	0	0	1	0	0	3	0
	%	0.4	0.4	0.0	0.0	0.0	0.0	1.1	0.0	0.0	1.0	0.0
81–90	Frequency	6	2	0	0	0	0	1	0	1	2	0
	%	0.3	0.2	0.0	0.0	0.0	0.0	1.1	0.0	3.1	0.7	0.0
91–100	Frequency	3	1	0	0	0	0	1	0	0	1	0
	%	0.2	0.1	0.0	0.0	0.0	0.0	1.1	0.0	0.0	0.3	0.0
NA	Frequency	802	443	20	41	28	57	37	10	16	112	38
	%	44.3	46.3	33.3	67.2	84.8	38.0	41.1	66.7	50.0	38.4	31.4

C1-3 Necessary or not to get the approval of administrative manager of work unit in using the union funds

			Sum	State-owned/ State-holding enterprise	Collective-owned enterprise	Private enterprise	Cooperative enterprise	Limited liability corporation	Share Holding Corporation Ltd	Enterprise with Funds from Hong Kong, Macao and Taiwan	Foreign funded enterprise	Others	NA
Necessary	Frequency		515	230	19	32	20	36	24	4	5	94	51
	%		28.4	24.0	31.7	52.5	60.6	24.0	26.7	26.7	15.6	32.2	42.1
Not necessary	Frequency		1116	657	35	17	10	101	63	8	22	148	55
	%		61.6	68.7	58.3	27.9	30.3	67.3	70.0	53.3	68.8	50.7	45.5
NA	Frequency		180	70	6	12	3	13	3	3	5	50	15
	%		9.9	7.3	10.0	19.7	9.1	8.7	3.3	20.0	15.6	17.1	12.4

C1-4 Whether or not having ever experienced the situation of nondistinctiveness of union expense and administrative expense

		Sum	State-owned/ State-holding enterprise	Collective-owned enterprise	Private enterprise	Cooperative enterprise	Limited liability corporation	Share Holding Corporation Ltd	Enterprise with Funds from Hong Kong, Macao and Taiwan	Foreign funded enterprise	Others	NA
Have experienced	Frequency	393	213	7	19	11	30	22	0	4	58	29
	%	21.7	22.3	11.7	31.1	33.3	20.0	24.4	0.0	12.5	19.9	24.0
Have not experienced	Frequency	1197	652	48	30	18	105	64	12	25	176	67
	%	66.1	68.1	80.0	49.2	54.5	70.0	71.1	80.0	78.1	60.3	55.4
NA	Frequency	221	92	5	12	4	15	4	3	3	58	25
	%	12.2	9.6	8.3	19.7	12.1	10.0	4.4	20.0	9.4	19.9	20.7

C1-5 Whether or not facing revenue shortfall in conducting union activities

		Sum	State-owned/ State-holding enterprise	Collective-owned enterprise	Private enterprise	Cooperative enterprise	Limited liability corporation	Share Holding Corporation Ltd	Enterprise with Funds from Hong Kong, Macao and Taiwan	Foreign funded enterprise	Others	NA
Revenue shortfall is serious	Frequency	306	142	14	7	4	20	13	0	4	68	34
	%	16.9	14.8	23.3	11.5	12.1	13.3	14.4	0.0	12.5	23.3	28.1
Face revenue shortfall	Frequency	780	415	22	23	16	61	39	2	16	133	53
	%	43.1	43.4	36.7	37.7	48.5	40.7	43.3	13.3	50.0	45.5	43.8

Not face revenue shortfall so much	Frequency	517	301	19	21	7	50	29	8	9	55	18
	%	28.5	31.5	31.7	34.4	21.2	33.3	32.2	53.3	28.1	18.8	14.9
Not face revenue shortfall at all	Frequency	95	50	3	5	3	12	7	3	1	7	4
	%	5.2	5.2	5.0	8.2	9.1	8.0	7.8	20.0	3.1	2.4	3.3
NA	Frequency	113	49	2	5	3	7	2	2	2	29	12
	%	6.2	5.1	3.3	8.2	9.1	4.7	2.2	13.3	6.3	9.9	9.9

C2-1 The way to collect the membership dues

Deduction from the payroll	Frequency	759	393	28	31	13	57	38	9	17	136	37
	%	41.9	41.1	46.7	50.8	39.4	38.0	42.2	60.0	53.1	46.6	30.6
Direct payment by union members	Frequency	835	487	23	15	12	75	43	2	11	106	61
	%	46.1	50.9	38.3	24.6	36.4	50.0	47.8	13.3	34.4	36.3	50.4
Other means	Frequency	97	40	4	9	3	7	5	2	2	18	7
	%	5.4	4.2	6.7	14.8	9.1	4.7	5.6	13.3	6.3	6.2	5.8
NA	Frequency	120	37	5	6	5	11	4	2	2	32	16
	%	6.6	3.9	8.3	9.8	15.2	7.3	4.4	13.3	6.3	11.0	13.2

C2-2 The condition of union members' non-payment of the membership dues

Very serious	Frequency	38	17	4	0	0	2	2	0	0	9	4
	%	2.1	1.8	6.7	0.0	0.0	1.3	2.2	0.0	0.0	3.1	3.3
Relatively serious	Frequency	56	21	5	5	4	5	4	0	1	6	5
	%	3.1	2.2	8.3	8.2	12.1	3.3	4.4	0.0	3.1	2.1	4.1
The problem exists, but not very serious	Frequency	306	184	9	10	6	34	13	0	2	32	16
	%	16.9	19.2	15.0	16.4	18.2	22.7	14.4	0.0	6.3	11.0	13.2
The problem does not exist	Frequency	1238	679	39	33	17	97	66	13	24	200	70
	%	68.4	71.0	65.0	54.1	51.5	64.7	73.3	86.7	75.0	68.5	57.9
NA	Frequency	173	56	3	13	6	12	5	2	5	45	26
	%	9.6	5.9	5.0	21.3	18.2	8.0	5.6	13.3	15.6	15.4	21.5

C3-1 The condition of the work units' non-payment of the contribution of the trade union expense

		Ownership form of your enterprise							Enterprise with Funds from Hong Kong, Macao and Taiwan	Foreign funded enterprise	Others	NA
	Sum	State-owned/ State-holding enterprise	Collective-owned enterprise	Private enterprise	Cooperative enterprise	Limited liability corporation	Share Holding Corporation Ltd					
Very serious — Frequency	51	23	6	1	0	2	3	1	0	10	5	
%	2.8	2.4	10.0	1.6	0.0	1.3	3.3	6.7	0.0	3.4	4.1	
Relatively serious — Frequency	118	60	5	3	2	13	7	0	1	14	13	
%	6.5	6.3	8.3	4.9	6.1	8.7	7.8	0.0	3.1	4.8	10.7	
The problem exists, but not very serious — Frequency	311	178	11	17	9	37	15	1	0	29	14	
%	17.2	18.6	18.3	27.9	27.3	24.7	16.7	6.7	0.0	9.9	11.6	
The problem does not exist — Frequency	1159	633	37	34	16	86	60	11	28	194	60	
%	64.0	66.1	61.7	55.7	48.5	57.3	66.7	73.3	87.5	66.4	49.6	
NA — Frequency	172	63	1	6	6	12	5	2	3	45	29	
%	9.5	6.6	1.7	9.8	18.2	8.0	5.6	13.3	9.4	15.4	24.0	

C3-2 Attitude toward the regulation in the revised Trade Union Law: When an enterprise or undertaking delays allocating or refuses to allocate the contribution to the trade union, the trade unions may apply to the People's Court for an order for payment or compulsory enforcement

	Sum	State-owned/ State-holding enterprise	Collective-owned enterprise	Private enterprise	Cooperative enterprise	Limited liability corporation	Share Holding Corporation Ltd	Enterprise with Funds from Hong Kong, Macao and Taiwan	Foreign funded enterprise	Others	NA
Agree — Frequency	1204	638	41	36	19	108	61	9	24	194	74
%	66.5	66.7	68.3	59.0	57.6	72.0	67.8	60.0	75.0	66.4	61.2
Disagree — Frequency	454	255	15	19	11	31	25	3	4	64	27
%	25.1	26.6	25.0	31.1	33.3	20.7	27.8	20.0	12.5	21.9	22.3
NA — Frequency	153	64	4	6	3	11	4	3	4	34	20
%	8.4	6.7	6.7	9.8	9.1	7.3	4.4	20.0	12.5	11.6	16.5

C3-2-1 Whether or not having ever exercised the right actually

Have exercised	Frequency	34	14	2	1	1	3	1	0	0	10	2
	%	1.9	1.5	3.3	1.6	3.0	2.0	1.1	0.0	0.0	3.4	1.7
Have not exercised	Frequency	1577	858	53	52	28	134	87	12	25	236	92
	%	87.1	89.7	88.3	85.2	84.8	89.3	96.7	80.0	78.1	80.8	76.0
NA	Frequency	200	85	5	8	4	13	2	3	7	46	27
	%	11.0	8.9	8.3	13.1	12.1	8.7	2.2	20.0	21.9	15.8	22.3

C3-2-2 Whether or not considering to exercise this right in case non-payment or delay of payment is very serious

Want to exercise this right very much	Frequency	197	95	7	3	5	21	11	2	4	36	13
	%	10.9	9.9	11.7	4.9	15.2	14.0	12.2	13.3	12.5	12.3	10.7
Do not want to exercise this right, but if there are no other ways, have to exercise	Frequency	467	245	9	18	8	41	32	4	7	75	28
	%	25.8	25.6	15.0	29.5	24.2	27.3	35.6	26.7	21.9	25.7	23.1
Do not want to exercise this right	Frequency	710	400	30	29	12	53	32	3	7	106	38
	%	39.2	41.8	50.0	47.5	36.4	35.3	35.6	20.0	21.9	36.3	31.4
NA	Frequency	437	217	14	11	8	35	15	6	14	75	42
	%	24.1	22.7	23.3	18.0	24.2	23.3	16.7	40.0	43.8	25.7	34.7

C3-3 Attitude toward the way to entrust the collection of the contribution to taxation affairs department

1 Agree	Frequency	450	216	16	26	10	35	28	4	9	71	35
	%	24.8	22.6	26.7	42.6	30.3	23.3	31.1	26.7	28.1	24.3	28.9
2 Disagree	Frequency	1205	670	40	29	19	106	61	9	17	189	65
	%	66.5	70.0	66.7	47.5	57.6	70.7	67.8	60.0	53.1	64.7	53.7
NA	Frequency	156	71	4	6	4	9	1	2	6	32	21
	%	8.6	7.4	6.7	9.8	12.1	6.0	1.1	13.3	18.8	11.0	17.4

C3-3-1 Whether or not having ever used this way actually

		Ownership form of your enterprise									
	Sum	State-owned/State-holding enterprise	Collective-owned enterprise	Private enterprise	Cooperative enterprise	Limited liability corporation	Share Holding Corporation Ltd	Enterprise with Funds from Hong Kong, Macao and Taiwan	Foreign funded enterprise	Others	NA
1 Have used Frequency	52	11	1	4	3	6	8	0	2	9	8
%	2.9	1.1	1.7	6.6	9.1	4.0	8.9	0.0	6.3	3.1	6.6
2 Have not used Frequency	1492	824	52	45	25	127	74	12	23	231	79
%	82.4	86.1	86.7	73.8	75.8	84.7	82.2	80.0	71.9	79.1	65.3
NA Frequency	267	122	7	12	5	17	8	3	7	52	34
%	14.7	12.7	11.7	19.7	15.2	11.3	8.9	20.0	21.9	17.8	28.1

C3-3-2 (If you chose 2 in C3-3-1) whether or not having intention to use it in the future

	Sum	State-owned/State-holding enterprise	Collective-owned enterprise	Private enterprise	Cooperative enterprise	Limited liability corporation	Share Holding Corporation Ltd	Enterprise with Funds from Hong Kong, Macao and Taiwan	Foreign funded enterprise	Others	NA
Yes Frequency	183	96	6	8	4	13	9	2	2	35	8
%	12.3	11.7	11.5	17.8	16.0	10.2	12.2	16.7	8.7	15.2	10.1
No Frequency	1220	675	45	30	20	110	62	9	19	184	66
%	81.8	81.9	86.5	66.7	80.0	86.6	83.8	75.0	82.6	79.7	83.5
NA Frequency	89	53	1	7	1	4	3	1	2	12	5
%	6.0	6.4	1.9	15.6	4.0	3.1	4.1	8.3	8.7	5.2	6.3

C3-3-3 (If you chose 2 in C3-3) agree or disagree with the following reasons

1 Collection by the taxation affairs department is untrustworthy

	Sum	State-owned/State-holding enterprise	Collective-owned enterprise	Private enterprise	Cooperative enterprise	Limited liability corporation	Share Holding Corporation Ltd	Enterprise with Funds from Hong Kong, Macao and Taiwan	Foreign funded enterprise	Others	NA
Disagree Frequency	1092	605	34	25	17	92	58	8	15	178	60
%	90.6	90.3	85.0	86.2	89.5	86.8	95.1	88.9	88.2	94.2	92.3
Agree Frequency	113	65	6	4	2	14	3	1	2	11	5
%	9.4	9.7	15.0	13.8	10.5	13.2	4.9	11.1	11.8	5.8	7.7

2 Collection by the taxation affairs departments would create the image of trade unions' funds belong to government finance, and disadvantage in the trade unions' displaying its independency

Disagree	Frequency	518	289	21	8	12	44	29	2	4	75	34
	%	43.0	43.1	52.5	27.6	63.2	41.5	47.5	22.2	23.5	39.7	52.3
Agree	Frequency	687	381	19	21	7	62	32	7	13	114	31
	%	57.0	56.9	47.5	72.4	36.8	58.5	52.5	77.8	76.5	60.3	47.7

3 Primary trade unions have taken their inherent responsibility to collect the contribution for themselves. If they renounce some certain parts of the responsibility, it might be disadvantageous for mobilizing primary trade unions' enthusiasm

Disagree	Frequency	615	348	19	15	11	51	31	3	8	90	39
	%	51.0	51.9	47.5	51.7	57.9	48.1	50.8	33.3	47.1	47.6	60.0
Agree	Frequency	590	322	21	14	8	55	30	6	9	99	26
	%	49.0	48.1	52.5	48.3	42.1	51.9	49.2	66.7	52.9	52.4	40.0

4 Primary trade unions have taken their inherent responsibility to collect the contribution for themselves. If the collection is changed to be the contract matter between local trade union and taxation affairs department, it would be disadvantageous for the unity between local trade union and primary trade unions

Disagree	Frequency	719	394	21	20	12	64	36	5	9	113	45
	%	59.7	58.8	52.5	69.0	63.2	60.4	59.0	55.6	52.9	59.8	69.2
Agree	Frequency	486	276	19	9	7	42	25	4	8	76	20
	%	40.3	41.2	47.5	31.0	36.8	39.6	41.0	44.4	47.1	40.2	30.8

Part 5: Questions about the activity contents of the trade union

D1 Most important activities

1. The first most important activity

		Sum	State-owned/State-holding enterprise	Collective-owned enterprise	Private enterprise	Cooperative enterprise	Limited liability corporation	Share Holding Corporation Ltd	Enterprise with Funds from Hong Kong, Macao and Taiwan	Foreign funded enterprise	Others	NA
Negotiate with the administration/ management on the working conditions including wages, bonus, working hour and welfare, sign collective contracts	Frequency %	1175 64.9	661 69.1	40 66.7	45 73.8	20 60.6	113 75.3	66 73.3	10 66.7	22 68.8	141 48.5	57 47.1
Participate in the mediation and arbitration of labor disputes	Frequency %	74 4.1	36 3.8	4 6.7	3 4.9	2 6.1	7 4.7	2 2.2	0 0.0	3 9.4	13 4.5	4 3.3
Solicit members' opinions, present them to the administration/ management without delay, and request for the solutions	Frequency %	212 11.7	87 9.1	5 8.3	4 6.6	3 9.1	12 8.0	11 12.2	3 20.0	1 3.1	62 21.3	24 19.8

Ownership form of your enterprise

Promote the democratic management and disclosure of factory management affairs as the working body of the congress of workers and staff members	Frequency	151	98	3	2	3	4	2	0	1	31	7
	%	8.3	10.2	5.0	3.3	9.1	2.7	2.2	0.0	3.1	10.7	5.8
Assist and supervise the administration/management in properly dealing with social insurance	Frequency	14	5	2	0	0	0	0	0	1	6	0
	%	0.8	0.5	3.3	0.0	0.0	0.0	0.0	0.0	3.1	2.1	0.0
Assist the administration/management to execute the labor protection measures including the measures on working hour, occupational safety and health	Frequency	16	4	1	2	0	2	1	0	1	3	2
	%	0.9	0.4	1.7	3.3	0.0	1.3	1.1	0.0	3.1	1.0	1.7
Conduct education among members, encourage them to learn their rights and obligations	Frequency	19	5	2	0	0	1	1	0	0	9	1
	%	1.0	0.5	3.3	0.0	0.0	0.7	1.1	0.0	0.0	3.1	0.8

201

Ownership form of your enterprise

		Sum	State-owned/State-holding enterprise	Collective-owned enterprise	Private enterprise	Cooperative enterprise	Limited liability corporation	Share Holding Corporation Ltd	Enterprise with Funds from Hong Kong, Macao and Taiwan	Foreign funded enterprise	Others	NA
Handle new members' entrance formalities, manage the personal records of members	Frequency	9	4	0	0	0	1	0	0	0	3	1
	%	0.5	0.4	0.0	0.0	0.0	0.7	0.0	0.0	0.0	1.0	0.8
Cooperate with Party Committees and Communist Youth League Committees to carry out ideological and political education among members	Frequency	11	2	0	0	0	0	2	0	0	3	4
	%	0.6	0.2	0.0	0.0	0.0	0.0	2.2	0.0	0.0	1.0	3.3
Organize members to launch activities for vocational training and technical innovation	Frequency	7	3	0	1	0	1	1	0	0	1	0
	%	0.4	0.3	0.0	1.6	0.0	0.7	1.1	0.0	0.0	0.3	0.0

Appraise advanced workers and model workers	Frequency	4	2	1	0	0	0	1	0	0	0	0
	%	0.2	0.2	1.7	0.0	0.0	0.0	1.1	0.0	0.0	0.0	0.0
Understand members' living situations and their thoughts promptly	Frequency	5	3	0	0	0	1	0	0	0	1	0
	%	0.3	0.3	0.0	0.0	0.0	0.7	0.0	0.0	0.0	0.3	0.0
Safeguard women workers' rights including menstruation leave, maternity leave and child-care leave.	Frequency	1	0	0	0	0	0	0	1	0	0	0
	%	0.1	0.0	0.0	0.0	0.0	0.0	0.0	6.7	0.0	0.0	0.0
Implement family planning program												
Remove difficulties in members' living condition through mutual aid activities of mutual aid saving associations, mutual aid insurance, and Warmth Project.	Frequency	7	6	0	0	0	1	0	0	0	0	0
	%	0.4	0.6	0.0	0.0	0.0	0.7	0.0	0.0	0.0	0.0	0.0
Organize members to enjoy culture and sports activities												
NA	Frequency	105	41	2	4	5	7	3	1	3	18	21
	%	5.8	4.3	3.3	6.6	15.2	4.7	3.3	6.7	9.4	6.2	17.4

2. The second most important activity

		Ownership form of your enterprise									
	Sum	State-owned/ State-holding enterprise	Collective-owned enterprise	Private enterprise	Cooperative enterprise	Limited liability corporation	Share Holding Corporation Ltd	Enterprise with Funds from Hong Kong, Macao and Taiwan	Foreign funded enterprise	Others	NA
Negotiate with the administration/ management on the working conditions including wages, bonus, working hours and welfare, sign collective contracts — Frequency	47	34	2	0	2	2	2	0	1	3	1
%	2.6	3.6	3.3	0.0	6.1	1.3	2.2	0.0	3.1	1.0	0.8
Participate in the mediation and arbitration of labor disputes — Frequency	490	268	10	17	10	55	36	1	10	62	21
%	27.1	28.0	16.7	27.9	30.3	36.7	40.0	6.7	31.3	21.3	17.4
Solicit members' opinions, present them to the administration/ management without delay, and request for the solutions — Frequency	328	177	16	11	6	30	15	4	7	41	21
%	18.1	18.5	26.7	18.0	18.2	20.1	16.7	26.7	21.9	14.1	17.4

Promote the democratic management and disclosure of factory management affairs as the working body of the congress of workers and staff members	Frequency	467	279	20	10	2	35	19	4	1	70	27
	%	25.8	29.2	33.3	16.4	6.1	23.5	21.1	26.7	3.1	24.1	22.3
Assist and supervise the administration/management in properly dealing with social insurance	Frequency	76	26	3	6	2	3	3	3	3	21	6
	%	4.2	2.7	5.0	9.8	6.1	2.0	3.3	20.0	9.4	7.2	5.0
Assist the administration/management to execute the labor protection measures including the measures on working hours, occupational safety and health	Frequency	87	43	1	6	0	5	2	1	4	21	4
	%	4.8	4.5	1.7	9.8	0.0	3.4	2.2	6.7	12.5	7.2	3.3
Conduct education among members, encourage them to learn their rights and obligations	Frequency	63	18	3	5	2	5	3	0	1	17	9
	%	3.5	1.9	5.0	8.2	6.1	3.4	3.3	0.0	3.1	5.8	7.4

Ownership form of your enterprise

		Sum	State-owned/ State-holding enterprise	Collective-owned enterprise	Private enterprise	Cooperative enterprise	Limited liability corporation	Share Holding Corporation Ltd	Enterprise with Funds from Hong Kong, Macao and Taiwan	Foreign funded enterprise	Others	NA
Handle new members' entrance formalities, manage the personal records of members	Frequency	15	9	1	0	0	1	0	0	0	3	1
	%	0.8	0.9	1.7	0.0	0.0	0.7	0.0	0.0	0.0	1.0	0.8
Cooperate with Party Committees and Communist Youth League Committees to carry out ideological and political education among members	Frequency	48	21	0	0	1	2	2	0	1	18	3
	%	2.7	2.2	0.0	0.0	3.0	1.3	2.2	0.0	3.1	6.2	2.5
Organize members to launch activities for vocational training and technical innovation	Frequency	46	19	0	0	1	3	2	0	1	15	5
	%	2.5	2.0	0.0	0.0	3.0	2.0	2.2	0.0	3.1	5.2	4.1

Task		C1	C2	C3	C4	C5	C6	C7	C8	C9	C10	C11
Appraise advanced workers and model workers	Frequency	8	6	0	0	0	0	0	1	0	1	0
	%	0.4	0.6	0.0	0.0	0.0	0.0	0.0	6.7	0.0	0.3	0.0
Understand members' living situations and their thoughts promptly	Frequency	11	5	2	2	0	0	0	0	0	1	1
	%	0.6	0.5	3.3	3.3	0.0	0.0	0.0	0.0	0.0	0.3	0.8
Safeguard women workers' rights including menstruation leave, maternity leave and child-care leave.	Frequency	5	1	1	0	0	0	1	0	0	1	1
	%	0.3	0.1	1.7	0.0	0.0	0.0	1.1	0.0	0.0	0.3	0.8
Implement family planning program												
Remove difficulties in members' living condition through mutual aid activities of mutual aid saving associations, mutual aid insurance, and Warmth Project.	Frequency	20	12	0	0	1	3	2	0	0	1	1
	%	1.1	1.3	0.0	0.0	3.0	2.0	2.2	0.0	0.0	0.3	0.8
Organize members to enjoy culture and sports activities												
NA	Frequency	98	39	1	4	6	5	3	1	3	16	20
	%	5.4	4.1	1.7	6.6	18.2	3.4	3.3	6.7	9.4	5.5	16.5

3. The third most important activity

		Sum	State-owned/ State-holding enterprise	Collective-owned enterprise	Private enterprise	Cooperative enterprise	Limited liability corporation	Share Holding Corporation Ltd	Enterprise with Funds from Hong Kong, Macao and Taiwan	Foreign funded enterprise	Others	NA
Negotiate with the administration/ management on the working conditions including wages, bonus, working hours and welfare, sign collective contracts	Frequency	21	10	1	1	0	2	1	0	0	5	1
	%	1.2	1.0	1.7	1.6	0.0	1.3	1.1	0.0	0.0	1.7	0.8
Participate in the mediation and arbitration of labor disputes	Frequency	27	17	2	0	1	2	1	0	0	4	0
	%	1.5	1.8	3.3	0.0	3.0	1.3	1.1	0.0	0.0	1.4	0.0
Solicit members' opinions, present them to the administration/ management without delay, and request for the solutions	Frequency	261	147	7	7	6	24	21	0	4	36	9
	%	14.4	15.4	11.7	11.5	18.2	16.1	23.3	0.0	12.5	12.4	7.4

Promote the democratic management and disclosure of factory management affairs as the working body of the congress of workers and staff members	Frequency	379	245	14	3	2	35	23	3	5	34	15
	%	21.0	25.6	23.3	4.9	6.1	23.5	25.6	20.0	15.6	11.7	12.4
Assist and supervise the administration/management in properly dealing with social insurance	Frequency	147	60	3	11	4	19	7	2	2	28	11
	%	8.1	6.3	5.0	18.0	12.1	12.8	7.8	13.3	6.3	9.6	9.1
Assist the administration/management to execute the labor protection measures including the measures on working hour, occupational safety and health	Frequency	260	136	7	12	6	27	8	3	4	42	16
	%	14.4	14.2	11.7	19.7	18.2	18.1	8.9	13.3	12.5	14.4	13.2
Conduct education among members, encourage them to learn their rights and obligations	Frequency	125	47	5	5	3	9	9	2	4	26	15
	%	6.9	4.9	8.3	8.2	9.1	6.0	10.0	13.3	12.5	8.9	12.4

Ownership form of your enterprise

		Sum	State-owned/State-holding enterprise	Collective-owned enterprise	Private enterprise	Cooperative enterprise	Limited liability corporation	Share Holding Corporation Ltd	Enterprise with Funds from Hong Kong, Macao and Taiwan	Foreign funded enterprise	Others	NA
Handle new members' entrance formalities, manage the personal records of members	Frequency %	68 3.8	26 2.7	4 6.7	7 11.5	1 3.0	3 2.0	2 2.2	0 0.0	1 3.1	18 6.2	6 5.0
Cooperate with Party Committees and Communist Youth League Committees to carry out ideological and political education among members	Frequency %	89 4.9	48 5.0	2 3.3	2 3.3	0 0.0	5 3.4	3 3.3	0 0.0	2 6.3	19 6.5	8 6.6
Organize members to launch activities for vocational training and technical innovation	Frequency %	180 10.0	100 10.4	5 8.3	4 6.6	2 6.1	14 9.4	9 10.0	3 20.0	4 12.5	30 10.3	9 7.4

Item	Measure											
Appraise advanced workers and model workers	Frequency	44	24	0	1	1	2	1	0	0	10	5
	%	2.4	2.5	0.0	1.6	3.0	1.3	1.1	0.0	0.0	3.4	4.1
Understand members' living situations and their thoughts promptly	Frequency	55	25	5	2	0	1	2	1	2	12	5
	%	3.0	2.6	8.3	3.3	0.0	0.7	2.2	6.7	6.3	4.1	4.1
Safeguard women workers' rights including menstruation leave, maternity leave, and child-care leave.	Frequency	17	9	0	0	0	1	1	1	1	3	1
	%	0.9	0.9	0.0	0.0	0.0	0.7	1.1	6.7	3.1	1.0	0.8
Implement family planning program												
Remove difficulties in members' living condition through mutual aid activities of mutual aid saving associations, mutual aid insurance, and Warmth Project.	Frequency	40	26	4	1	1	0	0	0	0	8	0
	%	2.2	2.7	6.7	1.6	3.0	0.0	0.0	0.0	0.0	2.7	0.0
Organize members to enjoy culture and sports activities												
NA	Frequency	96	37	1	5	6	5	2	1	3	16	20
	%	5.3	3.9	1.7	8.2	18.2	3.4	2.2	6.7	9.4	5.5	16.5

4. The fourth most important activity

			Ownership form of your enterprise									
		Sum	State-owned/ State-holding enterprise	Collective-owned enterprise	Private enterprise	Cooperative enterprise	Limited liability corporation	Share Holding Corporation Ltd	Enterprise with Funds from Hong Kong, Macao and Taiwan	Foreign funded enterprise	Others	NA
Negotiate with the administration/ management on the working conditions including wages, bonus, working hours and welfare, sign collective contracts	Frequency	9	6	1	0	0	1	0	0	0	0	1
	%	0.5	0.6	1.7	0.0	0.0	0.7	0.0	0.0	0.0	0.0	0.8
Participate in the mediation and arbitration of labor disputes	Frequency	27	17	0	2	0	2	1	0	1	3	1
	%	1.5	1.8	0.0	3.3	0.0	1.3	1.1	0.0	3.1	1.0	0.8
Solicit members' opinions, present them to the administration/ management without delay, and request for the solutions	Frequency	29	20	1	0	0	1	1	1	0	4	1
	%	1.6	2.1	1.7	0.0	0.0	0.7	1.1	6.7	0.0	1.4	0.8

	Frequency %										
Promote the democratic management and disclosure of factory management affairs as the working body of the congress of workers and staff members	179 9.9	110 11.5	6 10.0	2 3.3	3 9.1	19 12.8	6 6.7	0 0.0	2 6.3	23 7.9	8 6.6
Assist and supervise the administration/ management in properly dealing with social insurance	85 4.7	47 4.9	5 8.3	0 0.0	0 0.0	5 3.4	5 5.6	1 6.7	4 12.5	13 4.5	5 4.1
Assist the administration/ management to execute the labor protection measures including the measures on working hour, occupational safety and health	218 12.1	116 12.1	5 8.3	7 11.5	4 12.1	26 17.4	17 18.9	3 20.0	4 12.5	23 7.9	13 10.7
Conduct education among members, encourage them to learn their rights and obligations	98 5.4	46 4.8	4 6.7	3 4.9	3 9.1	9 6.0	4 4.4	2 13.3	2 6.3	15 5.2	10 8.3

213

		Ownership form of your enterprise							Enterprise with Funds from Hong Kong, Macao and Taiwan	Foreign funded enterprise	Others	NA
	Sum	State-owned/ State-holding enterprise	Collective-owned enterprise	Private enterprise	Cooperative enterprise	Limited liability corporation	Share Holding Corporation Ltd					
Handle new members' entrance formalities, manage the personal records of members	Frequency %	52 2.9	26 2.7	1 1.7	2 3.3	2 6.1	7 4.7	3 3.3	0 0.0	1 3.1	3 1.0	7 5.8
Cooperate with Party Committees and Communist Youth League Committees to carry out ideological and political education among members	Frequency %	120 6.6	52 5.4	3 5.0	4 6.6	5 15.2	10 6.7	4 4.4	0 0.0	1 3.1	30 10.3	11 9.1
Organize members to launch activities for vocational training and technical innovation	Frequency %	292 16.1	169 17.7	9 15.0	9 14.8	4 12.1	24 16.1	10 11.1	1 6.7	3 9.4	47 16.2	16 13.2
Appraise advanced workers and model workers	Frequency %	152 8.4	88 9.2	5 8.3	6 9.8	1 3.0	13 8.7	9 10.0	0 0.0	6 18.8	17 5.8	7 5.8

Understand members' living situations and their thoughts promptly	Frequency	171	80	7	9	4	10	11	3	3	42	2
	%	9.5	8.4	11.7	14.8	12.1	6.7	12.2	20.0	9.4	14.4	1.7
Safeguard women workers' rights including menstruation leave, maternity leave, and child-care leave.	Frequency	232	109	12	10	2	16	15	2	2	48	16
	%	12.8	11.4	20.0	16.4	6.1	10.7	16.7	13.3	6.3	16.5	13.2
Implement family planning program Remove difficulties in members' living condition through mutual aid activities of mutual aid saving associations, mutual aid insurance, and Warmth Project.	Frequency	49	33	0	2	0	1	2	1	0	7	3
	%	2.7	3.4	0.0	3.3	0.0	0.7	2.2	6.7	0.0	2.4	2.5
Organize members to enjoy culture and sports activities NA	Frequency	96	38	1	5	5	5	2	1	3	16	20
	%	5.3	4.0	1.7	8.2	15.2	3.4	2.2	6.7	9.4	5.5	16.5

5. The fifth most important activity

			Ownership form of your enterprise								
	Sum	State-owned/ State-holding enterprise	Collective-owned enterprise	Private enterprise	Cooperative enterprise	Limited liability corporation	Share Holding Corporation Ltd	Enterprise with Funds from Hong Kong, Macao and Taiwan	Foreign funded enterprise	Others	NA
Negotiate with the administration/ management on the working conditions including wages, bonus, working hours and welfare, sign collective contracts — Frequency	15	7	2	1	1	1	1	0	0	1	1
%	0.8	0.7	3.3	1.6	3.0	0.7	1.1	0.0	0.0	0.3	0.8
Participate in the mediation and arbitration of labor disputes — Frequency	20	13	2	0	1	1	0	0	0	1	2
%	1.1	1.4	3.3	0.0	3.0	0.7	0.0	0.0	0.0	0.3	1.7
Solicit members' opinions, present them to the administration/ management without delay, and request for the solutions — Frequency	23	15	0	0	1	0	0	0	2	5	0
%	1.3	1.6	0.0	0.0	3.0	0.0	0.0	0.0	6.3	1.7	0.0

Promote the democratic management and disclosure of factory management affairs as the working body of the congress of workers and staff members	Frequency	21	14	1	0	0	2	1	0	0	2	1
	%	1.2	1.5	1.7	0.0	0.0	1.3	1.1	0.0	0.0	0.7	0.8
Assist and supervise the administration/ management in properly dealing with social insurance	Frequency	78	43	5	0	3	9	0	0	0	14	4
	%	4.3	4.5	8.3	0.0	9.1	6.0	0.0	0.0	0.0	4.8	3.3
Assist the administration/ management to execute the labor protection measures including the measures on working hours, occupational safety and health	Frequency	53	35	2	1	0	2	3	1	1	5	3
	%	2.9	3.7	3.3	1.6	0.0	1.3	3.3	6.7	3.1	1.7	2.5
Conduct education among members, encourage them to learn their rights and obligations	Frequency	53	30	1	1	0	4	2	0	1	7	7
	%	2.9	3.1	1.7	1.6	0.0	2.7	2.2	0.0	3.1	2.4	5.8

Ownership form of your enterprise

		Sum	State-owned/ State-holding enterprise	Collective-owned enterprise	Private enterprise	Cooperative enterprise	Limited liability corporation	Share Holding Corporation Ltd	Enterprise with Funds from Hong Kong, Macao and Taiwan	Foreign funded enterprise	Others	NA
Handle new members' entrance formalities, manage the personal records of members	Frequency	33	17	1	1	0	2	1	2	2	5	2
	%	1.8	1.8	1.7	1.6	0.0	1.3	1.1	13.3	6.3	1.7	1.7
Cooperate with Party Committees and Communist Youth League Committees to carry out ideological and political education among members	Frequency	45	26	0	1	0	6	2	0	0	7	3
	%	2.5	2.7	0.0	1.6	0.0	4.0	2.2	0.0	0.0	2.4	2.5
Organize members to launch activities for vocational training and technical innovation	Frequency	134	77	4	1	5	12	8	0	0	22	5
	%	7.4	8.0	6.7	1.6	15.2	8.0	8.9	0.0	0.0	7.6	4.2
Appraise advanced workers and model workers	Frequency	94	53	2	3	1	5	3	0	1	15	11
	%	5.2	5.5	3.3	4.9	3.0	3.3	3.3	0.0	3.1	5.2	9.2

Understand members' living situations and their thoughts promptly	Frequency	123	52	2	8	3	16	8	0	2	22	10
	%	6.8	5.4	3.3	13.1	9.1	10.7	8.9	0.0	6.3	7.6	8.3
Safeguard women workers' rights including menstruation leave, maternity leave, and child-care leave. Implement family planning program	Frequency	220	103	7	9	2	26	16	1	5	41	10
	%	12.2	10.8	11.7	14.8	6.1	17.3	17.8	6.7	15.6	14.1	8.3
Remove difficulties in members' living condition through mutual aid activities of mutual aid saving associations, mutual aid insurance, and Warmth Project. Organize members to enjoy culture and sports activities	Frequency	797	427	30	31	12	59	43	10	15	129	41
	%	44.1	44.6	50.0	50.8	36.4	39.3	47.8	66.7	46.9	44.3	34.2
NA	Frequency	100	45	1	4	4	5	2	1	3	15	20
	%	5.5	4.7	1.7	6.6	12.1	3.3	2.2	6.7	9.4	5.2	16.7

D2 Implementation of the equal consultations and signing collective contracts

D2-1 Whether or not having signed collective contracts with the administration of work unit

			Ownership form of your enterprise						Enterprise with			
		Sum	State-owned/ State-holding enterprise	Collective-owned enterprise	Private enterprise	Cooperative enterprise	Limited liability corporation	Share Holding Corporation Ltd	Funds from Hong Kong, Macao and Taiwan	Foreign funded enterprise	Others	NA
1 Has signed	Frequency	1134	698	40	39	19	112	62	9	15	109	31
	%	62.6	72.9	66.7	63.9	57.6	74.7	68.9	60.0	46.9	37.3	25.6
2 Has not signed	Frequency	470	180	16	17	8	32	25	5	14	119	54
	%	26.0	18.8	26.7	27.9	24.2	21.3	27.8	33.3	43.8	40.8	44.6
NA	Frequency	207	79	4	5	6	6	3	1	3	64	36
	%	11.4	8.3	6.7	8.2	18.2	4.0	3.3	6.7	9.4	21.9	29.8

D2-1-1 (If you chose 1 in D2-1) whether or not the draft of the collective contract has been passed through the discussion at the congress of workers and staff members

		Sum	State-owned/ State-holding enterprise	Collective-owned enterprise	Private enterprise	Cooperative enterprise	Limited liability corporation	Share Holding Corporation Ltd	Funds from Hong Kong, Macao and Taiwan	Foreign funded enterprise	Others	NA
Passed through the discussion at the congress of workers and staff members	Frequency	1002	649	40	25	12	100	53	7	8	83	25
	%	88.4	93.0	100.0	64.1	63.2	89.3	85.5	77.8	53.3	76.1	80.6
Not passed through the discussion at the congress of workers and staff members	Frequency	111	40	0	12	6	10	8	1	5	23	6
	%	9.8	5.7	0.0	30.8	31.6	8.9	12.9	11.1	33.3	21.1	19.4
NA	Frequency	21	9	0	2	1	2	1	1	2	3	0
	%	1.9	1.3	0.0	5.1	5.3	1.8	1.6	11.1	13.3	2.8	0.0

D2-1-2 (If you chose 1 in D2-1) whether or not the content of the collective contract has been announced to the entire workers

Announced	Frequency	1033	659	40	28	17	100	51	8	14	90	0
	%	91.1	94.4	100.0	71.8	89.5	89.3	82.3	88.9	93.3	82.6	0.0
Not announced	Frequency	82	28	0	10	2	10	10	1	0	16	5
	%	7.2	4.0	0.0	25.6	10.5	8.9	16.1	11.1	0.0	14.7	16.1
NA	Frequency	19	11	0	1	0	2	1	0	1	3	0
	%	1.7	1.6	0.0	2.6	0.0	1.8	1.6	0.0	6.7	2.8	0.0

D2-1-3 (If "announced") whether or not the following means of the announcement have been used

1 Announced at a meeting

Did not	Frequency	530	320	24	16	14	57	20	6	11	48	14
	%	51.3	48.6	60.0	57.1	82.4	57.0	39.2	75.0	78.6	53.3	53.8
Did	Frequency	503	339	16	12	3	43	31	2	3	42	12
	%	48.7	51.4	40.0	42.9	17.6	43.0	60.8	25.0	21.4	46.7	46.2

2 Distributed the copies of the collective agreements to the workers and staff members

Did not	Frequency	685	427	30	17	13	67	39	7	7	57	21
	%	66.3	64.8	75.0	60.7	76.5	67.0	76.5	87.5	50.0	63.3	80.8
Did	Frequency	348	232	10	11	4	33	12	1	7	33	5
	%	33.7	35.2	25.0	39.3	23.5	33.0	23.5	12.5	50.0	36.7	19.2

3 Read out the collective agreements in front of the entire workers

Did not	Frequency	697	439	30	18	10	69	33	5	13	61	19
	%	67.5	66.6	75.0	64.3	58.8	69.0	64.7	62.5	92.9	67.8	73.1
Did	Frequency	336	220	10	10	7	31	18	3	1	29	7
	%	32.5	33.4	25.0	35.7	41.2	31.0	35.3	37.5	7.1	32.2	26.9

4 Displayed the collective agreements on a wall

		Sum	State-owned/ State-holding enterprise	Collective-owned enterprise	Private enterprise	Cooperative enterprise	Limited liability corporation	Share Holding Corporation Ltd	Enterprise with Funds from Hong Kong, Macao and Taiwan	Foreign funded enterprise	Others	NA
Did not	Frequency	799	507	33	22	11	72	39	7	12	77	19
	%	77.3	76.9	82.5	78.6	64.7	72.0	76.5	87.5	85.7	85.6	73.1
Did	Frequency	234	152	7	6	6	28	12	1	2	13	7
	%	22.7	23.1	17.5	21.4	35.3	28.0	23.5	12.5	14.3	14.4	26.9

D2-1-4 (If you chose 1 in D2-1) whether or not having organized the Collective Contracts Surveillance and Inspection Group

		Sum	State-owned/ State-holding enterprise	Collective-owned enterprise	Private enterprise	Cooperative enterprise	Limited liability corporation	Share Holding Corporation Ltd	Enterprise with Funds from Hong Kong, Macao and Taiwan	Foreign funded enterprise	Others	NA
Organized	Frequency	697	477	25	10	11	73	25	6	6	48	16
	%	61.5	68.3	62.5	25.6	57.9	65.2	40.3	66.7	40.0	44.0	51.6
Not organized	Frequency	363	182	13	25	7	36	30	2	6	50	12
	%	32.0	26.1	32.5	64.1	36.8	32.1	48.4	22.2	40.0	45.9	38.7
NA	Frequency	74	39	2	4	1	3	7	1	3	11	3
	%	6.5	5.6	5.0	10.3	5.3	2.7	11.3	11.1	20.0	10.1	9.7

D3 Mediation and arbitration of labor disputes

D3-1 Whether or not having established the Labour Dispute Mediation Committee in the work unit

		Sum	State-owned/ State-holding enterprise	Collective-owned enterprise	Private enterprise	Cooperative enterprise	Limited liability corporation	Share Holding Corporation Ltd	Enterprise with Funds from Hong Kong, Macao and Taiwan	Foreign funded enterprise	Others	NA
Established	Frequency	1085	662	29	25	17	109	60	8	18	120	37
	%	59.9	69.2	48.3	41.0	51.5	72.7	66.7	53.3	56.2	41.2	30.6
Not established	Frequency	491	197	25	29	10	34	23	6	10	110	47
	%	27.1	20.6	41.7	47.5	30.3	22.7	25.6	40.0	31.2	37.8	38.8
NA	Frequency	234	98	6	7	6	7	7	1	4	61	37
	%	12.9	10.2	10.0	11.5	18.2	4.7	7.8	6.7	12.5	21.0	30.6

Ownership form of your enterprise

D3-2 Major causes of the labor disputes (choose three)

Conclusion of labor contracts	Frequency	433	243	18	10	6	34	27	2	6	65	22
	%	23.9	25.4	30.0	16.4	18.2	22.7	30.0	13.3	18.8	22.3	18.2
Dismissal of workers and staff members	Frequency	561	313	17	25	10	49	32	6	11	74	24
	%	31.0	32.7	28.3	41.0	30.3	32.7	35.6	40.0	34.4	25.3	19.8
Workers and staff members' voluntary resigning	Frequency	246	135	7	10	8	22	13	5	9	34	3
	%	13.6	14.1	11.7	16.4	24.2	14.7	14.4	33.3	28.1	11.6	2.5
Labor remuneration	Frequency	878	466	32	34	19	83	58	9	12	119	46
	%	48.5	48.7	53.3	55.7	57.6	55.3	64.4	60.0	37.5	40.8	38.0
Insurance and welfare	Frequency	467	243	19	14	6	43	25	4	5	80	28
	%	25.8	25.4	31.7	23.0	18.2	28.7	27.8	26.7	15.6	27.4	23.1
Labor protection, occupational safety and health	Frequency	330	197	8	14	2	35	17	3	5	32	17
	%	18.2	20.6	13.3	23.0	6.1	23.3	18.9	20.4	15.6	11.0	14.0
Vocational training	Frequency	88	39	3	6	3	6	7	0	3	15	6
	%	4.9	4.1	5.0	9.8	9.1	4.0	7.8	0.0	9.4	5.1	5.0
Working hours, rest and vacation	Frequency	421	244	10	15	6	38	23	4	7	53	21
	%	23.2	25.5	16.7	24.6	18.2	25.3	25.6	26.7	21.9	18.2	17.4
Protection of female workers' rights and interests	Frequency	174	99	4	8	2	9	7	0	3	27	15
	%	9.6	10.3	6.7	13.1	6.1	6.0	7.8	0.0	9.4	9.2	12.4
Other reasons	Frequency	39	19	2	1	1	3	3	0	1	9	0
	%	2.2	2.0	3.3	1.6	3.0	2.0	3.3	0.0	3.1	3.1	0.0
NA	Frequency	490	227	15	14	9	32	13	4	10	109	57
	%	27.1	23.7	25.0	23.0	27.3	21.3	14.4	26.7	31.3	37.3	47.1

D3-3 The number of labor disputes in the work unit from 1999 to 2003

		Sum	State-owned/ State-holding enterprise	Collective-owned enterprise	Private enterprise	Cooperative enterprise	Limited liability corporation	Share Holding Corporation Ltd	Enterprise with Funds from Hong Kong, Macao and Taiwan	Foreign funded enterprise	Others	NA
											Ownership form of your enterprise	
0	Frequency	634	310	22	11	3	51	27	3	7	128	72
	%	35.0	32.4	36.7	18.0	9.1	34.0	30.0	20.0	21.9	43.8	59.5
1	Frequency	122	70	4	4	3	11	9	0	2	17	2
	%	6.7	7.3	6.7	6.6	9.1	7.3	10.0	0.0	6.3	5.8	1.7
2	Frequency	109	58	5	5	1	13	5	0	6	15	1
	%	6.0	6.1	8.3	8.2	3.0	8.7	5.6	0.0	18.8	5.1	0.8
3	Frequency	75	38	3	2	2	12	7	0	0	9	2
	%	4.1	4.0	5.0	3.3	6.1	8.0	7.8	0.0	0.0	3.1	1.7
4	Frequency	32	21	1	0	0	3	2	0	2	2	1
	%	1.8	2.2	1.7	0.0	0.0	2.0	2.2	0.0	6.3	0.7	0.8
5	Frequency	44	30	1	2	0	3	0	0	2	5	1
	%	2.4	3.1	1.7	3.3	0.0	2.0	0.0	0.0	6.3	1.7	0.8
6	Frequency	17	16	0	0	0	0	1	0	0	0	0
	%	0.9	1.7	0.0	0.0	0.0	0.0	1.1	0.0	0.0	0.0	0.0
7	Frequency	13	6	2	0	1	2	2	0	0	0	0
	%	0.7	0.6	3.3	0.0	3.0	1.3	2.2	0.0	0.0	0.0	0.0
8	Frequency	7	4	0	2	0	0	0	0	0	1	0
	%	0.4	0.4	0.0	3.3	0.0	0.0	0.0	0.0	0.0	0.3	0.0
9	Frequency	2	1	0	0	0	0	0	0	0	0	1
	%	0.1	0.1	0.0	0.0	0.0	0.0	0.0	0.0	0.0	0.0	0.8
10	Frequency	29	14	2	1	0	1	4	0	0	6	1
	%	1.6	1.5	3.3	1.6	0.0	0.7	4.4	0.0	0.0	2.1	0.8
11	Frequency	5	3	0	0	0	1	1	0	0	0	0
	%	0.3	0.3	0.0	0.0	0.0	0.7	1.1	0.0	0.0	0.0	0.0

		C1	C2	C3	C4	C5	C6	C7	C8	C9	C10	C11
12	Frequency	8	3	0	1	2	0	1	0	0	1	0
	%	0.4	0.3	0.0	1.6	6.1	0.0	1.1	0.0	0.0	0.3	0.0
13	Frequency	6	4	0	1	0	0	1	0	0	0	0
	%	0.3	0.4	0.0	1.6	0.0	0.0	1.1	0.0	0.0	0.0	0.0
14	Frequency	2	2	0	0	0	0	1	0	0	0	0
	%	0.1	0.2	0.0	0.0	0.0	0.0	1.1	0.0	0.0	0.0	0.0
15	Frequency	5	0	0	0	0	2	1	1	0	1	0
	%	0.3	0.0	0.0	0.0	0.0	1.3	1.1	6.7	0.0	0.3	0.0
16	Frequency	0	0	0	0	0	0	0	0	0	0	0
	%	0.0	0.0	0.0	0.0	0.0	0.0	0.0	0.0	0.0	0.0	0.0
17	Frequency	5	0	0	0	0	0	2	0	0	0	3
	%	0.3	0.0	0.0	0.0	0.0	0.0	2.2	0.0	0.0	0.0	2.5
18	Frequency	0	0	0	0	0	0	0	0	0	0	0
	%	0.0	0.0	0.0	0.0	0.0	0.0	0.0	0.0	0.0	0.0	0.0
19	Frequency	1	1	0	0	0	0	0	0	0	0	0
	%	0.1	0.1	0.0	0.0	0.0	0.0	0.0	0.0	0.0	0.0	0.0
20	Frequency	11	8	0	1	0	2	0	0	0	0	0
	%	0.6	0.8	0.0	1.6	0.0	1.3	0.0	0.0	0.0	0.0	0.0
Over 20	Frequency	19	16	0	0	0	1	0	0	0	1	1
	%	1.0	1.7	0.0	0.0	0.0	0.7	0.0	0.0	0.0	0.3	0.8
NA	Frequency	665	352	20	31	21	48	27	11	13	106	36
	%	36.7	36.8	33.3	50.8	63.6	32.0	30.0	73.3	40.6	36.3	29.8

D3-3-1 The percentage of the following situations

1 Winning of the workers and staff members

		C1	C2	C3	C4	C5	C6	C7	C8	C9	C10	C11
0	Frequency	0	0	0	0	0	0	0	0	0	0	0
	%	0.0	0.0	0.0	0.0	0.0	0.0	0.0	0.0	0.0	0.0	0.0
1–10	Frequency	43	28	0	0	1	4	2	0	1	7	0
	%	8.4	9.5	0.0	0.0	11.1	2.0	2.8	0.0	8.3	12.1	0.0
11–20	Frequency	19	14	1	0	1	78	56	0	0	1	0
	%	3.7	4.7	5.6	0.0	11.1			0.0	0.0	1.7	0.0

Ownership form of your enterprise

		Sum	State-owned/State-holding enterprise	Collective-owned enterprise	Private enterprise	Cooperative enterprise	Limited liability corporation	Share Holding Corporation Ltd	Enterprise with Funds from Hong Kong, Macao and Taiwan	Foreign funded enterprise	Others	NA
21–30	Frequency	23	14	0	1	0	0	6	0	0	2	0
	%	4.5	4.7	0.0	5.3	0.0	0.0	16.7	0	0	3.4	0.0
31–40	Frequency	24	15	2	0	2	3	1	0	0	1	0
	%	4.7	5.1	11.1	0.0	22.2	5.9	2.8	0.0	0.0	1.7	0.0
41–50	Frequency	43	22	1	3	1	5	2	0	2	7	0
	%	8.4	7.5	5.6	15.8	11.1	9.8	5.6	0.0	16.7	12.1	0
51–60	Frequency	18	10	1	1	0	1	3	0	0	2	0
	%	3.5	3.4	5.6	5.3	0.0	2.0	8.3	0.0	0.0	3.4	0.0
61–70	Frequency	18	11	1	2	0	2	0	0	0	0	2
	%	3.5	3.7	5.6	10.5	0.0	3.9	0.0	0.0	0.0	0.0	15.4
71–80	Frequency	18	12	0	0	0	1	1	0	1	3	0
	%	3.5	4.1	0.0	0.0	0.0	2.0	2.8	0.0	8.3	5.2	0.0
81–90	Frequency	10	1	0	1	0	0	3	0	0	2	3
	%	2.0	0.3	0.0	5.3	0.0	0.0	8.3	0.0	0.0	3.4	23.1
91–100	Frequency	2	2	0	0	0	0	0	0	0	0	0
	%	0.4	0.7	0.0	0.0	0.0	0.0	0.0	0.0	0.0	0.0	0
NA	Frequency	294	166	12	11	4	34	17	1	8	33	8
	%	57.4	56.3	66.7	57.9	44.4	66.7	47.2	100.0	66.7	56.9	61.5

2 Winning of the employers

		1	2	3	4	5	6	7	8	9	10	11
0	Frequency	0	0	0	0	0	0	0	0	0	0	0
	%	0.0	0.0	0.0	0.0	0.0	0.0	0.0	0.0	0.0	0.0	0.0
1–10	Frequency	41	23	1	0	0	5	6	0	1	5	0
	%	8.0	7.8	5.6	0.0	0.0	9.8	16.7	0.0	8.3	8.6	0.0
11–20	Frequency	16	9	1	0	0	1	0	0	1	3	1
	%	3.1	3.1	5.6	0.0	0.0	2.0	0.0	0.0	8.3	5.2	7.7
21–30	Frequency	24	16	1	2	1	2	1	0	0	0	1
	%	4.7	5.4	5.6	10.5	11.1	3.9	2.8	0.0	0.0	0.0	7.7
31–40	Frequency	16	11	1	1	0	1	2	0	0	0	0
	%	3.1	3.7	5.6	5.3	0.0	2.0	5.6	0.0	0.0	0.0	0.0
41–50	Frequency	49	29	2	1	0	4	3	0	2	8	0
	%	9.6	9.8	11.1	5.3	0.0	7.8	8.3	0.0	16.7	13.8	0.0
51–60	Frequency	11	8	0	0	0	1	1	0	0	1	0
	%	2.1	2.7	0.0	0.0	0.0	2.0	2.8	0.0	0.0	1.7	0.0
61–70	Frequency	16	10	0	1	0	1	2	0	0	2	0
	%	3.1	3.4	0.0	5.3	0.0	2.0	5.6	0.0	0.0	3.4	0.0
71–80	Frequency	17	13	0	0	1	0	2	0	0	1	0
	%	3.3	4.4	0.0	0.0	11.1	0.0	5.6	0.0	0.0	1.7	0.0
81–90	Frequency	10	5	1	0	1	1	1	0	0	1	0
	%	2.0	1.7	5.6	0.0	11.1	2.0	2.8	0.0	0.0	1.7	0.0
91–100	Frequency	1	0	1	0	0	0	0	0	0	0	0
	%	0.2	0.0	5.6	0.0	0.0	0.0	0.0	0.0	0.0	0.0	0.0
NA	Frequency	311	171	10	14	6	35	18	1	8	37	11
	%	60.7	58.0	55.6	73.7	66.7	68.6	50.0	100.0	66.7	63.8	84.6

3 Partly winning of both sides

			Ownership form of your enterprise						Enterprise with Funds from Hong Kong, Macao and Taiwan			
		Sum	State-owned/State-holding enterprise	Collective-owned enterprise	Private enterprise	Cooperative enterprise	Limited liability corporation	Share Holding Corporation Ltd		Foreign funded enterprise	Others	NA
0	Frequency	0	0	0	0	0	0	0	0	0	0	0
	%	0.0	0.0	0.0	0.0	0.0	0.0	0.0	0.0	0.0	0.0	0.0
1–10	Frequency	38	22	1	1	1	3	3	0	0	6	1
	%	7.4	7.5	5.6	5.3	11.1	5.9	8.3	0.0	0.0	10.3	7.7
11–20	Frequency	18	12	0	0	1	1	1	0	0	3	0
	%	3.5	4.1	0.0	0.0	11.1	2.0	2.8	0.0	0.0	5.2	0.0
21–30	Frequency	9	8	1	0	0	0	0	0	0	0	0
	%	1.8	2.7	5.6	0.0	0.0	0.0	0.0	0.0	0.0	0.0	0.0
31–40	Frequency	9	6	1	1	0	1	0	0	0	0	0
	%	1.8	2.0	5.6	5.3	0.0	2.0	0.0	0.0	0.0	0.0	0.0
41–50	Frequency	46	25	2	5	1	4	5	0	0	3	1
	%	9.5	8.5	11.1	26.3	11.1	7.8	13.9	0.0	0.0	5.2	7.7
51–60	Frequency	5	4	0	0	1	0	0	0	0	0	0
	%	1.0	1.4	0.0	0.0	11.1	0.0	0.0	0.0	0.0	0.0	0.0
61–70	Frequency	3	1	0	0	0	1	1	0	0	0	0
	%	0.6	0.3	0.0	0.0	0.0	2.0	2.8	0.0	0.0	0.0	0.0
71–80	Frequency	2	2	0	0	0	0	0	0	0	0	0
	%	0.4	0.7	0.0	0.0	0.0	2.0	0.0	0.0	0.0	0.0	0.0
81–90	Frequency	1	0	0	0	0	1	0	0	0	0	0
	%	0	0.0	0.0	0.0	0.0	2.0	0.0	0.0	0.0	0.0	0.0

91–100	Frequency	0	0	0	0	0	0	0	0	0	0	0
	%	0.0	0.0	0.0	0.0	0.0	0.0	0.0	0.0	0.0	0.0	0.0
NA	Frequency	380	215	13	12	5	40	26	1	12	46	11
	%	74.2	72.9	72.3	63.2	55.6	78.4	72.2	100.0	100.0	79.3	84.6

D4 Mutual Aid Supplementary Insurance

D4-1 Whether or not providing mutual aid supplementary insurance for the union members

1 Provide	Frequency	826	494	24	23	17	70	40	9	12	108	29
	%	45.6	51.6	40.0	37.7	51.5	46.7	44.4	60.0	37.5	37.0	24.0
2 Not provide	Frequency	586	281	23	27	7	54	36	3	13	101	41
	%	32.4	29.4	38.3	44.3	21.2	36.0	40.0	20.0	40.6	34.6	33.9
NA	Frequency	399	182	13	11	9	26	14	3	7	83	51
	%	22.0	19.0	21.7	18.0	27.3	17.3	15.6	20.0	21.9	28.4	42.1

D4-2 (If you chose 1 D4-1) whether or not providing the following kinds of mutual aid supplementary insurances

1 Annuity mutual aid supplementary insurance

Not provide	Frequency	3	208	11	12	9	26	17	4	8	54	14
	%	43.9	42.1	45.8	52.2	52.9	37.1	42.5	44.4	66.7	50.0	48.3
Provide	Frequency	463	286	13	11	8	44	23	5	4	54	15
	%	56.1	57.9	54.2	47.8	47.1	62.9	57.5	55.6	33.3	50.5	51.7

2 Medical mutual aid supplementary insurance

Not provide	Frequency	183	87	4	11	8	21	14	1	4	27	6
	%	22.2	17.6	16.7	47.8	47.1	30.0	35.0	11.1	33.3	25.0	20.7
Provide	Frequency	643	407	20	12	9	49	26	8	8	81	23
	%	77.8	82.4	83.3	52.2	52.9	70.0	65.0	88.9	66.7	75.0	79.3

3 Death and mortuary mutual aid supplementary insurance

		Ownership form of your enterprise									
	Sum	State-owned/State-holding enterprise	Collective-owned enterprise	Private enterprise	Cooperative enterprise	Limited liability corporation	Share Holding Corporation Ltd	Enterprise with Funds from Hong Kong, Macao and Taiwan	Foreign funded enterprise	Others	NA
Not provide Frequency	685	389	21	22	14	59	33	9	11	100	27
%	82.9	78.7	87.5	95.7	82.4	84.3	82.5	100.0	91.7	92.6	93.1
Provide Frequency	141	105	3	1	3	11	7	0	1	8	2
%	17.1	21.3	12.5	4.3	17.6	15.7	17.5	0.0	8.3	7.4	6.9

4 Unemployment mutual aid supplementary insurance

	Sum	State-owned/State-holding enterprise	Collective-owned enterprise	Private enterprise	Cooperative enterprise	Limited liability corporation	Share Holding Corporation Ltd	Enterprise with Funds from Hong Kong, Macao and Taiwan	Foreign funded enterprise	Others	NA
Not provide Frequency	567	328	17	21	14	46	23	7	9	80	22
%	68.6	66.4	70.8	91.3	82.4	65.7	57.5	77.8	75.0	74.1	75.9
Provide Frequency	259	166	7	2	3	24	17	2	3	28	7
%	31.4	33.6	29.2	8.7	17.6	34.3	42.5	22.2	25.0	25.9	24.1

5 Industrial injury mutual aid supplementary insurance

Not provide	Frequency	584	349	18	19	7	42	26	6	9	88	20
	%	70.7	70.6	75.0	82.6	41.2	60.0	65.0	66.7	75.0	81.5	69.0
Provide	Frequency	242	145	6	4	10	28	14	3	3	20	9
	%	29.3	29.4	25.0	17.4	58.8	40.0	35.0	33.3	25.0	18.5	31.0

6 Unexpected calamity mutual aid supplementary insurance

Not provide	Frequency	545	311	17	17	11	53	30	7	10	68	21
	%	66.0	63.0	70.8	73.9	64.7	75.7	75.0	77.8	83.3	63.0	72.4
Provide	Frequency	281	183	7	6	6	17	10	2	2	40	8
	%	34.0	37.0	29.2	26.1	35.3	24.3	25.0	22.2	16.7	37.0	27.6

D4-3 Whether or not having built up a record for workers with living difficulties

Built	Frequency	1293	758	44	17	15	116	68	7	16	178	74
	%	71.4	79.2	73.3	27.9	45.5	77.3	75.6	46.7	50.0	61.0	61.2
Not built	Frequency	297	113	11	35	12	23	16	5	12	55	15
	%	16.4	11.8	18.3	57.4	36.4	15.3	17.8	33.3	37.5	18.8	12.4
NA	Frequency	221	86	5	9	6	11	6	3	4	59	32
	%	12.2	9.0	8.3	14.8	18.2	7.3	6.7	20.0	12.5	20.2	26.4

Part 6: Questions about the relationship between the primary trade union committee and other actors

E1-1 Perception of the image of the trade union among the members

			Ownership form of your enterprise								
		Sum	State-owned/ State-holding enterprise	Collective-owned enterprise	Private enterprise	Cooperative enterprise	Limited liability corporation	Share Holding Corporation Ltd	Enterprise with Funds from Hong Kong, Macao and Taiwan	Foreign funded enterprise	Others	NA
Very good	Frequency	214	126	7	4	1	19	9	2	3	32	11
	%	11.8	13.2	11.7	6.6	3.0	12.7	10.0	13.3	9.4	11.0	9.1
Good	Frequency	922	523	34	25	10	78	54	3	20	121	54
	%	50.9	54.6	56.7	41.0	30.3	52.0	60.0	20.0	62.5	41.4	44.6
Fair	Frequency	538	254	17	24	17	46	23	9	7	105	36
	%	29.7	26.5	28.3	39.3	51.5	30.7	25.6	60.0	21.9	36.0	29.8
Bad	Frequency	22	14	1	1	0	0	2	0	0	3	1
	%	1.2	1.5	1.7	1.6	0.0	0.0	2.2	0.0	0.0	1.0	0.8
Very bad	Frequency	2	0	0	1	0	0	0	0	0	1	0
	%	0.1	0.0	0.0	1.6	0.0	0.0	0.0	0.0	0.0	0.3	0.0
NA	Frequency	113	40	1	6	5	7	2	1	2	30	19
	%	6.2	4.2	1.7	9.8	15.2	4.7	2.2	6.7	6.3	10.3	15.7

E1-21 The methods having ever been used to understand the opinions and demands of the members' home visitation

		Sum	State-owned/ State-holding enterprise	Collective-owned enterprise	Private enterprise	Cooperative enterprise	Limited liability corporation	Share Holding Corporation Ltd	Enterprise with Funds from Hong Kong, Macao and Taiwan	Foreign funded enterprise	Others	NA
Has not used	Frequency	1164	571	42	49	26	100	54	11	27	193	91
	%	64.3	59.7	70.0	80.3	78.8	66.7	60.0	73.3	84.4	66.1	75.2
Has used	Frequency	647	386	18	12	7	50	36	4	5	99	30
	%	35.7	40.3	30.0	19.7	21.2	33.3	40.0	26.7	15.6	33.9	24.8

E1-22 Questionnaire survey

Has not used	Frequency	1138	550	43	49	26	102	58	13	19	204	74
	%	62.8	57.5	71.7	80.3	78.8	68.0	64.4	86.7	59.4	69.9	61.2
Has used	Frequency	673	407	17	12	7	48	32	2	13	88	47
	%	37.2	42.5	28.3	19.7	21.2	32.0	35.6	13.3	40.6	30.1	38.8

E1-23 Round-table discussion on special topic

Has not used	Frequency	732	310	39	37	19	60	36	9	16	149	57
	%	40.4	32.4	65.0	60.7	57.6	40.0	40.0	60.0	50.0	51.0	47.1
Has used	Frequency	1079	647	21	24	14	90	54	6	16	143	64
	%	59.6	67.6	35.0	39.3	42.4	60.0	60.0	40.0	50.0	49.0	52.9

E1-24 Telephone counseling

Has not used	Frequency	1446	721	50	55	29	132	68	14	27	247	103
	%	79.8	75.3	83.3	90.2	87.9	88.0	75.6	93.3	84.4	84.6	85.1
Has used	Frequency	365	236	10	6	4	18	22	1	5	45	18
	%	20.2	24.7	16.7	9.8	12.1	12.0	24.4	6.7	15.6	15.4	14.9

E1-25 Reception day of trade union chairman

Has not used	Frequency	1614	840	54	59	32	138	82	14	29	257	109
	%	89.1	87.8	90.0	96.7	97.0	92.0	91.1	93.3	90.6	88.0	90.1
Has used	Frequency	197	117	6	2	1	12	8	1	3	35	12
	%	10.9	12.2	10.0	3.3	3.0	8.0	8.9	6.7	9.4	12.0	9.9

E1-26 Opinion box

Ownership form of your enterprise

		Sum	State-owned/State-holding enterprise	Collective-owned enterprise	Private enterprise	Cooperative enterprise	Limited liability corporation	Share Holding Corporation Ltd	Enterprise with Funds from Hong Kong, Macao and Taiwan	Foreign funded enterprise	Others	NA
Has not used	Frequency	1433	743	52	49	21	112	79	10	28	252	87
	%	79.1	77.6	86.7	80.3	63.6	74.7	87.8	66.7	87.5	86.3	71.9
Has used	Frequency	378	214	8	12	12	38	11	5	4	40	34
	%	20.9	22.4	13.3	19.7	36.4	25.3	12.2	33.3	12.5	13.7	28.1

E2-1 Whether or not having had any cases that delegations or over 10 representatives bring in a bill at members' congress/members' assembly

		Sum	State-owned/State-holding enterprise	Collective-owned enterprise	Private enterprise	Cooperative enterprise	Limited liability corporation	Share Holding Corporation Ltd	Enterprise with Funds from Hong Kong, Macao and Taiwan	Foreign funded enterprise	Others	NA
There are	Frequency	582	370	9	8	8	39	25	2	9	76	36
	%	32.1	38.7	15.0	13.1	24.2	26.0	27.8	13.3	28.1	26.0	29.8
There are not	Frequency	800	395	36	31	14	82	51	7	15	128	41
	%	44.2	41.3	60.0	50.8	42.4	54.7	56.7	46.7	46.9	43.8	33.9
NA	Frequency	429	192	15	22	11	29	14	6	8	88	44
	%	23.7	20.1	25.0	36.1	33.3	19.3	15.6	40.0	25.0	30.1	36.4

E3-1 Demand to the higher-level trade union organizations to do

Convey the interests and demands of workers and staff members more effectively	Frequency	698	374	24	18	10	63	39	5	8	116	41
	%	38.5	39.1	40.0	29.5	30.3	42.0	43.3	33.3	25.0	39.7	33.9
Actively engage in establishing laws and regulations concerning vital interests of workers and staff members	Frequency	532	307	16	19	6	41	28	3	14	66	32
	%	29.4	32.1	26.7	31.1	18.2	27.3	31.1	20.0	43.8	22.6	26.4
Provide basic-level trade unions with theoretical policies and legal consultations	Frequency	282	137	8	15	7	29	17	4	5	44	16
	%	15.6	14.3	13.3	24.6	21.2	19.3	18.9	26.7	15.6	15.1	13.2
Others	Frequency	16	8	0	1	1	0	1	0	0	5	0
	%	0.9	0.8	0.0	1.6	3.0	0.0	1.1	0.0	0.0	1.7	0.0
NA	Frequency	283	131	12	8	9	17	5	3	5	61	32
	%	15.7	13.7	20.0	13.1	27.3	11.3	5.6	20.0	15.6	20.9	26.4

E4-1 Whether or not having established party organizations in the work unit

1 Established	Frequency	1638	903	56	40	23	138	84	10	27	256	101
	%	90.4	94.4	93.3	65.6	69.7	92.0	93.3	66.7	84.4	87.7	83.5
2 Not established	Frequency	59	7	1	16	8	6	4	4	3	9	1
	%	3.3	0.7	1.7	26.2	24.2	4.0	4.4	26.7	9.4	3.1	0.8
NA	Frequency	114	47	3	5	2	6	2	1	2	27	19
	%	6.3	4.9	5.0	8.2	6.1	4.0	2.2	6.7	6.3	9.2	15.7

E4-1 (If you chose 1 in E4-1) whether or not the following cadres being the members of the party committee of work unit

1. Trade union chairman

		Sum	State-owned/State-holding enterprise	Collective-owned enterprise	Private enterprise	Cooperative enterprise	Limited liability corporation	Share Holding Corporation Ltd	Enterprise with Funds from Hong Kong, Macao and Taiwan	Foreign funded enterprise	Others	NA
Is not the member	Frequency	403	131	19	22	10	25	19	3	5	115	54
	%	24.6	14.5	33.9	55.0	43.5	18.1	22.6	30.0	18.5	44.9	53.5
Is the member	Frequency	1235	772	37	18	13	113	65	7	22	141	47
	%	75.4	85.5	66.1	45.0	56.5	81.9	77.4	70.0	81.5	55.1	46.5

2. Trade union vice-chairman

		Sum	State-owned/State-holding enterprise	Collective-owned enterprise	Private enterprise	Cooperative enterprise	Limited liability corporation	Share Holding Corporation Ltd	Enterprise with Funds from Hong Kong, Macao and Taiwan	Foreign funded enterprise	Others	NA
Is not the member	Frequency	1513	833	53	32	21	127	78	8	24	243	94
	%	92.4	92.2	94.6	80.0	91.3	92.0	92.9	80.0	88.9	94.9	93.1
Is the member	Frequency	125	70	3	8	2	11	6	2	3	13	7
	%	7.6	7.8	5.4	20.0	8.7	8.0	7.1	20.0	11.1	5.1	6.9

3. Other committee members of the primary trade union committee

		Sum	State-owned/State-holding enterprise	Collective-owned enterprise	Private enterprise	Cooperative enterprise	Limited liability corporation	Share Holding Corporation Ltd	Enterprise with Funds from Hong Kong, Macao and Taiwan	Foreign funded enterprise	Others	NA
Is not the member	Frequency	1493	838	50	33	19	125	73	8	24	231	92
	%	91.1	92.8	89.3	82.5	82.6	90.6	86.9	80.0	88.9	90.2	91.1
Is the member	Frequency	145	65	6	7	4	13	11	2	3	25	9
	%	8.9	7.2	10.7	17.5	17.4	9.4	13.1	20.0	11.1	9.8	8.9

E4-2 Whether or not having established a party group or party branch in the primary trade union

Established	Frequency	1250	690	43	25	16	111	69	8	23	194	71
	%	69.0	72.1	71.7	41.0	48.5	74.0	76.7	53.3	71.9	66.4	58.7
Not established	Frequency	282	140	11	20	7	18	13	5	4	47	17
	%	15.6	14.6	18.3	32.8	21.2	12.0	14.4	33.3	12.5	16.1	14.0
NA	Frequency	279	127	6	16	10	21	8	2	5	51	33
	%	15.4	13.3	10.0	26.2	30.3	14.0	8.9	13.3	15.6	17.5	27.3

E5-1 Whether or not the following trade union cadres having participated in a board of directors as the representatives of workers and staff members

1. Trade union chairman

Has not participated	Frequency	1248	654	40	42	22	73	50	11	23	239	94
	%	69.0	68.3	66.7	68.9	66.7	48.7	55.6	73.3	71.9	82.1	77.7
Has participated	Frequency	562	303	20	19	11	77	40	4	9	52	27
	%	31.0	31.7	33.3	31.1	33.3	51.3	44.4	26.7	28.1	17.9	22.3

2. Trade union vice-chairman

Has not participated	Frequency	1747	921	56	59	30	144	88	15	32	283	119
	%	96.5	96.2	93.3	96.7	90.9	96.0	97.8	100.0	100.0	97.3	98.3
Has participated	Frequency	63	36	4	2	3	6	2	0	0	8	2
	%	3.5	3.8	6.7	3.3	9.1	4.0	2.2	0.0	0.0	2.7	1.7

3. Other committee members of the primary trade union committee

		Sum	State-owned/State-holding enterprise	Collective-owned enterprise	Private enterprise	Cooperative enterprise	Limited liability corporation	Share Holding Corporation Ltd	Enterprise with Funds from Hong Kong, Macao and Taiwan	Foreign funded enterprise	Others	NA
Has not participated	Frequency	1717	913	55	59	27	137	85	15	31	276	119
	%	94.9	95.4	91.7	96.7	81.8	91.3	94.4	100.0	96.9	94.8	98.3
Has participated	Frequency	93	44	5	2	6	13	5	0	1	15	2
	%	5.1	4.6	8.3	3.3	18.2	8.7	5.6	0.0	3.1	5.2	1.7

E5-1-1 (If a trade union cadre is participating in a board of directors) the procedure to elect him/her

		Sum	State-owned/State-holding enterprise	Collective-owned enterprise	Private enterprise	Cooperative enterprise	Limited liability corporation	Share Holding Corporation Ltd	Enterprise with Funds from Hong Kong, Macao and Taiwan	Foreign funded enterprise	Others	NA
Elected by the congress of workers and staff members	Frequency	302	166	12	7	11	43	16	2	2	28	15
	%	49.8	51.4	57.1	35.0	68.8	52.4	36.4	50.0	20.0	48.3	51.7
Elected by the trade union committee	Frequency	57	38	1	3	1	9	1	1	1	1	1
	%	9.4	11.8	4.8	15.0	6.3	11.0	2.3	25.0	10.0	1.7	3.4
Not passed through the election	Frequency	131	63	2	6	2	21	14	0	4	11	8
	%	21.6	19.5	9.5	30.0	12.5	25.6	31.8	0.0	40.0	19.0	27.6
NA	Frequency	117	56	6	4	2	9	13	1	3	18	5
	%	19.3	17.3	28.6	20.0	12.5	11.0	29.5	25.0	30.0	31.0	17.2

E5-2 Whether or not the following trade union cadres having participated in a board of supervisors as the representatives of workers and staff members

1. Trade union chairman

Has not participated	Frequency	1472	780	51	50	25	102	60	14	26	259	105
	%	81.3	81.5	85.0	82.0	75.8	68.0	66.7	93.3	81.3	89.0	86.8
Has participated	Frequency	338	177	9	11	8	48	30	1	6	32	16
	%	18.7	18.5	15.0	18.0	24.2	32.0	33.3	6.7	18.8	11.0	13.2

2. Trade union vice-chairman

Has not participated	Frequency	1648	855	56	57	29	131	80	13	30	278	119
	%	91.0	89.3	93.3	93.4	87.9	87.3	88.9	86.7	93.8	95.5	98.3
Has participated	Frequency	162	102	4	4	4	19	10	2	2	13	2
	%	9.0	10.7	6.7	6.6	12.1	12.7	11.1	13.3	6.3	4.5	1.7

3. Other committee members of the primary trade union committee

Has not participated	Frequency	1664	880	51	58	27	131	82	13	29	275	118
	%	91.9	92.0	85.0	95.1	81.8	87.3	91.1	86.7	90.6	94.5	97.5
Has participated	Frequency	146	77	9	3	6	19	8	2	3	16	3
	%	8.1	8.0	15.0	4.9	18.2	12.7	8.9	13.3	9.4	5.5	2.5

E5-2-1 (If a trade union cadre is participating in a board of supervisors) the procedure to elect him/her

		Sum	State-owned/State-holding enterprise	Collective-owned enterprise	Private enterprise	Cooperative enterprise	Limited liability corporation	Share Holding Corporation Ltd	Enterprise with Funds from Hong Kong, Macao and Taiwan	Foreign funded enterprise	Others	NA
									Ownership form of your enterprise			
Elected by the congress of workers and staff members	Frequency	298	165	12	5	8	42	23	2	3	25	13
	%	55.5	56.3	66.7	33.3	50.0	54.5	54.8	66.7	42.9	54.3	65.0
Elected by the trade union committee	Frequency	71	47	1	4	1	8	6	0	1	2	1
	%	13.2	16.0	5.6	26.7	6.3	10.4	14.3	0.0	14.3	4.3	5.0
Not passed through the election	Frequency	110	53	2	4	4	21	8	0	1	12	5
	%	20.5	18.1	11.1	26.7	25.0	27.3	19.0	0.0	14.3	26.1	25.0
NA	Frequency	58	28	3	2	3	6	5	1	2	7	1
	%	10.8	9.6	16.7	13.3	18.8	7.8	11.9	33.3	28.6	15.2	5.0

E6-1 Whether or not the primary trade union committee are doing any activities jointly with other mass organizations such as the local Women's Federation, Communist Youth League, or the Aging Committee

		Sum	State-owned/State-holding enterprise	Collective-owned enterprise	Private enterprise	Cooperative enterprise	Limited liability corporation	Share Holding Corporation Ltd	Enterprise with Funds from Hong Kong, Macao and Taiwan	Foreign funded enterprise	Others	NA
Doing activities jointly	Frequency	841	450	28	24	16	62	44	4	10	146	57
	%	46.4	47.0	46.7	39.3	48.5	41.3	48.9	26.7	31.3	50.0	47.1
Doing activities solely	Frequency	417	233	16	13	7	48	17	3	11	55	14
	%	23.0	24.3	26.7	21.3	21.2	32.0	18.9	20.0	34.4	18.8	11.6
NA	Frequency	553	274	16	24	10	40	29	8	11	91	50
	%	30.5	28.6	26.7	39.3	30.3	26.7	32.2	53.3	34.4	31.2	41.3

E6-2 Neighborhood activities in which the trade union participated actively in 2003

Provide human power and material resources for the utilities of the neighborhood community	Frequency	315	172	7	10	31	17	5	4	48	18
	%	17.4	18.0	11.7	16.4	20.7	18.9	33.3	12.5	16.4	14.9
Hold various social activities and public welfare activities of health promotion and enlightenment jointly with the neighborhood community	Frequency	495	262	16	13	38	25	2	10	83	31
	%	27.3	27.4	26.7	21.3	25.3	27.8	13.3	31.3	28.4	25.6
Open the trade union's facilities to the neighborhood community	Frequency	51	32	1	1	7	2	0	0	6	1
	%	2.8	3.3	1.7	1.6	4.7	2.2	0.0	0.0	2.1	0.8
Organize the trade union activists to do volunteer work in the leisure time	Frequency	142	66	6	3	15	9	2	1	24	13
	%	7.8	6.9	10.0	4.9	10.0	10.0	13.3	3.1	8.2	10.7
Others	Frequency	26	10	3	0	1	3	0	0	9	0
	%	1.4	1.0	5.0	0.0	0.7	3.3	0.0	0.0	3.1	0.0
Have never participated in any activities of neighborhood community	Frequency	253	139	8	15	22	13	1	9	37	7
	%	14.0	14.5	13.3	24.6	14.7	14.4	6.7	28.1	12.7	5.8
NA	Frequency	529	276	19	19	36	21	5	8	85	51
	%	29.2	28.8	31.7	31.1	24.0	23.3	33.3	25.0	29.1	42.1

E7-1 Whether or not the trade union has ever worked hard to be reported in the following media

1. Newspapers and magazines published by local trade unions

		Sum	State-owned/ State-holding enterprise	Collective-owned enterprise	Private enterprise	Cooperative enterprise	Limited liability corporation	Share Holding Corporation Ltd	Enterprise with Funds from Hong Kong, Macao and Taiwan	Foreign funded enterprise	Others	NA
Has not worked	Frequency	1339	682	50	46	26	111	66	12	27	224	95
	%	74.0	71.3	83.3	75.4	78.8	74.0	73.3	80.0	84.4	77.0	78.5
Has worked	Frequency	471	275	10	15	7	39	24	3	5	67	26
	%	26.0	28.7	16.7	24.6	21.2	26.0	26.7	20.0	15.6	23.0	21.5

2. Local newspapers and magazines

		Sum	State-owned/ State-holding enterprise	Collective-owned enterprise	Private enterprise	Cooperative enterprise	Limited liability corporation	Share Holding Corporation Ltd	Enterprise with Funds from Hong Kong, Macao and Taiwan	Foreign funded enterprise	Others	NA
Has not worked	Frequency	1464	763	53	51	31	116	75	15	27	231	102
	%	80.9	79.7	88.3	83.6	93.9	77.3	83.3	100.0	84.4	79.4	84.3
Has worked	Frequency	346	194	7	10	2	34	15	0	5	60	19
	%	19.1	20.3	11.7	16.4	6.1	22.7	16.7	0.0	15.6	20.6	15.7

3. Local radio and television stations

Has not worked	Frequency	1535	814	55	54	28	122	69	14	29	255	95
	%	84.8	85.1	91.7	88.5	84.8	81.3	76.7	93.3	90.6	87.6	78.5
Has worked	Frequency	275	143	5	7	5	28	21	1	3	36	26
	%	15.2	14.9	8.3	11.5	15.2	18.7	23.3	6.7	9.4	12.4	21.5

4. Newspapers and magazines published by All-China Federation of Trade Unions

Has not worked	Frequency	1661	868	60	56	32	130	84	15	31	276	109
	%	91.8	90.7	100.0	91.8	97.0	86.7	93.3	100.0	96.9	94.8	90.1
Has worked	Frequency	149	89	0	5	1	20	6	0	1	15	12
	%	8.2	9.3	0.0	8.2	3.0	13.3	6.7	0.0	3.1	5.2	9.9

5. National newspapers and magazines

Has not worked	Frequency	1723	911	57	61	33	134	88	15	32	278	114
	%	95.2	95.2	95.0	100.0	100.0	89.3	97.8	100.0	100.0	95.5	94.2
Has worked	Frequency	87	46	3	0	0	16	2	0	0	13	7
	%	4.8	4.8	5.0	0.0	0.0	10.7	2.2	0.0	0.0	4.5	5.8

6. National radio and television stations

		Ownership form of your enterprise							Enterprise with Funds from Hong Kong, Macao and Taiwan	Foreign funded enterprise	Others	NA
	Sum	State-owned/State-holding enterprise	Collective-owned enterprise	Private enterprise	Cooperative enterprise	Limited liability corporation	Share Holding Corporation Ltd					
Has not worked	Frequency	1773	938	59	60	33	140	89	15	32	286	121
	%	98.0	98.0	98.3	98.4	100.0	93.3	98.9	100.0	100.0	98.3	100.0
Has worked	Frequency	37	19	1	1	0	10	1	0	0	5	0
	%	2.0	2.0	1.7	1.6	0.0	6.7	1.1	0.0	0.0	1.7	0.0

E7-1-1 Whether or not the following media have ever reported on your trade union
1. Newspapers and magazines published by local trade unions

Did not	Frequency	1329	672	50	49	26	112	66	12	22	228	92
	%	73.4	70.2	83.3	80.3	78.8	74.7	73.3	80.0	68.8	78.4	76.0
Did a report	Frequency	481	285	10	12	7	38	24	3	10	63	29
	%	26.6	29.8	16.7	19.7	21.2	25.3	26.7	20.0	31.3	21.6	24.0

2. Local newspapers and magazines

Did not	Frequency	1429	739	55	53	31	119	70	15	24	227	96
	%	79.0	77.2	91.7	86.9	93.9	79.3	77.8	100.0	75.0	78.0	79.3
Did a report	Frequency	381	218	5	8	2	31	20	0	8	64	25
	%	21.0	22.8	8.3	13.1	6.1	20.7	22.2	0.0	25.0	22.0	20.7

3. Local radio and television stations

Did not	Frequency	1526	805	57	54	25	118	71	14	28	255	99
	%	84.3	84.1	95.0	88.5	75.8	78.7	78.9	93.3	87.5	87.6	81.8
Did a report	Frequency	284	152	3	7	8	32	19	1	4	36	22
	%	15.7	15.9	5.0	11.5	24.2	21.3	21.1	6.7	12.5	12.4	18.2

4. Newspapers and magazines published by All-China Federation of Trade Unions

Did not	Frequency	1693	890	59	57	32	136	87	15	29	279	109
	%	93.5	93.0	98.3	93.4	97.0	90.7	96.7	100.0	90.6	95.9	90.1
Did a report	Frequency	117	67	1	4	1	14	3	0	3	12	12
	%	6.5	7.0	1.7	6.6	3.0	9.3	3.3	0.0	9.4	4.1	9.9

5. National newspapers and magazines

		Sum	State-owned/ State-holding enterprise	Collective-owned enterprise	Private enterprise	Cooperative enterprise	Limited liability corporation	Share Holding Corporation Ltd	Enterprise with Funds from Hong Kong, Macao and Taiwan	Foreign funded enterprise	Others	NA
											Ownership form of your enterprise	
Did not	Frequency	1739	916	59	60	32	139	87	15	31	285	115
	%	96.1	95.7	98.3	98.4	97.0	92.7	96.7	100.0	96.9	97.9	95.0
Did a report	Frequency	71	41	1	1	1	11	3	0	1	6	6
	%	3.9	4.3	1.7	1.6	3.0	7.3	3.3	0.0	3.1	2.1	5.0

6. National radio and television stations

		Sum	State-owned/ State-holding enterprise	Collective-owned enterprise	Private enterprise	Cooperative enterprise	Limited liability corporation	Share Holding Corporation Ltd	Enterprise with Funds from Hong Kong, Macao and Taiwan	Foreign funded enterprise	Others	NA
Did not	Frequency	1785	944	60	61	33	143	87	15	31	290	121
	%	98.6	98.6	100.0	100.0	100.0	95.3	96.7	100.0	96.9	99.7	100.0
Did a report	Frequency	25	13	0	0	0	7	3	0	1	1	0
	%	1.4	1.4	0.0	0.0	0.0	4.7	3.3	0.0	3.1	0.3	0.0

E7-2 The organizations that are worth contacting with to convey the opinions of primary trade unions and the members and to solve the problems effectively

1. The first

Organization												
Administrative organizations in the work unit	Frequency	1036	564	25	33	15	97	54	9	20	155	64
	%	57.2	58.9	41.7	54.1	45.5	64.7	60.0	60.0	62.5	53.1	52.9
Party organizations in the work unit	Frequency	194	121	8	3	3	9	5	2	2	33	8
	%	10.7	12.6	13.3	4.9	9.1	6.0	5.6	13.3	6.3	11.3	6.6
Local government where the work unit locates	Frequency	35	7	0	2	3	3	3	0	1	11	5
	%	1.9	0.7	0.0	3.3	9.1	2.0	3.3	0.0	3.1	3.8	4.1
Party committee where the work unit locates	Frequency	15	5	1	0	0	2	2	0	1	4	0
	%	0.8	0.5	1.7	0.0	0.0	1.3	2.2	0.0	3.1	1.4	0.0
Deputies of the People's Congress/ Commissars of the Political Consultative Conference where the work unit locates	Frequency	5	2	1	0	0	1	0	0	0	0	1
	%	0.3	0.2	1.7	0.0	0.0	0.7	0.0	0.0	0.0	0.0	0.8
Local federation of trade unions where the work unit locates	Frequency	37	19	1	1	2	2	3	0	0	8	1
	%	2.0	2.0	1.7	1.6	6.1	1.3	3.3	0.0	0.0	2.7	0.8
Higher-level government	Frequency	13	4	1	1	0	2	1	1	0	2	1
	%	0.7	0.4	1.7	1.6	0.0	1.3	1.1	6.7	0.0	0.7	0.8
Higher-level Party Committee	Frequency	19	8	2	0	1	1	2	0	1	4	0
	%	1.0	0.8	3.3	0.0	3.0	0.7	2.2	0.0	3.1	1.4	0.0

Ownership form of your enterprise

		Sum	State-owned/ State-holding enterprise	Collective-owned enterprise	Private enterprise	Cooperative enterprise	Limited liability corporation	Share Holding Corporation Ltd	Enterprise with Funds from Hong Kong, Macao and Taiwan	Foreign funded enterprise	Others	NA
Deputies of the higher-level People's Congress/ Commissars of the higher-level Political Consultative Conference	Frequency	0	0	0	0	0	0	0	0	0	0	0
	%	0.0	0.0	0.0	0.0	0.0	0.0	0.0	0.0	0.0	0.0	0.0
Higher-level federations of trade unions	Frequency	24	13	3	0	0	2	2	1	2	1	0
	%	1.3	1.4	5.0	0.0	0.0	1.3	2.2	6.7	6.3	0.3	0.0
Central government	Frequency	4	1	2	0	0	0	1	0	0	0	0
	%	0.2	0.1	3.3	0.0	0.0	0.0	1.1	0.0	0.0	0.0	0.0
Central Party Committee	Frequency	11	7	0	0	0	0	1	1	0	1	1
	%	0.6	0.7	0.0	0.0	0.0	0.0	1.1	6.7	0.0	0.3	0.8
Deputies of the National People's Congress/ Commissars of the Chinese People's Political Consultative Conference	Frequency	4	1	0	0	0	0	0	0	0	2	1
	%	0.2	0.1	0.0	0.0	0.0	0.0	0.0	0.0	0.0	0.7	0.8
All-China Federation of Trade Unions	Frequency	10	6	0	1	0	1	0	0	0	1	1
	%	0.6	0.6	0.0	1.6	0.0	0.7	0.0	0.0	0.0	0.3	0.8

Public celebrities/ Scholars/ Democratic parties	Frequency	1	1	0	0	0	0	0	0	0	0	0
	%	0.1	0.1	0.0	0.0	0.0	0.0	0.0	0.0	0.0	0.0	0.0
Local media	Frequency	2	2	0	0	0	0	0	0	0	0	0
	%	0.1	0.2	0.0	0.0	0.0	0.0	0.0	0.0	0.0	0.0	0.0
National media	Frequency	8	5	0	1	0	0	2	0	0	0	0
	%	0.4	0.5	0.0	1.6	0.0	0.0	2.2	0.0	0.0	0.0	0.0
NA	Frequency	393	191	16	19	9	30	14	1	5	70	38
	%	21.7	20.0	26.7	31.1	27.3	20.0	15.6	6.7	15.6	24.0	31.4

2. The second

Administrative organizations in the work unit	Frequency	150	88	7	3	2	8	8	0	3	21	10
	%	8.3	9.2	11.7	4.9	6.1	5.3	8.9	0.0	9.4	7.2	8.3
Party organizations in the work unit	Frequency	813	471	15	12	7	74	37	4	11	136	46
	%	44.9	49.2	25.0	19.7	21.2	49.3	41.1	26.7	34.4	46.6	38.0
Local government where the work unit locates	Frequency	84	20	7	9	5	10	4	0	2	14	13
	%	4.6	2.1	11.7	14.8	15.2	6.7	4.4	0.0	6.3	4.8	10.7
Party committee where the work unit locates	Frequency	50	27	1	2	0	3	5	0	0	5	7
	%	2.8	2.8	1.7	3.3	0.0	2.0	5.6	0.0	0.0	1.7	5.8
Deputies of the People's Congress/ Commissars of the Political Consultative Conference where the work unit locates	Frequency	22	12	1	1	0	0	2	0	0	6	0
	%	1.2	1.3	1.7	1.6	0.0	0.0	2.2	0.0	0.0	2.1	0.0
Local federation of trade unions where the work unit locates	Frequency	95	36	3	8	3	7	6	1	5	21	5
	%	5.2	3.8	5.0	13.1	9.1	4.7	6.7	6.7	15.6	7.2	4.1

Ownership form of your enterprise

		Sum	State-owned/State-holding enterprise	Collective-owned enterprise	Private enterprise	Cooperative enterprise	Limited liability corporation	Share Holding Corporation Ltd	Enterprise with Funds from Hong Kong, Macao and Taiwan	Foreign funded enterprise	Others	NA
Higher-level government	Frequency	54	14	5	5	3	7	9	1	2	5	3
	%	3.0	1.5	8.3	8.2	9.1	4.7	10.0	6.7	6.3	1.7	2.5
Higher-level Party Committee	Frequency	64	42	2	1	1	2	1	2	2	8	3
	%	3.5	4.4	3.3	1.6	3.0	1.3	1.1	13.3	6.3	2.7	2.5
Deputies of the higher-level People's Congress/Commissars of the higher-level Political Consultative Conference	Frequency	5	1	0	0	0	1	1	1	0	1	0
	%	0.3	0.1	0.0	0.0	0.0	0.7	1.1	6.7	0.0	0.3	0.0
Higher-level federations of trade unions	Frequency	73	44	1	2	1	8	2	1	2	8	4
	%	4.0	4.6	1.7	3.3	3.0	5.3	2.2	6.7	6.3	2.7	3.3
Central government	Frequency	9	4	1	1	0	0	1	1	0	1	0
	%	0.5	0.4	1.7	1.6	0.0	0.0	1.1	6.7	0.0	0.3	0.0
Central Party Committee	Frequency	7	3	0	1	1	0	0	0	0	2	0
	%	0.4	0.3	0.0	1.6	3.0	0.0	0.0	0.0	0.0	0.7	0.0
Deputies of the National People's Congress/Commissars of the Chinese People's Political Consultative Conference	Frequency	5	2	1	0	0	1	0	0	0	1	0
	%	0.3	0.2	1.7	0.0	0.0	0.7	0.0	0.0	0.0	0.3	0.0

		1	2	3	4	5	6	7	8	9	10	11
All-China Federation of Trade Unions	Frequency	19	10	0	0	0	1	3	2	0	3	0
	%	1.0	1.0	0.0	0.0	0.0	0.7	3.3	13.3	0.0	1.0	0.0
Public celebrities/ Scholars/ Democratic parties	Frequency	2	1	0	0	0	1	0	0	0	0	0
	%	0.1	0.1	0.0	0.0	0.0	0.7	0.0	0.0	0.0	0.0	0.0
Local media	Frequency	8	5	1	0	0	0	1	1	0	0	0
	%	0.4	0.5	1.7	0.0	0.0	0.0	1.1	6.7	0.0	0.0	0.0
National media	Frequency	2	1	0	0	0	1	0	0	0	0	0
	%	0.1	0.1	0.0	0.0	0.0	0.7	0.0	0.0	0.0	0.0	0.0
NA	Frequency	349	176	15	16	10	26	10	1	5	60	30
	%	19.3	18.4	25.0	26.2	30.3	17.3	11.1	6.7	15.6	20.5	24.8

3. The third

		1	2	3	4	5	6	7	8	9	10	11
Administrative organizations in the work unit	Frequency	77	33	2	7	3	6	6	0	2	12	6
	%	4.3	3.4	3.3	11.5	9.1	4.0	6.7	0.0	6.3	4.1	5.0
Party organizations in the work unit	Frequency	106	55	6	1	0	11	8	0	2	14	9
	%	5.9	5.7	10.0	1.6	0.0	7.3	8.9	0.0	6.3	4.8	7.4
Local government where the work unit locates	Frequency	94	42	6	3	2	11	6	2	3	14	5
	%	5.2	4.4	10.0	4.9	6.1	7.3	6.7	13.3	9.4	4.8	4.1
Party committee where the work unit locates	Frequency	47	28	1	1	0	2	1	0	1	10	3
	%	2.6	2.9	1.7	1.6	0.0	1.3	1.1	0.0	3.1	3.4	2.5
Deputies of the People's Congress/ Commissars of the Political Consultative Conference where the work unit locates	Frequency	14	8	0	2	0	0	1	0	0	1	2
	%	0.8	0.8	0.0	3.3	0.0	0.0	1.1	0.0	0.0	0.3	1.7

		Sum	State-owned/ State-holding enterprise	Collective-owned enterprise	Private enterprise	Cooperative enterprise	Limited liability corporation	Share Holding Corporation Ltd	Enterprise with Funds from Hong Kong, Macao and Taiwan	Foreign funded enterprise	Others	NA
												Ownership form of your enterprise
Local federation of trade unions where the work unit locates	Frequency	242	115	9	8	3	29	9	0	4	40	25
	%	13.4	12.0	15.0	13.1	9.1	19.3	10.0	0.0	12.5	13.7	20.7
Higher-level government	Frequency	73	26	5	6	4	5	5	0	3	10	9
	%	4.0	2.7	8.3	9.8	12.1	3.3	5.6	0.0	9.4	3.4	7.4
Higher-level Party Committee	Frequency	139	87	1	2	2	9	7	1	1	22	7
	%	7.7	9.1	1.7	3.3	6.1	6.0	7.8	6.7	3.1	7.5	5.8
Deputies of the higher-level People's Congress/ Commissars of the higher-level Political Consultative Conference	Frequency	3	0	0	0	0	0	1	1	0	1	0
	%	0.2	0.0	0.0	0.0	0.0	0.0	1.1	6.7	0.0	0.3	0.0
Higher-level federations of trade unions	Frequency	484	273	8	16	7	34	22	6	11	87	20
	%	26.7	28.5	13.3	26.2	21.2	22.7	24.4	40.0	34.4	29.8	16.5
Central government	Frequency	9	1	1	0	0	1	1	0	0	3	2
	%	0.5	0.1	1.7	0.0	0.0	0.7	1.1	0.0	0.0	1.0	1.7
Central Party Committee	Frequency	9	7	0	0	0	1	1	0	0	0	0
	%	0.5	0.7	0.0	0.0	0.0	0.7	1.1	0.0	0.0	0.0	0.0

Deputies of the National People's Congress/Commissars of the Chinese People's Political Consultative Conference	Frequency	6	6	0	0	0	0	0	0	0	0	0
	%	0.3	0.6	0.0	0.0	0.0	0.0	0.0	0.0	0.0	0.0	0.0
All-China Federation of Trade Unions	Frequency	28	12	1	2	1	6	1	1	0	1	3
	%	1.5	1.3	1.7	3.3	3.0	4.0	1.1	6.7	0.0	0.3	2.5
Public celebrities/Scholars/Democratic parties	Frequency	2	1	1	0	0	0	0	0	0	0	0
	%	0.1	0.1	1.7	0.0	0.0	0.0	0.0	0.0	0.0	0.0	0.0
Local media	Frequency	47	25	2	1	0	3	3	1	0	9	3
	%	2.6	2.6	3.3	1.6	0.0	2.0	3.3	6.7	0.0	3.1	2.5
National media	Frequency	47	25	1	0	2	2	5	2	1	8	1
	%	2.6	2.6	1.7	0.0	6.1	1.3	5.6	13.3	3.1	2.7	0.8
NA	Frequency	384	213	16	12	9	30	13	1	4	60	26
	%	21.2	22.3	26.7	19.7	27.3	20.0	14.4	6.7	12.5	20.5	21.5

E8 The major impediments of the development of trade union work

1. The trade union cadres' enthusiasm is not high

Is not a major impediment	Frequency	1177	641	38	36	18	94	53	9	19	196	73
	%	65.0	67.0	63.3	59.0	54.5	62.7	58.9	60.0	59.4	67.4	60.3
Is a major impediment	Frequency	633	316	22	25	15	56	37	6	13	95	48
	%	35.0	33.0	36.7	41.0	45.5	37.3	41.1	40.0	40.6	67.4	39.7

2. The trade union cadres' knowledge and competence are not sufficient

		Sum	State-owned/ State-holding enterprise	Collective-owned enterprise	Private enterprise	Cooperative enterprise	Limited liability corporation	Share Holding Corporation Ltd	Enterprise with Funds from Hong Kong, Macao and Taiwan	Foreign funded enterprise	Others	NA
Is not a major impediment	Frequency	1079	539	39	35	18	88	43	9	16	202	90
	%	59.6	56.3	65.0	57.4	54.5	58.7	47.8	60.0	50.0	69.4	74.4
Is a major impediment	Frequency	731	418	21	26	15	62	47	6	16	89	31
	%	40.4	43.7	35.0	42.6	45.5	41.3	52.2	40.0	50.0	30.6	25.6

3. Activities do not meet the needs of workers and staff members

		Sum	State-owned/ State-holding enterprise	Collective-owned enterprise	Private enterprise	Cooperative enterprise	Limited liability corporation	Share Holding Corporation Ltd	Enterprise with Funds from Hong Kong, Macao and Taiwan	Foreign funded enterprise	Others	NA
Is not a major impediment	Frequency	1484	780	49	52	28	117	70	11	29	238	110
	%	82.0	81.5	81.7	85.2	84.8	78.0	77.8	73.3	90.6	81.8	90.9
Is a major impediment	Frequency	326	177	11	9	5	33	20	4	3	53	11
	%	18.0	18.5	18.3	14.8	15.2	22.0	22.2	26.7	9.4	18.2	9.1

4. Lack in the awareness of the position and roles of the trade union by the administration of the work unit

		Sum	State-owned/ State-holding enterprise	Collective-owned enterprise	Private enterprise	Cooperative enterprise	Limited liability corporation	Share Holding Corporation Ltd	Enterprise with Funds from Hong Kong, Macao and Taiwan	Foreign funded enterprise	Others	NA
Is not a major impediment	Frequency	904	486	31	32	13	72	38	10	15	144	63
	%	49.9	50.8	51.7	52.5	39.4	48.0	42.2	66.7	46.9	49.5	52.1
Is a major impediment	Frequency	906	471	29	29	20	78	52	5	17	147	58
	%	50.1	49.2	48.3	47.5	60.6	52.0	57.8	33.3	53.1	50.5	47.9

5. Lack in the awareness of the position and roles of the trade union by the party organizations of the work unit

Is not a major impediment	Frequency	1343	724	48	55	30	110	59	12	25	198	82
	%	74.2	75.7	80.0	90.2	90.9	73.3	65.6	80.0	78.1	68.0	67.8
Is a major impediment	Frequency	467	233	12	6	3	40	31	3	7	93	39
	%	25.8	24.3	20.0	9.8	9.1	26.7	34.4	20.0	21.9	32.0	32.2

6. Lack of support from higher-level trade unions

Is not a major impediment	Frequency	1574	853	51	52	27	127	72	12	25	245	110
	%	87.0	89.1	85.0	85.2	81.8	84.7	80.0	80.0	78.1	84.2	90.9
Is a major impediment	Frequency	236	104	9	9	6	23	18	3	7	46	11
	%	13.0	10.9	15.0	14.8	18.2	15.3	20.0	20.0	21.9	15.8	9.1

7. Financial difficulties

Is not a major impediment	Frequency	1005	554	27	39	17	88	47	8	23	137	65
	%	55.5	57.9	45.0	63.9	51.5	58.7	52.2	53.3	71.9	47.1	53.7
Is a major impediment	Frequency	805	403	33	22	16	62	43	7	9	154	56
	%	44.5	42.1	55.0	36.1	48.5	41.3	47.8	46.7	28.1	52.9	46.3
	Frequency	1	0	0	0	0	0	0	0	0	1	0
	%	0.1	0.0	0.0	0.0	0.0	0.0	0.0	0.0	0.0	0.3	0.0

Index

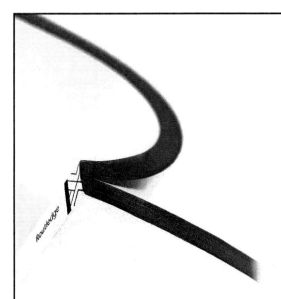

ROUTLEDGE
INTERNATIONAL
HANDBOOKS

Routledge International Handbooks is an outstanding, award-winning series that provides cutting-edge overviews of classic research, current research and future trends in Social Science, Humanities and STM.

Each *Handbook*:

- is introduced and contextualised by leading figures in the field
- features specially commissioned original essays
- draws upon an international team of expert contributors
- provides a comprehensive overview of a sub-discipline.

Routledge International Handbooks aim to address new developments in the sphere, while at the same time providing an authoritative guide to theory and method, the key sub-disciplines and the primary debates of today.

If you would like more information on our on-going *Handbooks* publishing programme, please contact us.

Tel: +44 (0)20 701 76566
Email: reference@routledge.com

www.routledge.com/reference

Biomechanics and Human Movement Science
Edited by Youlian Hong and Roger Bartlett

The Routledge Companion to Nonprofit Marketing
Edited by Adrian Sargeant and Walter Wymer

The Routledge Companion to Fair Value and Financial Reporting
Edited by Peter Walton

Routledge Handbook of Globalization Studies
Edited by Bryan S. Turner

Sexuality, Health and Rights
Edited by Peter Aggleton and Richard Parker